CAPTURING KALTENBRUNNER

THE PURSUIT, CAPTURE, AND TRIAL OF HITLER'S HIDDEN GESTAPO CHIEF

ROBERT E. MATTESON

SPECIAL AGENT, COUNTER INTELLIGENCE CORPS,
80TH INFANTRY DIVISION, THIRD ARMY

EDITED BY SUMNER W. MATTESON AND FREDRIC L. MATTESON

LITTLE CREEK PRESS
MINERAL POINT, WISCONSIN

Copyright © 2025 Robert E. Matteson

All rights reserved. No part of this publication may be reproduced, distributed, or transmitted in any form or by any means, including photocopying, recording, digital scanning, or other electronic or mechanical methods, without the prior written permission of the publisher, except in the case of brief quotations embodied in critical reviews and certain other noncommercial uses permitted by copyright law. For permission requests or other information, please send correspondence to the following address:

Little Creek Press
5341 Sunny Ridge Road
Mineral Point, WI 53565

With support from Blackburnian Press, LLC

ORDERING INFORMATION
Quantity sales. Special discounts are available on quantity purchases by corporations, associations, and others. For details, contact info@littlecreekpress.com

Orders by US trade bookstores and wholesalers.
Please contact Little Creek Press or Ingram for details.

Printed in the United States of America

Cataloging-in-Publication Data
Names: Robert E. Matteson, author
Title: Capturing Kaltenbrunner: The Pursuit, Capture, and Trial of Hitler's Hidden Gestapo Chief
Description: Mineral Point, WI Little Creek Press, 2025
Identifiers: LCCN: 2025907187 | ISBN: 978-1-955656-98-6
Classification: BIOGRAPHY & Autobiography / Military
HISTORY / Wars & Conflicts / World War II / European Theater
HISTORY / Modern / 20th Century / Holocaust

Book design by Little Creek Press

Cover photo credit: United States Holocaust Memorial Museum, courtesy of Archiv der KZ-Gedenkstaette Mauthausen

This book is dedicated to Alfred Etcheverry, who took
my place on 13 January 1945 during the Battle of the Bulge
and was killed. Etch had wanted to get at and feel the central
experience of war. In a way, his wish was granted but not
in the way he would have chosen, for he loved life.

—Robert E. Matteson, 1993

Also, we dedicate our father's work to the memory of
our late brother, Robert E. Matteson Jr., who kept the fire lit
and the dance going with his open-hearted embrace of
life until he passed on Valentine's Day, 2021.

—Sumner and Fredric Matteson, 2025

Alfred Etcheverry

Robert E. Matteson, Jr.

From Hiroshima, to Nanjing, to Pearl Harbor, to the killing fields of the eastern front, the Second World War was a global catastrophe—and a tear in the fabric of humanity. Somewhere near the center of the darkness was the Holocaust itself, an event that continues to haunt Western society's historical memory just as experiences of trauma may haunt individual memory.

—Jeremy Eichler,
TIMES'S ECHO, Music, Memory, and the Second World War

TABLE OF CONTENTS

Foreword 1
Preface 8
Introduction 35

★ ★ ★

Chapter One. Gathering Intelligence .39
Chapter Two. Closing In 69
Chapter Three. Capture and Interrogation 77
Chapter Four. Testing Security 87
Chapter Five. War Crimes and the Trial of the Century 97
Chapter Six. Perspectives 115
Chapter Seven. Coda 139

★ ★ ★

Appendix A. Excerpts from the *Last Valhalla of the Nazis* by Geoffrey Bocca 146
Appendix B. Testimony of Ernst Kaltenbrunner, 12 October, 9–10 November 1945 149
Appendix C. War Letters, July 1944 – October 1945 181
Appendix D. "SECRET" CIC Report, 8 June 1945 240
Appendix E. Robert B. Persinger on 6 May 1945 Liberation of Ebensee Concentration Camp – October 2009 Email to Sumner Matteson 243
Appendix F. Compiled Emails from Samuel Goetz to Sumner Matteson, 29 November 2009 – 29 April 2010, Regarding Nazi Concentration Camps, Especially Ebensee in Austria 245

Appendix G. Email from Phyllis Bausher, Daughter of Sydney Bruskin – Robert Matteson's Interpreter and Traveling Companion in the Final Days of the War 250

Appendix H. Lloyd Roach Letter to Jane Matteson, 15 January 2000 252

Appendix I. George Griebenow Letter to Robert E. Matteson, 7 November 1978 254

Appendix J. 1945 Letters to Marion Etcheverry from Thomas McMillen and Robert Matteson 256

Appendix K. Kaltenbrunner Recollections, September 19, 1978 260

★ ★ ★

Acknowledgments 264
About the Author 266
Notes 270
Index 292

Wildensee Route to Kaltenbrunner Hideout, 11-12 May 1945. Etching by Altauseee artist Christl Kerry and purchased by Matteson during one of several post-war visits to the region with his wife, Jane.

"Mr. Matteson has had a truly remarkable career. During World War II, he was a combat officer and led the platoon which captured the notorious German General Kaltenbrunner.... I think you will find him a very interesting person."

—Supreme Court Chief Justice Warren E. Burger,
26 August 1982 letter to Lev Nikolaevich,
chairman of the Supreme Court of the Soviet Union,
regarding a pending visit by Robert E. Matteson to Moscow

FOREWORD
by Sumner and Fredric Matteson

The world continues to be fascinated by the people and events of World War II, in large part because of widespread racial persecution, as well as the subjugation of entire nations, that led to the Holocaust—elements still at play in the world today. This account* of the capture of SS General Ernst Kaltenbrunner—in charge of the Reich Security Main Office (*Reichssicherheitshauptamt-RSHA*),[1] which included the Secret State Police (*Geheime Staatspolizei*), more commonly known by its acronym, Gestapo, as well as the internal and foreign political intelligence services, known as the SD (*Sicherheitsdienst*), and one of the most powerful SS men alive after Hitler's and Himmler's suicides, was originally self-published for family and friends in 1993 by the man who captured Kaltenbrunner, Counter Intelligence Corps (CIC) Special Agent Robert E. Matteson.[2]

*Edited with additional text from our father's 1980 self-published booklet titled The War Years 1940–1946. We believe the original manuscript on Kaltenbrunner, self-published in 1993, was simply an edited version of The War Years, which in turn was partly based on a typed 1946 personal account describing Kaltenbrunner's capture and aftermath. We have occasionally inserted brackets when editing a sentence. Additionally, we adhered to his spelling of Altaussee as "Alt Aussee"—a common spelling at the time. Footnotes, presented as endnotes in their entirety at the book's end, often include updated source materials not available to our father when he wrote his account. We have also added a "Preface" comprised of our father's earlier writings to allow for a fuller portrait of the man. Finally, we added ten appendices to complement his original lone appendix—excerpts from a 1964 article on the Alpine National Redoubt, the reported last stronghold of the German army. These ten appendices include, among others, excerpts from the original post-war interrogations of Kaltenbrunner and selected wartime letters from our father to our mother during his overseas service.

A final word about the use of "Hidden" in the subtitle. Father was always telling us that Kaltenbrunner was a mysterious figure and that after Heydrich was assassinated, Adolf Hitler made it clear that he didn't want the same to happen to his fellow Austrian compatriot, Ernst Kaltenbrunner. Hitler did not want any pictures, photographs, or images of Kaltenbrunner in the public. To keep Kaltenbrunner safe, Hitler wanted to keep him as secretive and "hidden" as possible, to keep him from being assassinated as had happened to his predecessor, Heydrich. So when Robert Matteson went looking for him, he knew the name and notoriety but had no picture or photograph—his image and likeness were that hidden. It wasn't until Dad was in Kaltenbrunner's very house that he saw a picture of him on Frau Kaltenbrunner's living room mantle for the first time. An image that had been hidden from the world until then.

Life's uncertainty is fraught with potential peril. Tragedy hit our father's life when he was a young man. At age 19, he lost his older brother to pneumonia, and two years later, in 1936, both of his parents died in a sudden automobile accident in South Florida. These traumatic events may have driven this humble, reserved man to "get the most out of life," aware of life's brevity, and to sometimes courageously risk his life, such as when he trudged alone (in disguise as a lost Austrian hiker) across an exposed snowy plateau and up the steps of an Alpine hut where Kaltenbrunner (also in disguise as deceased Wehrmacht doctor, Dr. Josef Unterwogen) hid out with Nazi guards in the early, still morning of 12 May 1945.

Matteson's drive to capture the notorious and much-feared Kaltenbrunner may also have been influenced by the sudden death of close CIC colleague Alfred Etcheverry four months earlier. "Etch" had been asked by Robert to take his place at a Luxembourg town meeting with an informant so that he, Robert, could interview a potential CIC applicant. Etcheverry was killed when the town was shelled. He had foreshadowed this possibility. Less than a month before he died, he penned a powerful letter to his wife (the letter shared by Etch's son, Nicholas, 53 years later with Robert's widow, Jane, and discovered in our father's archives). We present this letter below.

December 14, 1944

My beloved wife,

In a few days, or possibly even a few hours, I shall be going into action.

It is never far from my thoughts that I may not see you again—you and our blessed babies. And since it is not given us to know at what obscure spot on the map or at whatever meaningless moment my time will come, I have thought it best to write—to write now while I am still sound and well—some few things about myself, about us, and our children.

If I should die, it will be no one's responsibility but my own that it was so willed. This is my war, my army—one in which, in a peculiar sense, I elected to serve. So easy it would have been to have requested limited service, even to have evaded the draft altogether. But I could never have brought myself to such a course last winter—so many lifetimes ago. And I could not bring myself to it today. For I would be severely judged and by mankind condemned if, having seen the inevitability of this struggle, having urged that other men give their lives in the resolution of it, I were content with a lesser sacrifice.

However confused is our picture of the world today, how blurred the lines of the conflict, yet I am certain that I fight on the side of men of good will everywhere in the world. No more than that. For men of ill will were not born so, and may, by time, and by God's good grace, be redeemed. It is for men everywhere—whoever they are, wherever they may be—that I am fighting.

And in death, it is at least possible that I may accomplish as much, or more, than in life. For I recognize that my life, to date, as judged by conventional standards, has made but a very small contribution to the world. My professional career has been a disappointment; it may be that it would never have come to the fruition of which I have dreamed.

In one respect only do I feel my life to have been a glorious success. That has been your love for me and mine for you, the years we have spent together, the children we have brought into the world. I do not think I idolize you blindly, and yet I honestly believe that if I had sought the whole world over, I would never have found anyone to compare with you in all the qualities I hold most dear. Your gentleness, your strength, your passion, your understanding—you, in fact, have brought me such happiness as I never believed possible. And no one can rob me of it. It is mine for eternity.

There is one request I would make of you, and that a curious one. It is this: that if you have known as much happiness as I have during the last seven years, you do not content yourself to live on the memory of it. You were made to love and be loved. You cannot, or should not, exist on your thoughts, on old letters, and fading photographs. Some time—not now when your heart is broken, as is mine while I write, but later—you will discover other people, another person. Love him, show him and the world what our years of happy life together have taught you.

As for Chonty [Michelle] and Nick, there is not much for me to say that we have not talked of many times and that you do not know. But if I could wish for one thing only for them, it is this: make them strong. Let them see life as it is, neither prettified on the one hand or sordid on the other and the two in uneasy equilibrium but whole and healthy. Teach them that quality of toughness that we have both so often admired in your mother. Let them know that there is nothing so mean or so unpleasant that they will be degraded in the doing of it. And if you can, and this is a difficult job, keep alive in them forever that child's sense of wonder about the world and everything in it, that "Well, where have you been?" look.

That's about all, I guess. It's not very much, but I've never had to say much to you that your heart didn't already know.

God bless you and keep you safe, my darling.

Always,

Your Etch

("The Luxembourgers erected a war memorial in Goesdorf dedicated to my father and to the widows and war orphans of World War 2. My brother and I were overwhelmed by the kindness of the Luxembourg group who arranged this and the ceremony they organised. You can see the memorial on this website: http://www.uswarmemorials.org/html/monument_details.php?SiteID=783&MemID=1083."
—Etch's daughter, Michelle Etcheverry Pearce, in email to
   S. Matteson, October 2014.)

Ernst Kaltenbrunner, a lawyer by training, was carefully picked by Himmler to succeed RSHA chief SS General Reinhard Heydrich, who was ambushed and fatally wounded on 27 May 1942 by two British-trained Czech patriots in Prague, and who died in a Prague hospital on 4 June 1942. Fearing another assassination attempt, fellow Austrian Hitler at first kept Kaltenbrunner's identity a secret except to those within the top Nazi inner circle.[3]

Kaltenbrunner, married with three children, had an extra-marital affair with Countess Gisela von Westarp, who gave birth in a renovated cowshed to twins in March 1945. Less than two months later, Matteson, with four Austrian guides and a small number of accompanying GIs, began to ascend the Dead Mountain Range (*Totes Gebirge*) from the town of Alt Aussee, Austria, to confront and capture Kaltenbrunner.

"It is fitting," wrote our father in the book's original 1993 Foreword, "that this story be told now as we approach the fiftieth [now, at this writing, 80th] anniversary of the end of World War II, the fiftieth [at this writing, 80th] anniversary of the capture and trial of Kaltenbrunner at the end of the bloodiest century in world history, [and] the [aftermath] of a century of totalitarianism centering around

Joseph Stalin and Adolf Hitler, who were responsible for the cold-blooded deaths of millions of innocent people," including six million Jews during WWII.

Also, in 2022, had he been alive, he would have reminded us of history repeating itself to a degree by the massacres of Ukrainian civilians, including the indiscriminate shelling of Ukrainian towns and cities and the killing of children by Russian forces under autocrat Vladimir Putin. And equally awful, he would have been horrified by the news and images from the Hamas murder of Jewish women, men, and children on Saturday, 7 October 2023, near the Gaza border in southern Israel. But he also would have decried the age-old perpetuation of the cycle of vengeance as thousands of Palestinian civilians, including infants, lost their lives during horrific Israeli retaliatory bombing strikes and errant Hamas missiles within Gaza.

(Though ages old, the present conflict can likely be traced back to the 1967 Middle East War when Israel annexed Palestinian land, and the fenced-in Palestinian people at Gaza were subjected to a diminished and impoverished existence, setting the stage for decades of violence on both sides.)

★ ★ ★

One of the many components of this story's rich complexity, but not revealed here in this book, is that after the war, Matteson felt an obligation to stay in touch with Etch's two young children, which he did for nearly 50 years ... and on the other side of the Atlantic to do the same—quietly—with Kaltenbrunner's twins, who were born two months before war's end. He felt it vitally important to stay in touch with these innocents.

Our father's Foreword concluded: "It is also fitting that this story be told now as I approach the end of my life, I being 78 and in an advanced stage of Parkinson's disease. This was probably the most memorable experience of my life...."

Robert E. Matteson passed away less than a year later in January 1994, but living on is his life's philosophy, which he summarized to his family this way: "One should never overlook the fact that, as in backgammon, tennis, and other games in life, good fortune by itself isn't enough. One must, oneself, plan for, create, and then take advantage of the opportunities that arise. In keeping with this general philosophy, there is a lot to be said for the old adage: 'nothing ventured, nothing gained.' One needs to 'search for adventure and service' and thus create opportunities in order, I believe, to have a happy life. And by a 'happy life,' I mean to realize to the fullest extent possible the potential that is imminent in each of us."

The icon above each chapter heading is the patch representing the U.S Army's battle-tested 80th "Blue Ridge" Infantry Division of General George S. Patton's Third Army.

PREFACE

A boy's will is the wind's will.

—Longfellow

There are events—challenging, tragic, even comical—in our father's life that predisposed him early to being battle-tested and war-ready and later seriously tested his mettle in wartime experiences overseas. Now, let us review these events through our father's words—excerpts from his self-published A Search for Adventure and Service, Part I—The Early Years 1914-1940; Part II—The War Years 1940-1946[4]—Sumner and Fredric Matteson

Roscoe Finch Jr. and Carl Hensel were two of my best boyhood friends. We all lived in the same block on Lincoln Avenue between Avon and Grotto. Our house was between Carl Hensel's and Roscoe Finch's. Carl Hensel's backyard was our playground. Roscoe and Carl were two of the best junior athletes

Roscoe Finch Jr. (left), Carl Hensel (right)

in St. Paul. Roscoe won the Junior Athletic Cup at the SPA [St. Paul Academy] in 1927, and Carl won it in 1929. The game that we played the most was "M&F," standing for "Matteson and Finch." It was an adaptation of Cops and Robbers and Robin Hood.

M&F was played in the Carl Hensel backyard—our athletic playground—where there was a giant elm tree from which we hung ropes and swung from the tree to grape trellises and to garage roofs. The object of the game was to try and capture members of the other side, and if a person's foot touched ground, he was an automatic POW and placed in what we called the dungeon, which was a vegetable cellar under the Hensel garage.

Without doubt, Roscoe Finch was the most unusual, dramatic, and almost legendary figure in our neighborhood gang. He was born August 2, 1913. He was one or two years older than the rest of us—tall, muscular, blue-eyed. His mother called him "Buddy Boy," and he was her idol. He was the oldest of four children, the other three being girls—Jane, Peggy, and Betty....

My earliest remembrance of Roscoe was when he first moved into our neighborhood in 1920. His house at 776 Lincoln Avenue was a little more elegant than some of the others in the neighborhood. It was white with a long front porch with white columns. Roscoe must have been seven years old at the time. From the very first day that he moved into "our territory," he established his physical dominance. At first he was a little on the heavy side, and the rest of us could escape his vengeance by outrunning him. But there was no doubt at all about his general athletic prowess. In football, baseball, hockey, tennis, boxing, he excelled. Roscoe was well coordinated and unusually strong....

My initial physical encounter with Roscoe [occurred] one warm July day at Lindstrom, a Swedish village 40 miles northeast of St. Paul. The Finches had taken a cottage there at Kline's Resort, along with about ten other St. Paul families.

Among the ten families, each of whom had its own four-room cottage and outhouse, was the Foley family—Dr. Frederick Foley, his wife, and two beautiful daughters, Jessie Ann and Betty. The resort's common tennis court—and I mean common—was situated on the edge of the cow pasture in front of the Foley cottage and the hand water pump. On one sunny day, Jessie Ann was sitting on the green wooden bench by the tennis court, combing her beautiful, long, auburn hair. Roscoe and I were playing tennis. Roscoe, as the saying went in the 1920s, had a heavy "crush" on Jessie Ann. That day, I beat Roscoe in tennis, but what made it unbearable to Roscoe was that Jessie Ann was a spectator. I somehow sensed that Roscoe, as a result, was suffering a deep humiliation.

I quietly walked off the court toward our cottage but soon noticed that Roscoe walked after me. I quickened my pace. Roscoe quickened his pace. I started to run. Roscoe started to run. I entered the screen porch of our cottage with Roscoe only five yards behind me. I quickly locked the screen door and went into the innermost room, locking the wooden door as I went. I locked all the other doors and got my BB pump gun out of the closet. Then I took my station in a chair in the middle of the room and awaited the worst.

I could hear Roscoe at the screen door snorting like a mad bull. With one jerk, he pulled the screen door open, forcing the iron hook out of the frame. The wooden frame door gave him more of a problem, but not much. He solved this by putting his foot against the wall of the cottage and, with a mighty heave, pulled the frame of the door from its setting. There I was with my one-shot BB gun, trapped like a fox in its den.

As he entered my lair, I fired the one shot into his chest. That only infuriated him the more. It was like a bull stung by a bee or BB. I backed out of the door onto the porch and, as I did, ran into a long, green wooden bench. I looked around to see what it was, and just then, Roscoe let loose with a right to my jaw. The next thing I knew, after I had regained consciousness, was that I was lying on a cot on the porch with Roscoe standing over me, holding in one hand a dripping ice cream cone and in the other his favorite record—gifts to propitiate me and the wrath of my mother.

What had happened was that Mother had returned from shopping in the nearby village of Lindstrom and was greeted by screams from Sumner, my younger brother [the editor's uncle—Sumner III], who was jumping up and down crying, "Roscoe has killed Bobby! Roscoe has killed Bobby!" Mother fainted, according to Sumner, but that may have been an embellishment he sometimes added to his own vivid stories.

For some reason, the only person in the world Roscoe feared was my mother. Perhaps it was because she swung a wicked hairbrush. I spent a lot of my younger days side-stepping that hairbrush. It so improved my footwork that later on I won the heavyweight boxing title not only at Camp Owakonze in Canada but at Carleton College.

In any event—for whatever reason—Roscoe feared my mother. But, on that particular day, his sudden change of attitude might have been caused more by the realization that he might have killed me than by fear of my mother—for Roscoe and I were the best of friends.

I would be remiss in my treatment of my friend Roscoe if I didn't acknowledge a great debt I owed him. It was Halloween—the evening preceding All Saints' Day—the year was 1929, the beginning of my freshman or third form year at the St. Paul Academy. As was our wont on this sacred eve, the neighborhood gang raised hell.

On that particular night, we had evened our score with Mr. Horace Thompson, who (with good reason) had not taken kindly to the damage our "M&F" game had done to his garage roof, by pelting him with rotten eggs and ripe tomatoes when he answered the doorbell and, as Carl Hensel remembers, dumping a can of garbage on his front porch. He, also with very good reason, was furious—to say the least—and chased us for two blocks over one backyard fence after another. I was amazed at his agility and endurance.

I ended up with Roscoe by the Conger Drug Store at Grand and Grotto. We had eluded "Gokey," as he was later called. Our next target was the city streetcar system. The object was to tie up all traffic on Grand Avenue. So when the next large yellow streetcar stopped to discharge a passenger, I quickly climbed up the back onto the roof. I pulled the trolley off the wire, thus effectively stopping the motor.

It wasn't long before there was a line of streetcars stretching to St. Albans [church in St. Paul]. And it wasn't very long before a police squad car drew up, and two heavy-set policemen emerged, shouting for me to put the trolley back on the wire and to come down. I was reluctant to entertain such a summons—in part, I guess, because it was Halloween and in greater part because I wasn't exactly sure what would happen next. So I did nothing. The two policemen were too heavy to climb up and get me, so they took rocks and threw them at me. One went through the plate glass window of Conger's Drug Store, but none hit me, for I ran the length of the streetcar and jumped off. As I hit the cement between the rails, I felt pain in my ankles, and I couldn't move. Just then Roscoe—fast as a deer—moved out of the shadows from where he had been a silent spectator and, taking me up in his arms, darted down the alley toward Avon Street. I shall always be indebted to Roscoe for that great service. He kept me from an early police record.

In June 1935, it was off to Camp Owakonze [in Ontario, Canada] as a counselor for the second season. To me, the highlight of the season was a ten-day canoe trip on which Bat Barrett, Bill Horsting, and I took nine "middlers" down the Seine River. It was along the old Dawson route of 1868 from Port Arthur to Winnipeg.

On reaching the Seine River dam at the outlet of Lac des Mille Lacs, one of the middlers, Sammy Mendel of Chicago, bet me $25 that I couldn't swim through the gate of the dam. There were three gates, but only the center one was open.

I jumped into the water above the dam—not, however, having made up my mind to do it. As I swam near the open gate, I was suddenly caught up in the fast current, and my mind was made up for me. In no time at all, I was in the vortex and being swept through the gate. I tried to grab the side but to no avail. Down the chute I went and over a six-foot falls.

The impact of the water was so strong it knocked my false tooth out [original tooth lost during a collegiate boxing match]. I remember being held down in the dark depths by the force of the water coming off the chute and over the falls. Then, after what seemed an eternity, I began to see light, yellowish water. My head bobbed up, and then down I went again. I thought I had had it, but about one-tenth of a mile downstream, I came up again, and this time I was able to get ashore.

Sammy Mandel ran down the bank thinking I had drowned, but no such luck. I was there to collect my $25.

I had won the bet but had lost my false tooth. The $25, I was to learn later, didn't even cover the cost of a replacement.

On Friday afternoon, March 13, 1936, I was sitting in [Carleton College's] Willis Hall in English class when I received an unexpected summons to the dean's office. When I arrived, Dean Blayney was looking unusually somber. He said that he had just received word from St. Paul that my mother and father had been in an automobile accident in Florida and that my father had been killed and my mother seriously injured. He said that the car had hit a gasoline truck and gone up in flames.

The fact was, as I was to learn later, that the reverse had happened—my mother was killed and my father very badly burned. In addition, Mr. Sidney Porter, vice-president of the Inland Steel Company of Chicago, who was driving the car, had been killed and his wife injured, though not critically. The car was a LaSalle owned by Mr. Porter. They were driving from the Hillsboro Club at Pompano Beach, Florida, to Miami on Friday morning, March 13.

Sixteen miles north of Miami at Hollandale, Mr. Porter tried to pass a large gasoline truck driven by Tom Tennet of Detroit. The truck swerved to the left, just as the Porter car was passing, in order to avoid a telephone wire that had dropped down over the road. The Porter car sideswiped the truck, exploding the gasoline. Whether my mother and Mr. Porter died instantly, I don't know. My father was severely burned, and Mrs. Porter suffered broken bones and second-degree burns....

Charles D. Matteson and Adelaide H. Matteson

I went immediately to St. Paul. My brother Sumner was in the fifth form at the St. Paul Academy [older brother Dick had died two years earlier from pneumonia]. Friends began to gather at the house.... Someone bought me an airplane ticket to Florida. I was in a daze. I couldn't comprehend what was happening. It was impossible to believe that my mother was dead.

At first, the story was that she had survived but had died crawling back into the flames to save my father. It would have been like her to do that, but I was never able to establish whether or not it was true....

I arrived at the Miami airport at 6 p.m. and was driven north to the Hollywood Beach Hotel. The word was that my father was in the local hospital and that I should wait until morning to see him.... The next morning, I received a call from the hospital saying there was no need to go there, that my father had died during the early morning hours. I was told that it was a blessing since he had been badly disfigured and would have been an invalid the rest of his life. He would have been 67 in September and my mother 57 in August. This was the first real vacation trip they had taken in the 29 years they had been married....

In her January and February 1936 letters to Sumner and myself, written from the Hillsboro Club in Florida, she said, "Your father talks and laughs so much with them [the Brittons from Winnetka] that it does my heart good. He has been so much better this last week and seems to love it here.... The people here call him 'Papa' and me 'Dolly' after Dolly Madison." Then, in another, "We are really having a lovely time—I never have seen such a change in a person in a week as in Mr. Matteson. He is so jolly, talks to everyone, and enjoys the beach and swimming. There are a great many very interesting people here whom he likes.... We are really having a marvelous time and much better than I expected."

Finally, on March 3rd, "Yesterday we went on a picnic to Hobe Sound, which is 120 miles, with the Sidney Porters from Evanston. They have a wonderful car, and we just flew along. Hobe Sound is a beautiful place.... Everyone knows each other so well, and there are so many nice people to have a good time with...."

My mother's last letter from Florida to Sumner and me reflected how happy my father seemed to be and what a good time my mother was having. She was in her element, making all kinds of new friends with people from New York, Connecticut, Chicago, and Minneapolis....

It was a tragic event—more tragic in the case of my mother than my father. She was only 56 years old and would have had 20 or 25 more years of a happy life.

She would have known that I had married a girl who was very much like her and whom she would have loved to be with. She might have lived to about 1960 and thus would have had the great joy—particularly for her—of grandchildren. She would have loved to visit us in Philadelphia and Washington, D.C., and particularly to visit us at Lake Namakagon during the summer. In my father's case, it was tragic too, for he had had a very difficult last 12 years business and health-wise, and was only then, for the first time during this period, beginning to enjoy life again. But he was 66, and the ravages of a heart attack, ulcers, and a stroke had taken their toll. He had come close to death twice in 1935 and was a partial invalid, requiring a full-time registered nurse (Mae Peterson) during most of 1935.

Mother must have had some kind of premonition that she wouldn't return from this vacation in Florida, for she left behind a letter addressed "To My Dear Family," which began, "I do not wish to be taken away from my home but laid in my bed until it is time to go to church. I want a simple service at St. Clement's—no choir—with Mr. Atwill [minister, St. Clement's Church in St. Paul] and Dr. Haupt to conduct the service.... I wish no flowers except white flowers on the altar and on the casket. I wish them to be simple....

"I want someone who will be good to my children to take care of them.... Please keep up your interest in the church and remember no one loved you as your mother."

My immediate task the morning of March 15th, when my father died, was to arrange for the two bodies to be taken to the railroad station for the long, sad trip home. I didn't wish to view the bodies. I wanted to remember my mother and father as I had last seen them....

Letters, telegrams, telephone calls, flowers, and people were pouring into 791 Lincoln [home]. A wonderful group of women were handling everything.... As Mother had wished, there was a simple funeral service at our family church, St. Clement's, with Mr. Atwill ... officiating. The service was on Wednesday afternoon, March 18th. Douglas Atwill (in the next year, 1937, to become Bishop Atwill) and Mrs. Atwill were two of Mother's dearest friends.... The church was packed, with people standing along the aisles. There was a graveside internment service at Oakland Cemetery where [brother] Dick and Grandmother Hickcox had already been buried.

By accident more than by design, Sumner and I still have a few of the letters that poured in during March and April 1936. "By accident" because during the war, when I was not there, the house at 791 Lincoln was sold, and most of the memorabilia—silver cups, medals, letters, and photos—went with it. The following are some representative quotes: "I never have been so shocked as when I was handed the wire, and I cannot yet believe that it is true and that you two dear boys have to face this awful loss. You know your dear mother was my best friend—like my sister—and I always felt that your home was another home to me—and nothing in St. Paul will ever seem the same to me without her there and your father. I never knew a lovelier character nor a person who had as many friends of all kinds—and you were all so happy together."

Another said: "You have suffered a double loss in losing both parents, but I cannot but feel that it was a mercy that your father did not survive the accident as I understand he could not have been well again and, without your dear mother's devotion, could not have been happy. I have known your mother ever since she was a slip of a girl about 14 years old. She was one of the most unselfish and kindhearted persons I have ever known, and I believe had more friends than any other woman in St. Paul. Even so, her family and home always came first."

And another: "You [Sumner] and Bobby have been called upon to endure so much anxiety and sorrow these last few years, and you have shown so much courage in the way you have taken everything.... I loved your mother and father very much, and I shall always be grateful for having had them as friends."

And: "I know you know how much I loved your wonderful mother and splendid father. No one can take your mother's special place in my heart. How proud you will always be of such parents."

[Also]: "Constantly we think of the fine things which your mother did to make life happier for others, and there are so many of these to remember that her example is truly a Christian one.... All of her good deeds must point for us a path—it is an inspiration."

Bishop Douglas Atwill ... gave perhaps the most comprehensive eulogy in the *St. Clement's Chimes*, March 21, 1936:[5] "A life filled with loving deeds came to its earthly close on Friday of last week with the death of Adelaide Hickcox Matteson. It is not often that superlatives may be used without a sense of exaggeration, but when we think of Mrs. Matteson's character and life, even superlatives seem to be inadequate:

> The most sympathetic person I have ever known.
> The kindliest soul of my acquaintance.
> The most thoughtful woman in all my experience.

"All of these things and many others have been said of her, and still there is left a lack in the description of what she was and what her life meant to her friends.... Her thoughtfulness, her generous acts of kindness, her untiring willingness to give of her own strength to another's need, her understanding sympathy, and her unswerving loyalty, all of which were felt wherever the wide circle of her friendship and her associations reached, made an invaluable contribution to the character of our own parish life....

"Nearly everyone in the parish knew Mrs. Matteson, and all who knew her loved her. The accident which brought death to her makes us sorrowful, but even in the midst of sorrow, there is gratitude for the privilege, and for the blessings, of her presence with us throughout these many years."

These next final selections cover the war period from late August 1943 to 3 May 1945, setting the stage for Robert E. Matteson's Introduction.
—*Sumner and Fredric*

I was ordered to my local draft board in Faribault, Minnesota, on August 23rd, 1943. There, I was put in charge of a contingent of selected men from Local Board No. 1 for the trip by train to Fort Snelling, Minnesota.... When we arrived at Fort Snelling, we were issued our GI olive drab fatigues and uniform and assigned a barracks. During the first days, we were examined and given the Army Intelligence Test. The theory was that this would help determine in what branch of the Army we would be placed. I scored 145 on the IQ test and, it was thought, would therefore be assigned to Intelligence.

But we were soon to find out that it wasn't the tests or one's aptitude that determined the assignment. It was where manpower was most needed.... In my case, I soon learned I was going to be sent to Camp Callan near La Jolla, California, for basic training in anti-aircraft artillery.

My two weeks at Fort Snelling were so dull that I decided to enliven them. Every morning, we were up at 5:30 a.m., shaved and showered, and lined up in front of the barracks for the 6 a.m. morning report. Then we marched off in a single column to breakfast. After breakfast, we were given half an hour to make our beds, clean the barracks, [and] put our shoes in line "with the toes out and shoelaces in." We then assembled in formation to march off to our various morning work assignments. My first week's assignment was to peel potatoes. So on the third day, as we marched off to the potato shed, instead of right-facing into the shed, I marched straight ahead and out into the woods where I had parked my car. I changed my clothes and spent the day playing golf with Jane. I felt a little like my boyhood friend, Roscoe Finch.

The trick was to be back by the 10 p.m. bed check, which I made just in time. Nobody knew the difference. However, I was being very foolish, for if I had been caught, it would have seriously marred my army record. AWOL (absent without leave) is a violation of the first order....

At Camp Callan, anti-artillery training basic training lasted 17 weeks, which carried into January 1944.... The drill at Camp Callan was similar to that at Fort Snelling, except that instead of peeling potatoes, I was [a] latrine orderly. I was also instructed on how to handle the huge 90-mm anti-aircraft guns. I was assigned to "B" Battery, 52 A.A.R.T. Battalion. The usual schedule was: 6 a.m. reveille; 6:45 breakfast; 7:30 close order drill; then four hours on map reading; dinner at 12:30; 10 minutes to hear the news; more instruction; 5:15 retreat; 5:30 mess; free for the evening until 9 p.m. bed check, and lights out at 11:00 p.m.

I had latrine orderly duty from 5:30 a.m. to 9:30 p.m. once every three days. When the captain came through, I said, "Sir, Private Matteson reports the latrine of the 1st platoon, Battery B, ready for inspection." I saluted, he saluted, the sergeant saluted. He looked around, said "good," and I would spend the rest of the day cleaning the bowls, mopping the floor, and cleaning the walls....

By November 15th, we had had six weeks of basic training. We were having more "physical hardening," learning how to throw hand grenades, taking our M-1 rifles apart (every five minutes it seemed), [and] going on night bivouacs and six-mile hikes with packs. Meal times were like prison. You weren't allowed to talk to anyone, and if you did, you would find yourself on K.P. [kitchen patrol] for the weekend. The idea was to eat as fast as you could and get out. As things got tougher, more were hospitalized, and some went AWOL. One of these was caught and had to spend 30 days in the guardhouse....

Since we were in anti-aircraft, heavy emphasis was placed on aircraft recognition. Every day after lunch, we were drilled on that. The reason for this was that half our planes in North Africa, we were told, were shot down by our own anti-aircraft. Another part of the drill was to crawl 100 yards under live machine gun bullets. Once in a while, a boy would lose his head—first figuratively and occasionally literally.

Jane's and my letter writing stopped November 15th when she arrived in La Jolla. The principal things that stood out during those last couple of months were my four weeks in the hospital and our final two weeks of simulated maneuvers on the nearby Borrego Desert. Charlie Bachman (son of the well-known Michigan State football coach) and I, to liven things up, had combined to capture the enemy headquarters by scaling a rocky cliff along the ocean at night. I cut my leg, a deep gash below the knee.

I was hospitalized for a week in the camp hospital ... [but] soon after getting out for Christmas Day, infection set in, and I returned for three weeks until January 21st. Jane and [daughter] Daidie would come to visit me there, singing the latest song from the musical *Oklahoma*—"Oh, What a Beautiful Morning, Oh What a Beautiful Day." The result of my hospitalization was that I could rejoin my outfit for only the last nine days of maneuvers. Consequently, I was left behind when my anti-aircraft group left for other staging areas and eventually [for] somewhere in the Pacific. I had missed four weeks of basic training.

That one accident changed my entire army career. It was another example to me of how one's life is constantly affected by unforeseen accidents, not by planning.

Instead of going to the Pacific—to me, a less interesting theater of war and with anti-aircraft artillery, which held even less interest—I was suddenly, on February 3rd, ordered to report to the 80th Infantry Division, which was on desert maneuvers near Fort Yuma, Arizona. The reason? The Army, in February 1944, needed infantrymen more than anti-aircraft. The fact that I had had 17 weeks of anti-aircraft training and none in infantry didn't make any difference. Their final reason was that No. 128 on the list for Yuma had come down with measles, and I was the replacement to fill the quota. So spins the wheel of fortune that determines one's future life!

The 80th Infantry Division was on desert maneuvers 26 miles from Yuma, Arizona, and right on the Mexican border in the Mojave Desert. It was in its final toughening process. In February and March, it is hot during the day and cold at night. We lived in six-man tents when not on actual maneuvers. Desert maneuvers with the 80th Infantry Division proved to be the roughest part of my army career....

As I wrote Jane on February 18th, "It's been hell out here, but I know I'll look back on it as a great experience. We never sleep—maybe one or two hours a night. Everything is done in the dark, and it is unbelievably cold. When we do sleep, it is on rocks. We are given one blanket. There can be no fire...." The general program was to get up at 3:30 a.m., eat a cold breakfast (three cold pancakes, a cup of coffee, and a hard biscuit), and move up toward the main line of simulated resistance. We would hike for seven or eight hours and would then have "C" or "K" rations at 11:30 a.m.

After standing in a long line (each person 10 yards from the next) to get food, we would repeat the process to wash our mess kits. Following that, we would move forward, and after several miles, the order would come to "dig in; enemy up ahead." We had to dig foxholes up to our shoulders from a prone position in slag, with some young lieutenant standing over us, ordering us to dig deeper and harder.

The mountains we were in looked like piles of red cinders—no vegetation at all—and the higher we went, the colder it was. The wind howled, and often it rained. We kept going until about 7 p.m., when we had our evening meal. After that, we stood outpost guard until midnight. Then, and only then, were we allowed to sleep. But it was so cold we could only catnap. The officers had nice warm bedrolls that we, the privates, carried for them and laid out for them. After the first three days, we were allowed to make a fire and sleep on the burned-out coals....

One day on maneuvers, the clouds figuratively broke. I was ordered to report to division headquarters. My name had come up to be assigned to intelligence school at Camp Ritchie, Maryland.... I left for Camp Ritchie at 3:00 a.m., March 23rd, 1944.... At Camp Ritchie, we rose at 5:30 a.m. and attended classes from 7:30 a.m. until 5:30 p.m. seven days in a row, with the eighth day free. It was like heaven. There was no K.P., latrine duty, inspection, or guard duty. However, everyone else held a higher rank and had been in intelligence and in the army for a long time. One of my instructors pointed out that I was in a rank by myself—the only private.

The course covered a wide variety of intelligence subjects, not just photo-reconnaissance. One of our last assignments was a night reconnaissance through the very property we were later to buy [14 years later, Robert and Jane would buy 30 acres of land near Blue Ridge Summit—a mile or so from Camp Ritchie]....

On April 28th, 1944, I, along with others, was awarded a certificate by General Banfill, the commandant at Camp Ritchie, for satisfactorily completing the special course during the period March 25th to April 28th, 1944. About this time ... I received an invitation from the Special Branch of Military Intelligence to come to Washington, D.C., for an interview. After the interview, I received a letter dated May 22nd, 1944, from Major Porter Chandler of the Military Intelligence Division [MID] saying MID had put in an application for my assignment to the Special Branch as one of the quota of enlisted men....

I was now part of the G-2 (intelligence) of the 80th Division headquarters, a big step up from being rifleman with "B" Company of the 318th Regiment. The head of G-2 was Colonel Richard Fleischer of Philadelphia ... under him was Captain Coe Kerr, a nifty guy who had gone to Yale ... [and] the head of counter-intelligence was a Captain Thomas McMillen, a graduate of Harvard Law School and the son of a Republican congressman from Illinois....

Finally, the end of June, the word came that we were leaving July 1st for Europe. The curtain of censorship descended. Later, we were told we were going to Petty Pool near Chester, England.... On July 20th, 1944, came the plot against Hitler's life. It gave a great boost to the morale of the troops. My future acquaintance, SS General Ernst Kaltenbrunner, as chief of the RSHA had responsibility for rooting out the perpetrators of the plot.[6] This role brought Kaltenbrunner closer to Hitler's personal secretary and chief of the Nazi Party Chancery, Martin Bormann, a connection that increased Kaltenbrunner's influence with and access to Hitler during the last nine months of the war, though Himmler remained firmly in command as Reichsfuhrer SS until almost the very end.[7]

On July 31st, our stay in Petty Pool ended, and the word came down we were moving into the real war. We didn't know how or where, but we went by truck convoy to Southampton by way of Oxford. Our first contact with the war came sooner than we had expected when several Nazi V-2 [ballistic missiles] landed in the vicinity of our camp near Southampton.

On August 2nd, the big day arrived, and at night we took off for France on an LST—U.S. *Liberty Ship 512*. We left at 11:00 p.m. under a clear, moonlit sky and [on a] calm sea. We were escorted by submarines, cruisers, and overhead a squadron of planes....

We landed without incident [at Normandy] at noon August 3rd.... As we landed ... we saw for the first time the visible destruction of boats and tanks and the shattered West Wall. The fighting, starting with the first coordinated Allied offensive on July 25th, had moved inland but was not far away. At Utah, it was so peaceful we went in swimming off the LST, waiting for the tide to go out so that we could drive our vehicle onto the beach....

On August 5th, the chief of staff of the 80th, Colonel Fleischer—the G-2; and Sergeant Patrick and I set out on a tour of the front.... From St. Jores, we visited Perier's, which had been wiped out, Coutances (only the cathedral high [on] a hill was standing), and then Gavray, where I saw the first dead American—a Black American soldier lying beside a demolished half-track. It made a deep impression, as deep almost as the miles of dead bodies I was to see later at the Ebensee concentration camp. The smell of dead—mostly dead—cattle was terrible....

On August 13th, we made a major move to close the gap between Argentan and Falaise. Immediately, six of our reconnaissance troops were killed by mines one mile ahead of us. The objective was to trap 400,000 Germans, mostly the 7th Army. Our major worry at first was mines and booby traps. On every side was evidence of vehicles and personnel destroyed by them. As we moved through one town after another, the French turned out to cheer and sing the "Marseillaise" and give us wine, bread, eggs, and flowers. The Germans were caught between us in the south and the British and Canadians to the north. The destruction was unbelievable. On August 12th, Argentan was reached, and on August 19th, Falaise fell....

On August 17th, Captain Kerr and I were sent by General McBride on a mission to make contact with General Leclerc of the 2nd French Armored. We started at 4 a.m. over roads not yet cleared of mines. We passed the advanced elements of our recon troops and went on into Mortree, where we found the headquarters of the 2nd French Armored. The troops were Moroccan with red berets and fezzes. From a hill we could see Argentan, which was still held by the Nazis. Above it were 20 planes we thought were American. But all of a sudden, the planes swept in over us, spraying the field we were in with machine gun bullets. I dove behind a stalk of grain just in time to see bullets kick up a line of dust where I had been standing nine feet away. The planes were German FW-190s, not U.S. P-47s. We reported back to General McBride and then moved into the area of Argentan with heavy artillery pounding away all night.

On August 18th, many of the Germans pulled back to a line east of Paris and the Seine River. But some Germans still held out in the Argentan area, and 88-mm fire was heavy. With the British on our left and the U.S. 90th Infantry Division on our right, the 80th finally cleaned out the remaining resistance. Prisoners kept streaming in all day. Most of them were Poles and Russians who had been pressed into service. They were glad it was all over. Some of the SS escaped to the north. We were finally out of the Normandy Peninsula. It was one of the decisive victories of the war....

On September 4th, four of us took off in a jeep for a town near Nancy in eastern France. It was a replica of what the Nazis had done in Lidice in Czechoslovakia after the assassination of Reinhard Heydrich, Kaltenbrunner's predecessor. The Free French (FFI) had dared to resist the first Nazis. In return, the Nazis had cut off their hands and set fire to the little town. The population had been terrorized, and farm buildings set afire. As we entered the town, we could see from the hill the SS withdrawing under U.S. artillery fire. Until then, it had been a peaceful, pretty, rural village on a small river. Now it was in ruins. An old man lay shot under his apple tree, his basket beside him. On the floor of the church was a young boy, his wrists slashed, his teeth knocked out, and a bullet in his chest.

The FFI had killed the Nazi mayor, and in retaliation, the SS tried to destroy the town....

On October 1st, General Patton visited us to hand out bronze stars to four of the very deserving infantrymen. As he read the citations, he broke into tears. It was paradoxical to see "old blood and guts" with his pearl-handled revolvers on each hip, crying like a baby.

Captain Tom McMillen

Captain Tom McMillen [promoted to Major by war's end], head of the 80th Counter Intelligence Corps (CIC), spoke to me on 11 October 1944 about transferring into the CIC to take the place of a CIC man killed at Pont-à-Mousson. There wasn't time to send back to the States for a trained CIC replacement.... October 14th was a significant day in my army career. I transferred from Headquarters G-2 to Special Agent Axtell's CIC team, which was attached to the 318th Infantry Regiment in the vicinity of Jeandelaincourt. With Ax were very able CIC agents—Bob Rainey from Peoria, Illinois, and John Klimek from Wisconsin, who spoke eight languages. Ax was from Binghamton, New York. He was an able lawyer who had gone to Cornell. At that point, CIC and Civil Affairs (CA) had not yet assumed the importance they would later. CA didn't do much more than oversee the burial of dead cows and advise the local French officials. CIC's job was to screen the local populace and root out those who were Nazi sympathizers and collaborators....

I was very much impressed by the simplicity of French rural life. As I wrote Jane October 27th: "Everything is done by hand—plowing of the fields, the laundry done in the community water trough, the processing of grapes, the baking of bread, the slaughter of hogs and cattle. On the streets now you can see the Christmas geese being fattened for Christmas dinner. The geese, squawking loudly, take delight in chasing the small children. The new wine is awful, and the Mirabelle from small plums is so potent it burns all the way down.

"There is the old town crier dressed in a special uniform and armed with a drum, marching down the street and calling people to their doors and windows to listen to the latest local news. There are also the countless funeral processions. A carriage, covered with black cloth with gold border and drawn by a horse that looks like a circus horse, carries the casket. The mourners walk behind, silent as ships at night.... The trees have turned a dark red and gold, not as brilliant as they are in Minnesota but still too much that way not to remind me sharply of home...."

On November 26th, we moved from Villers and Faulquemont to Longeville, where I contacted Mr. Mouth, one of the Maquis or resistance types. He was living, like many others of the resistance, in a room dug into the side of a hill. It was perfectly concealed. I had to lower myself through a trap door. Inside there was a radio, electric lights, guns, books, maps of the area. Mouth came out only at night. Others were living in the block houses of the Maginot Line, which we had passed as we entered Longeville. From Longeville, only eight kilometers from the German border ... 120 families had been sent east to Nazi concentration camps. A Dr. Frentzen from Faulquemont had given injections and broken the fingers and arms of French boys who wanted to evade military service with the Germans.

On November 27th, I drove into St. Avold, a pretty little resort town of 6,000 people. We took up headquarters at the vacated Nazi Kreisleiter's house. Soon after we started functioning, a German agent turned himself in. He reported that 30 time bombs had been left behind in various houses and buildings, set to go off in six days. In six days, 12 went off, blowing the houses sky high.... I had left to go into Bening, an outpost town. Returning that night with five prisoners across a muddy field was like what I had imagined no-man's land to be. Shells were coming over from both sides, whining overhead in the night or swooshing in with a *kerplunk* as they landed nearby. For three nights in a row, I had to return in the dark over that same road.

On December 5th, my CIC unit moved from Bad Homburg to Merlebach, a town of 18,000 people only three kilometers from the German border. We set up our headquarters in a German bakery where we had both beds and bread—huge loaves of brown bread just out of the oven. The road in was under direct observation, and 88-mm fire chased us all the way. U.S. casualties had risen sharply. In five weeks, the November–December offensive had cost the U.S. 64,000 casualties, almost half of them on a 12-mile front in the 1st Army area just north of us. There were 12,000 victims of trench foot, many incapacitated for life. Shipments of proper footwear and winter clothing had been bypassed in the interest of more ammunition and gasoline. As in all wars, the infantry riflemen bore the brunt of the enemy fire and, thus, of the casualties. In this case, the percentage was 85 to 90% of the casualties.

On December 16th, Alfred Etcheverry, a new CIC recruit from New York, joined us as we started a big move south.... The infantry, as usual, was to do the dirty work, opening the holes and taking the heavy losses. But the tentative word on December 16th also was that there were indications of a possible large Hitler counter-offensive to the north on the 1st and 9th Army fronts, with the Germans using as many as 16 divisions....

About this time, also, I was cautioned by the army censor for the umpteenth time that I was saying too much in my letters. Also, about this time, I had a letter from Chuck Bachman, who had been with me at Camp Callan. He was with an anti-aircraft unit on some island in the Netherland East Indies. If it hadn't been for the ... infected leg, that's where I would have been. I thanked my lucky stars for being in the most interesting theater of operations. About the same time, I ran into Riegel from my old "B" Company, 318th Infantry at Yuma. He told me that my entire platoon, except for three men, had been wiped out by an ambush while on combat patrol in eastern France. Again, fate had looked kindly on me. I had been sent, instead, to Camp Ritchie and intelligence school.

On December 16th, the German Ardennes offensive began. It began against the U.S. 1st Army and, particularly, its VIII Corps. It struck at the most vulnerable point in the entire Allied defense. It was directed by Field Marshal Gerd von Rundstedt. By December 19th, Hitler's forces had achieved a breakthrough into Luxembourg and Belgium below Trier in the Ardennes region.... It was Hitler's last gasp—an attempt to split the Americans and British and drive to the English Channel. The Germans were using captured American jeeps, uniforms, weapons as spearheads to confuse and disorganize us in attacks from our rear. To trap them, we asked them to identify themselves by the use of baseball names, which they could not do, and thus, most of them were arrested. The leader of these jeep parties was Lieutenant Colonel Otto Skorzeny, a subordinate of SS General Ernst Kaltenbrunner....

[Approaching Christmas] Axtell and I moved fast to catch up to our 318th Infantry Regiment of the 80th [Division], which was attacking north between Luxembourg City and Trier at midnight. We moved into Vichten [Luxembourg]. Here, the 80th relieved the 28th Division, which had taken the brunt of [a] counterattack in this section. Their 110th Regiment had been entirely wiped out, along with part of the 111th and 112th, by General Hasso von Manteuffel's 5th Panzer Army. Over 600 tanks had been massed by Rundstedt for the Battle of the Bulge....

The Allied Plan was for the 1st Army to drive south and meet up with the 3rd Army driving north, trapping 16 divisions, including five Panzer Divisions, and thus breaking the back of German resistance on this western front. General Patton was there to take personal command. The word was that German tanks were 20 miles into Belgium and had surrounded Bastogne, a little to the north of us....

By December 22nd, six divisions, including ours, the 80th, were driving into the German flank. Over 133,000 vehicles turned the entire 3rd Army around.... The 26th Infantry Division was now on our left and the fabulous 4th Armored Division on our right, but the 80th was in front as the point....

December 24th, the skies cleared, and 5,000 planes descended on the Germans, making havoc of their long supply lines and advancing tanks.... On Christmas Eve, we heard the good news that the German offensive was stopped, but their resistance was fanatical. Our losses were heavy. Prisoners were streaming in all day. Snow was falling, and as I passed PW cages, I could hear the German prisoners singing "Tannenbaum O Tannenbaum" and other Christmas songs.

For the first time, we picked up members of the Volkssturm (People's Army) who had been drafted as a last resort. On Christmas Day, I had dinner at the regimental command post. I was promoted and given charge of the CIC unit covering the 318th, with John Klimek and Alfred Etcheverry as my team....

On December 26th, Bastogne, which was held by General McAuliffe's 101st Airborne, was relieved by our 4th Armored Division, and von Rundstedt reported to Hitler that the "last gamble" of the Nazis had been lost. *The New York Times* military correspondent termed this the Battle of the Bulge— "the greatest battle American troops ever fought."

★ ★ ★

The three of us [Matteson, Klimek, Etcheverry] stayed with Josel and Elise Jacoby [in Vichten], native farmers about 35 years old. We occupied the best room in their humble abode—the living room to the right of the entrance door. It had a wood and coal stove and mattresses on the floor. They appeared to be honored to have Americans staying with them and did all they could to provide us with wood, water, apples, [and] eggs. There was no running water and no electricity, but we had a Coleman lantern and a pump.... Everything of value was buried underground. The Jacobys had a truck which they dismantled and buried piece by piece. When we arrived ... they dug it up and reassembled it.

New Year's Eve, we celebrated in Vichten at the Jacobys, drinking quetsch, which is like bathtub gin—so raw you can't hold it in your mouth. Etcheverry, who was a Yale drama major and had some minor parts on Broadway, practiced his French on the Jacobys....

[Etch greeted the New Year with a sunny outlook. This letter below from 1 January 1945, comes from a selection of Etch's letters to his wife, Marion. Their daughter, Michelle Etcheverry Pearce, shared these with Sumner in October 2014.]

My darling,

A new year and I hope it will be a happier one for all of us. Some of the boys up the road a piece asked us to drop in last night for some New Year cheer, but it's pretty cold nights, the roads are slippery, night comes down early, and—most important of all— we would have had to bring our own liquor, so we didn't go....

It's a surpassingly beautiful day, and I have been barging about in the jeep with business as the excuse but the countryside as the real object of my interest. Gently sculptured hills frosted with snow, blue-white and tinsel-sparkling with evergreen fingers groping down their slopes and into every secret place.

Clear-running ice-fringed brooks between red willow branches. The fir boughs powdered white and the scarlet clusters of some unknown berry trees against the crisp blue sky. A day for a sleigh instead of a jeep and the tinkle of bells instead of the dull shudder of artillery. The snow is kind, tenderly rounding the bloated and mishappen carcass of a horse lying by the wayside while its mate or its friend, understanding nothing, watches forlornly and patiently for someone who will come and lead it back to its stall. And the earth is forgetful, bubbling secretly beneath the snow, and waiting for the sun to quicken it to new life....

On reading this note over, it sounds very much like a "posterity letter." I'm sorry, but it was fun writing it.

All my love, my darling.

Always,

Your Etch

On January 5th [1945], I decided to make our CIC headquarters in Heiderscheider Grund, a town of 50 people beside the Sauer River. We found a cottage along the narrow street that belonged to two old crones and moved in. With them lived two refugees and a dachshund named Waldi. Waldi liked to stay in our room because it was warm, and we liked to have him because he chased away the mice and rats. In front of the cottage was a little brook of clear, clean, cold water from which we all got our drinking water....

Klimek and I were making regular trips to Goesdorf, high on top of a hill on the other side of the river. Goesdorf was surrounded on three sides by steep hills but was not protected from the north, and there were no woods. The Nazis held the ground to the north and east, their outposts being within 1,500 yards of the town. On January 11th, the day that I was officially promoted to Special Agent in CIC, Klimek and I visited Dahl, which was within rifle shot of the Germans in Nocher. As usual, we contacted the resistance man, Salentiny, in Goesdorf and interrogated the ones in Dahl who had been friendly with the Nazis. The deep snow made it difficult for the tanks and infantry to move, except along the road, which was under constant surveillance and fire.

We returned to find that Captain McMillen had brought us bottles of Cinzano, peach liqueur, wine, cognac and vermouth, and two hunks of beef, four chickens, and four loaves of bread. On Sunday, the villagers put on their Sunday clothes and walked up and down the village street before going to the tiny church. However, because of the nearby Germans, they spent most of the time in their cellars.

The two old crones cooked our meals. They had ruddy faces, teeth missing in front ... but they had perpetual smiles on their faces and a twinkle in their eyes. They gave us the best of what they had, and we shared what we had with them. Their hands were so hard and rough that they picked up live coals barehanded when the coals fell from the stove onto the floor. They spent Sunday afternoons, with heads nodding, in front of the stove.

January 13th turned out to be a black day in our lives.

I had been called back to Division HQ to interview a CIC applicant. Our new agent, Alfred Etcheverry, took my place and went to Goesdorf. When I returned to our cottage, I found Captain McMillen and John Vance waiting for me. McMillen had received word that either Klimek or Etcheverry had been killed in Goesdorf just an hour before by a mortar shell. It was my guess that it was Etcheverry because Klimek had always made the point of taking cover in some building in Goesdorf while I contacted the Battalion S-2 [staff officer responsible for security and intelligence matters] and Salentiny.

As it turned out, it was Etcheverry. He had contacted the S-2 and was talking to Jean Thilges and Salentiny in the barnyard in the center of the village. As he talked, two American tanks went by in the street, drawing mortar fire from the Germans, who had the street under direct observation. We learned that as the shells dropped, Etch had tried to take cover in the barn but was hit in the back of the head and through his arms and legs. He was killed instantly. Jean Thilges, one of the two civilians he had been talking with, was also killed.

It was a great shock.

As I wrote in my diary: "Etch had everything—a sense of humor, objective intelligence, was provocative, interested in all angles of every problem, progressive in his ideas, democratic in his outlook.

He had an unusual talent for dramatizing the ordinary. He wanted to feel the central experience of war. He had felt he hadn't known it yet. He was all the time trying to get at the meaning of it—to make it an assessment—to feel himself the feelings of the central actor on the scene. He was fair, just, kind, good-natured, and had one of those rare marriages of complete congeniality.... He is a friend at first sight. He has a zest for life and for different experiences. He is stimulating because he wants to explore every question to its roots and because there is nothing that doesn't hold interest or significance."

On January 14th, the next day, I wrote Jane describing both Klimek and Etch but was not allowed by the censor to say that Etch had been killed. I hoped, though, that it would prompt Jane to get in touch with his wife, Marion, which it did. About Klimek, I wrote: "The man of many languages—a Slav, large and rough, peasant parents, slow-moving, patient, slow to anger, deeply religious, generous and thoughtful. He loves his family and hates the war, which keeps him from them, with every fibre of his being."

Klimek was stunned, and it was many days before he was himself again.

By accident, I had been called back and escaped the same fate. Is there a rationality that decides who and when it should be? Etch had wanted to get at and feel the central experience of war. In a way, his wish was granted but not in the way he would have chosen, for he loved life....

[Three days before Etch died, he penned a letter to Marion that she received on the day of his death—13 January:]

January 10, 1945

My dearest wife,

It occurs to me that in my letters I have said very little about the war. I [have] written about the weather, the landscape, the people, but of the central reality—the monstrous business that keeps me from most of the things I love—almost nothing. I have been wondering why. Is it consideration for your sensibilities? Or those of the censor? Or is it because my impressions are still amorphous that I am waiting for some not-as-yet emergent awareness to make itself felt? I suspect it's all three but most of all the last.

Somewhere—just around the next corner perhaps—there must be something called War, a compound of all that I have read and heard. Of Tolstoi [sic] and Ralph Ingersoll, of pictures in Life, of my uncle Michel, of *All Quiet on the Western Front*, and *Journey's End*, of *Dere Mable* and *The Red Badge of Courage*, and I know not what else. Is there no clear distillation, I keep asking myself, of all that men have known of fear, of anger, of sorrow, and of savage exultation? Something which can be expressed in those three letters W-A-R? Something of which it can be said: This is it?

Now I am aware, as I have written you before, that I am not experiencing this war in the way that a rifleman experiences it. I have not crouched for days in a water-filled foxhole nor trampled through snow and freezing water to the point of collapse and beyond. I have never heard the crack of a rifle fired in anger. My bayonet has drawn no German blood. I have no bayonet.

But I have been cold and uncomfortable and sick. I have seen the lines of prisoners. I have seen the dead and touched their cold faces. I have ventured into shattered towns some scant hours after their capture. I have sat in a building and shivered as a near explosion strewed the floor with glass. This is not the whole business of war. But it is certainly not peace.

Yesterday in a cupboard of the room which is presently our home I came across a stack of letters. They were from a dozen different people but were written to only one, an Infantry private [name censored]. Since I don't know him and he doesn't know me, and it seems unlikely that either of us will ever have the pleasure, I sat down and read the whole stack. They were all from friends and relatives in a small town in Arkansas and from a girl in Texas. And the first thing that struck me about them was their incredible monotony.... But almost instantly it struck me what a snobbish, stupid thought had crossed my mind. I realized that these letters were brimming with life, with home, with the love of people whose hearts were aching with the want of their boy, their pal, their lover, but who nonetheless were going on with the business [of living].... Evidently he had pulled out in a hurry and had forgotten them....

I have been thinking a lot about [censored] and about the other people who go on living. Because I think that's the thing which strikes me most forcibly about war—how men build little fir shelters over their foxholes and bed them with straw, how people creep back to their blasted houses and stuff the windows with rags and rummage in the ruins for chairs or potatoes or dolls. They, and all the rest of us, go on sleeping and eating and defecating and working and playing. Living.

Maybe it will seem different if I am wounded or if one of my friends is killed. Maybe then I'll know what War is.

But to date, that's it.

I love you, my darling, and go on living—with you even when I'm far away.

Always,

Your Etch

The end of February, we moved our CIC office to Körperich and then Outscheid, not far from Bitburg in the German Rhineland. Hearing about a Kreisleiter adviser in the little town of Hamm, I walked with Klimek one mile into Hamm. The road was out. Hamm is a beautiful town of 60 people surrounded by high hills and the River Prum and dominated by a 12th-century medieval castle. As I came over the hill and saw it below, still smoking from a fire, it reminded me of a medieval castle in the time of Robin Hood. An 80-year-old forester of the count, who owned the castle, greeted me. He wore a dark green costume and had a white flowing beard. The forester's father, grandfather, etc., had each been the game warden and forester for the count's ancestors back to 1500. Around the castle was a woods in which they still hunted wild boar....

On April 17th, we moved into the vicinity of Chemnitz, close to Czechoslovakia. At this point, we were on the verge of linking up with the Soviets. Instead of moving to free Prague, General Patton was given orders to swing south toward Nuremberg and attack the Alpine Redoubt area, where intelligence showed the Nazis were to make their last stand [see Notes 16 and 18]. We had finally reached the "restraining line" dividing the U.S. and Soviet troops and territory.

With the 3rd Army, my unit swung south via Bamberg and reached Nuremberg in Bavaria. Sniping was still going on at night from the catacombs of the walled city. We found a complete list of all Nuremberg Gestapo members in the labyrinth of tunnels under the police presidium in the old part of the city....

On May 2nd, we moved into Braunau, Hitler's birthplace, just across the Inn River in Austria. By coincidence, it was here that I first heard that Hitler, Goebbels, and Eva Braun had committed suicide in the Führer's bunker in Berlin on April 30th. Mussolini was also reported dead, and all Italy and western Austria had surrendered. We were now headed for the Alpine Redoubt in Austria, which had not yet surrendered. We moved on fast to the Enns River and Steyr, where, on May 3rd, we met the Russians. We met them on the bridge over the Enns River and, after exchanging greetings, which neither understood, retired to our respective sides of the demarcation line.

With Hitler's death, the European phase of the war was, in reality, over. It had been the most deadly war in U.S. and world history.[8] Casualties on all sides were the highest ever. The Soviet Union led the list, with just over 8,668,000 military personnel killed in battle. All told, they lost more than 22,000,000, including civilians. Germany had 2,050,000 killed in battle but 1,903,000 missing; Poland, 325,000 killed in battle and at least 1.8 million civilians killed; the United Kingdom, nearly 400,000; Yugoslavia, 300,000; Romania, 300,000 military personnel killed; and France, 213,000. The United States, with 16,000,000 men under arms, had 292,000 battle deaths, including those in other theaters....

INTRODUCTION

This is a story of the final period in the life of SS General Ernst Kaltenbrunner, chief of the Reich Security Main Office (*Reichssicherheitshauptamt*—RSHA), which contained the Gestapo, Criminal Police, and Intelligence Services—both foreign and domestic (*Sicherheitsdienst*—SD) of the Nazi Reich. The RSHA had assumed such power at the end that all Nazi leaders were wary of it. Among its vast powers, not the least, was its responsibility for assigning people to the dreaded concentration camps and for coordinating the implementation of the annihilation of the European Jews.[9] Under Kaltenbrunner was Adolf Eichmann, the man charged with achieving the "Final Solution of the Jewish Question." Though the majority of the Jews who would die in the Holocaust were already dead by the time Kaltenbrunner came to Berlin in January 1943, Kaltenbrunner was deeply implicated in all annihilation operations that stretched into 1943 and 1944. William Shirer, in his 1984 book on the Nazis, referred to Kaltenbrunner as "the greatest killer of them all."[10]

A [major] reason for writing this story is the continuing public interest in the Nazi period of World War II and by the stream of books on this critical period of world history, including a book entitled *Ernst Kaltenbrunner: Ideological Soldier of the Third Reich.*[11] This account serves to help complete that story.

A more basic reason for writing about Kaltenbrunner and the RSHA is that it will serve to let us not forget too easily and too soon the bloodiest period in all annals. This story then deals with the

Left to right: Heinrich Himmler, Mauthausen camp commandant Franz Ziereis, Ernst Kaltenbrunner—at Mauthausen, likely summer 1942. Photo by Heinrich Hoffmann and given to Matteson at the start of the Nuremberg Trials. The photo was used as proof that Kaltenbrunner had knowledge of, and visited, a Nazi concentration camp. Photo courtesy of Wisconsin Veterans Museum—from Matteson's WW2 scrapbook titled "Kaltenbrunner + World War II + Nuremberg Trial."

capture and trial at Nuremberg of the yet little-known Nazi police-state leader, Ernst Kaltenbrunner, and his organization, the RSHA, one of the most diabolical organizations man has created.

The names of Reinhard Heydrich (who headed the RSHA from its creation in 1939 until his assassination by British-trained Czech agents in 1942) and Ernst Kaltenbrunner (who was its chief from 1943 until the war ended) are not well known to the general public. Their names and photographs were purposely kept out of public print by the Nazis because of the secret and sinister nature of their work. Even after I had found Kaltenbrunner hiding out in a cabin on top of the Dead Mountains in Austria in May 1945, and until the start of the Nuremberg Trial in November 1945, the American press persisted in publishing the wrong picture of Kaltenbrunner for the simple reason that they didn't have one.[12] When at the Nuremberg trial, I asked Heinrich Hoffmann, Hitler's personal photographer, for prints of Kaltenbrunner from his extensive official collection, Hoffmann at first could not produce a single negative.[13]

As Justice Robert Jackson, the United States prosecutor at the Nuremberg trial, said of him: "Kaltenbrunner, the grand inquisitor, took up the bloody mantle of Heydrich to stifle opposition and terrorize compliance, and buttressed the power of National Socialism on a foundation of guiltless corpses.... Where, for example, shall we find the hand that ran the concentration camps if it is not the hand of Kaltenbrunner?"[14]

Himmler and Heydrich, Berlin, 1938. *Scherl/Süddeutsche Zeitung*, Himmler and Heydrich, 1938, Alamy stock photo C45CB1.

Condemned to death and then sentenced to hang by the International Military Tribunal at Nuremberg, Ernst Kaltenbrunner, to the Nazis in power, was well known as a symbol of terror. Kaltenbrunner was "one of the most evil spirits among the little group who guided Germany's destiny in those days.... In the final phase, Kaltenbrunner spent several hours every day with the Führer and did all he could to work him up to continue the course upon which he had embarked so long ago."[15] As the American prosecution stated in its original trial brief, "He [Kaltenbrunner] wrote his name in blood—a name to be remembered as a symbol for cruelty, degradation, and death."

Alt Aussee, oil painting by the late Horst Jandl of Altaussee, Austria. Painting purchased by Robert and Jane Matteson. High-resolution photo of painting by Ned Foster.

CHAPTER ONE
Gathering Intelligence

As of 3 May 1945, my only information was that Kaltenbrunner was Number One on our CIC Automatic List, but we had no idea where he was. We also knew that there was something called the National [Alpine] Redoubt in the Salzburg-Berchtesgaden area where Hitler might make his last stand.[16]

On May 3rd, I, a special agent in charge of a CIC team, was covering the area of the 318th Regiment of the 80th Infantry Division, Third Army. Little did I know on May 3rd that Kaltenbrunner was in charge of the National Redoubt, that there was a large counterfeiting operation in the Ebensee concentration camp, that there was hidden art treasure in the Alt Aussee salt mine,[17] that there was an underwater rocket experiment station at Toplitzsee [lake high in the Austrian Alps], that Eichmann was in Alt Aussee reporting to Kaltenbrunner, that Otto Skorzeny was also there reporting to Kaltenbrunner, that puppet governors from all over Europe were hiding out there, that an artist colony took refuge in Alt Aussee, and that Prince Hohenlohe had his residence there.

The war was coming to a close, and the 80th Division had just been ordered back from its meeting place with the Russian troops at Steyr, Austria, on the Enns River to an area about 60 kilometers north of the center of the National Redoubt area. To us at that time, there was nothing mythical about either the Werwolves [Nazi resistance force operating behind enemy lines] or the National Redoubt. General Walter Bedell Smith, Eisenhower's chief of staff, stated that "the Alpine area contained the mysterious National Redoubt where we had every reason to believe the Nazis intended to make their last stand among the crags."

From the time that the Siegfried Line [German defensive line] was broken until the end of the war, all of our intelligence pointed to the area in the Austrian Alps that lay east, south, and southwest of Salzburg as the fortress for the final Götterdämmerung ["Twilight of the Gods," which means, in this context, ultimate destruction] for all remaining Nazi fanatics. Reconnaissance photographs revealed that the Nazis were installing bunkers, ammunition, and supply depots in this mountainous region. Interrogations of military and political prisoners alike indicated that the Berlin officers, high-ranking Nazi Party leaders, and SS troops were moving to the Redoubt, leaving the Wehrmacht to stem the Allied advance.

General Eisenhower, in his report to the Combined Chiefs of Staff on 26 April 1945, said, "Prior to the Allied advance across Central Germany, evidence had been received that the government was preparing to evacuate Berlin and move southward ultimately perhaps to Berchtesgaden in the National Redoubt, ... but with the Allied link-up on the Elbe [River], it was too late. An impossible barrier had been drawn across the country, and the way to the Redoubt was cut off. The possibility remained that it would be the scene of a desperate stand by the fanatical elements of the armies south of the dividing line, together with those which might retreat northward out of Italy."[18]

Kaltenbrunner had had a meeting at Königssee in April on this subject with General Paul Winter, Chief of Operations Staff South, and Field Marshal Albert Kesselring, who was in charge of the Wehrmacht forces in the south.[19] According to Eisenhower's account of the war, 100 divisions, including the bulk of the remaining armored divisions and SS, might be concentrated in the Redoubt. He described it as extending 240 miles in length and 80 miles in width—bounded on the north by the Bavarian plains, on the south by the Dolomites and the Carnic Alps, on the east by the Soviet frontier, and on the west by the western half of Austria and small parts of Germany (including Berchtesgaden) and northern Italy.

The First Lead on Kaltenbrunner's Whereabouts

On May 5th, Sydney Bruskin (Syd) of New Haven, Connecticut (a CIC agent interpreter working with me), and I happened to arrest a Nazi Ortsgruppenleiter, the party leader of the [Austrian] village of Vorchdorf who had indisputable information that August Eigruber, Gauleiter [Nazi Party District Leader] who also served as the Upper Austrian Defense Commissar, had two days previously passed through Vorchdorf on his way to the fashionable resort town of Gmunden on the Traunsee, a mountain lake in the foothills of the Austrian Alps, about 60 kilometers due east of Salzburg. A Gauleiter was considered "good fishing," for there were only seven in Austria but up to 90 in early spring in the Greater Reich. So though Gmunden was beyond our prescribed area, we started off in pursuit.

In Gmunden, we contacted the Austrian police and were told that during the past week, SS Obergruppenführer [General] Dr. Ernst Kaltenbrunner, Dr. Robert Ley (Reichsleiter, leader of the German Labor Front), and Eigruber had passed through Gmunden. This was our first lead on Kaltenbrunner. Also in this area, in April, was Baldur von Schirach, head of the Hitler youth and former Gauleiter of Vienna. But we didn't know this at the time. They were headed for the heart of the Redoubt in the Salzkammergut, a mountainous region extending from [Lake] Attersee through St. Wolfgang and Bad Ischl to Bad Aussee in the Steiermark [Styria, a state in southeast Austria].

The Ebensee Concentration Camp

"The morning reveille always began with loud yells; 'Get up! *Raus*! (Get out)'. They [SS] used rubber hoses to make us move faster. Occasionally, I suffered these painful blows to my weak, emaciated body.... By late March [1945], there was a hint of spring in the air. I caught a glimpse of some birds during roll call. The birds were freer than we were; they could simply fly over the fence and go their own ways. How I envied them! ... Sunday, May 6, 1945, was the day of my liberation: a day that will always live with me; a day forever etched in my memory. For the first time in almost three years, I was neither awakened by the shouts of either the *Kapo* or the block leader, nor did I receive any blows...."

—Samuel Goetz, author of *I Never Saw My Face* and 16-year-old Ebensee inmate. [20]

The chase was now getting hotter. We were in the Redoubt area. On May 6th, we reached Ebensee [in Austria] and the Ebensee concentration camp, as did a tank battalion [led by General Patton's 3rd Army 3rd Cavalry's Robert B. Persinger—see Appendix C]. The guards had left a few hours before we arrived. Ebensee, established in the autumn of 1943, was a subcamp of the Mauthausen concentration camp constructed under Kaltenbrunner's general supervision when he was the Higher SS and Police Leader for Vienna, Upper Austria and Salzburg; it seemed more horrible than Dachau or Ohrdruf. Bodies walked around that I would never had believed could exist. They were covered with sores and lice. Filth was indescribable. The rooms adjacent to the crematorium were piled high with nude, shrunken bodies. Over them was thrown lye to combat the stench and vermin.

Worse than the crematorium was the hospital. Here lay the sick and dying before being carted off to the crematorium. As we entered the hospital, the inmates put out their hands and begged for food. We had none to give them, and they broke down and sobbed, "We have been waiting for you for four, five, and six years; now you come empty-handed!" We couldn't make them understand that the American medical and military government would soon be moving in to care for them. The beds in the hospital were no beds at all. They were shelves covered with rags on which two or three inmates huddled like mice to keep warm. In another part of the enclosure was the burying ditch. Here, the excess of bodies that couldn't be handled by the crematorium

Hospital Inmate of Ebensee Concentration Camp, Austria. Photo by Sydney Bruskin, 6 May 1945. Courtesy of Phyllis Bausher, daughter of Sydney Bruskin.

were dumped by the wagonload into open pits filled with a chemical solution.

The Austrian Freedom Movement

May 7th brought us closer to the man who had primary responsibility for sending people to the concentration camps. We entered Bad Ischl, the home of Franz Lehar, composer of "The Merry Widow" waltz, and the former summer home of the Emperor Franz Joseph I. At this point, we were 16 kilometers farther into the Redoubt with no sign of resistance. Here, we ran into Sepp Plieseis, leader in the local Austrian Freedom Movement (Österreichische Freiheitsbewegung).

The Freedom Movement had sprung up in Austria in opposition to the Nazis and was of invaluable aid to us in CIC in tracking down the Nazi leaders. I know from my own experience that about 80 percent of the arrests of Intelligence, SS, Gestapo, and party leaders we made in Austria at that time were due directly from leads we received from the Austrian Freedom Movement.

Sepp Plieseis informed us that he had it on reliable authority that, at that moment, Kaltenbrunner and his wife were in Strobl, a town 10 kilometers west of Bad Ischl. He suggested that I accompany him in his car to Strobl and that we would be followed by a second car in which he said would be Archduke Anton of Habsburg and other members of the Freedom Movement. Although I was somewhat suspicious of this arrangement, which had been so quickly planned by this resistance leader, I accepted and told Syd to get busy organizing an informant net in Bad Ischl.

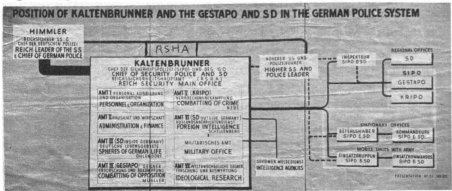

Diagram courtesy of Wisconsin Veterans Museum—from Matteson's WW2 scrapbook titled "Kaltenbrunner + World War II + Nuremberg Trial."

The Importance of Kaltenbrunner and the RSHA

Up to this time, the only information I had on Kaltenbrunner was that he was the highest priority on our CIC automatic arrest. Few people, even today, are cognizant of the RSHA, which included within its organization the well-publicized Gestapo (Geheime Staatspolizei) or Secret State Police, the Kripo (Kriminalpolizei) or Criminal Police, the Internal and Foreign SD (Sicherheitsdienst—SD-Inland and SD-Ausland) or Intelligence Services. In addition, the RSHA contained the unit that coordinated and kept statistical track of the annihilation of the European Jews under Eichmann. This unit was a section of the Gestapo. The sabotage section of the RSHA under Otto Skorzeny, were a part of the SD-Ausland.

Kaltenbrunner came from a family of master craftsmen based in the Upper Austrian village of Micheldorf near Braunau am Inn, Hitler's birthplace. Kaltenbrunner was born 4 October 1903 in Ried im Innkreis, Upper Austria. He attended elementary school in Raab and moved to Linz to attend Gymnasium (academic high school). In 1921, he began his law studies at the university in Graz, earning his degree as a doctor of jurisprudence in 1926. Kaltenbrunner's grandfather Karl was the first attorney in the family. Kaltenbrunner's father, Hugo Kaltenbrunner, and then Kaltenbrunner, also became lawyers.

During his university days, Kaltenbrunner joined a German nationalist dueling fraternity and was considered a skilled swordsman. Upon graduation, he practiced law in Linz for a few years, but by 1929 he had joined the Upper Austrian Home Guard (Heimwehr), a fascist paramilitary unit and then, in 1931, switched over to the Austrian Nazi Party and its paramilitary formation, the Schutzstaffel (SS) in Linz. Kaltenbrunner served both the Party and SS as a District Speaker and as a legal advisor; by 1933, he had become commander of the Linz SS Sturm [company]. After the Austrian government of Engelbert Dollfuss banned the Nazi Party and its formations throughout Austria in response to terrorist attacks in May 1933, Kaltenbrunner was arrested in January 1934. Incarcerated in a detention camp by the Dollfuss government for his activities in the now illegal Nazi Party, he was released in May 1934, but for tactical reasons refrained from participation in the July 1934 Nazi putsch in Austria, during which Dollfuss was murdered. An investigation of Kaltenbrunner's connection with Dollfuss was conducted by Dr. Benz, an Austrian police official. The investigation was never conclusive, but it is significant that when the German Army seized power in Austria, the name of Dr. Benz was the first on the purge list. Dr. Benz was murdered by Kaltenbrunner's SS men on the same day the invasion began.[21]

By 1937, Kaltenbrunner had become the leader of the underground SS throughout all of Austria and managed the SD intelligence network in the country. In the wake of Hitler's threats to Austrian Chancellor Kurt von Schuschnigg at Berchtesgaden on February 12, 1938, and increasing agitation thereafter by various Nazi formations in Austria, Schuschnigg agreed to name Nazi sympathizer Arthur Seyss-lnquart Minister of Interior. The Deutsche Polizei of 15 May 1943 admitted that Kaltenbrunner's SS was a decisive factor in the annexation, and for this, Kaltenbrunner was rewarded with the post of State Secretary for Security Matters in the new Nazi cabinet, established on March 11, 1938, under Seyss-lnquart's leadership.[22]

On the day of annexation, Hitler promoted Kaltenbrunner to brigadier general of the SS, and later that year, he was made Higher SS and Police Leader of Germany's Wehrkreis XVII, which comprised Vienna and the former Austrian provinces of Upper Austria, Lower Austria, Salzburg, and the northern half of the Burgenland.

In April 1941, Kaltenbrunner was promoted to major general in the SS and was awarded the high Nazi decorations: the Gold Nazi Party Badge and the Blutorden [Blood Order award]. In 1938, he had already been appointed a member of the Nazi Reichstag. On 30 January 1943, Hitler appointed Kaltenbrunner to one of the most influential positions in Nazi Germany, chief of the RSHA, a position known also as chief of Security Police [Sicherheitspolizei – SIPO] and Security Service [Sicherheitsdienst—SD].

In this position, as indicated earlier, he was successor to Heydrich, who had died of wounds sustained in an assassination attempt on 27 May 1942. So well did Kaltenbrunner perform his job as chief of the RSHA that on 9 December 1944, Hitler bestowed on him one of the highest military decorations—The Knights Cross of the War Merit Cross with Swords [Ritterkreuz des Kriegsverdienstkreuzes]. By that time, he had been promoted to the rank of SS general.

One of Kaltenbrunner's key accomplishments from the perspective of the SS was the unification of all Reich political intelligence agencies. After February 1944, the RSHA incorporated the Office Foreign Intelligence [Amt Auslands/Abwehr] of the High Command of the Armed Forces [Oberkommando der Wehrmacht—OKW], formerly under Admiral Wilhelm Canaris, who was executed under RSHA decree on 9 April 1945 for his connections with the conservative resistance against Hitler, even though there was no evidence that Canaris participated—either actively or passively—in the 20 July 1944 putsch.

Within the Nazi police state, the RSHA had become, toward the end, the most powerful and important agency in existence, responsible for all foreign and domestic intelligence (combining the functions of our FBI and CIA) for the elimination of all opposition to the totalitarian state within the Reich and occupied countries, and for espionage and sabotage at home and abroad. It had responsibility for the fate of prisoners incarcerated in the concentration camps and played a significant role in identifying, apprehending, and annihilating the European Jews.

Walter Schellenberg—former Nazi Party intelligence operative who testified as a witness at the Nuremberg Trials. Photo by Kurt Alber (Wikimedia Commons, CC-BY-SA 3.0).

As indicated earlier, the chief of the RSHA, from its formation in September 1939 until his assassination in June 1942, had been Reinhard Heydrich, "the Hangman," generally considered to be the most intelligent and ruthless man in the Nazi Reich. The chief of the RSHA—Heydrich's successor from January 1943 until the end of the war—was Kaltenbrunner.

Walter Schellenberg, chief of the Nazi Foreign Intelligence under Kaltenbrunner and confidant of Himmler, testified under oath at Nuremberg (18 November

Wilhelm Höttl—former Nazi Party intelligence operative who testified as a witness at the Nuremberg Trials. https://www.ns-archiv.de/imt/ps2601-ps2800/2738-ps.php

1945): "So powerful had Kaltenbrunner become toward the end that even Himmler feared him," remarked Schellenberg (Document number 1990-P.S. U.S. Chief of Consul).[23] Dr. Wilhelm Höttl, whom I later arrested in Alt Aussee and who was an American prosecution witness at Nuremberg as deputy chief of the Nazi Balkan Intelligence Net, stated in an interrogation at the Third Army Intelligence Center, "Kaltenbrunner ranked with Hitler, Himmler, and Bormann as one of the most powerful leaders in the Reich."

Strobl and the Arrest of Frau Kaltenbrunner

On May 7, 1945, the road between Bad Ischl and Strobl was clogged with remnants of the fanatic Sixth SS Panzer Army retreating before the Russians. But accompanied by personnel with the German Army uniform, we were not bothered. Anyway, the war was almost at an end, and the main bulk of the SS and Wehrmacht were glad to see the end of continued resistance. What worried us at that time were the Werwolves [*Werwolf* was the Nazi plan to create armed resistance beginning in 1944 behind enemy lines as the Allies marched farther into Germany], snipers, and the Underground Resistance.

In Strobl, we contacted the Bürgermeister, Hans Girbl, who, in a trembling voice, admitted that the Kaltenbrunner party had been staying at an estate at the outskirts of the town. We parked the two cars on the parkway at the entrance to the grounds and walked up to the house. As we approached, I noticed that several men in civilian clothes came out of the woods and were following us. I was soon to find out that they belonged to the Kaltenbrunner Dienststelle assigned to the protection of Kaltenbrunner.

At the house, I was greeted by a large, blonde woman of about 38 years who immediately admitted that she was Mrs. Ernst Kaltenbrunner. With her were three young children but no husband. I informed her that she was under arrest pending further interrogation. On a shelf in the living room, I found the first photograph of Kaltenbrunner. In the meantime, I noticed that the men in civilian clothes outside had gathered near the entrance. Escorting Mrs. Kaltenbrunner, we walked down to the car, still followed by the civilian men. At the car, they finally broke their silence. The leader, in perfect English, informed me that his group had been given personal instructions by General Kaltenbrunner to safeguard Mrs. Kaltenbrunner and the children. He said that only the day before, an order from General Eisenhower had come over the radio instructing all civilians to turn their weapons in to the local Bürgermeister. Like dutiful Germans, they had all surrendered their weapons and had no means of carrying out their orders; the will to resist was gone.

The First Description of Kaltenbrunner

I took Mrs. Kaltenbrunner back to Bad Ischl and from there back to the 80th Division CP [Company Post] at Vöcklabruck for interrogation. The information we were able to elicit from Mrs. Kaltenbrunner, a cold intellectual sort of person, was scanty. But with the information we had from our informant net in Bad Ischl, we were certain that the center of the National Redoubt area was in the vicinity of the mountain town of Alt Aussee, 30 kilometers south of Bad Ischl, well up in the Dead Mountain range of the Austrian Alps.

In addition to the photograph, Mrs. Kaltenbrunner did provide us with the following information: Kaltenbrunner, age 43, stood six feet, four inches tall, weighed 220 pounds, had deep scars on both sides of his face from duels at the University of Graz, and presented dark features and a powerful build. He had been at Strobl on May 3rd (really May 7th), she said, and had had a meeting there with various personalities. Finally, she said Kaltenbrunner did know the Alt Aussee area well from periodic summer visits during his previous tenure as the "Little Himmler" of Austria. On the basis of this information from Frau Kaltenbrunner, the G-2 [brigadier general, military intelligence] of the 80th Infantry Division was informed, and I was instructed to accompany Major Ralph Pearson and his task force (three platoons of tanks and infantry of the 2nd Battalion of the 318th Regiment) into Alt Aussee to safeguard the art treasure in the Alt Aussee salt mines. I didn't know then that the Austrian Freedom Movement (Albrecht Gaiswinkler) had alerted the headquarters of the 80th Infantry Division about the art treasures stored in the salt mines.

Postcard of Alt Aussee from Matteson's WW2 scrapbook titled "Kaltenbrunner + World War II + Nuremberg Trial." Courtesy of Wisconsin Veterans Museum..

Aerial view from the west of the Altausseer See and the town of Altaussee (Alt Aussee). Photo by Carsten Steger (Wikimedia Commons, CC-BY-SA 4.0).

Alt Aussee and Prince Chlodwig Hohenlohe

I left Vöcklabruck at 3:00 a.m. on May 9th, en route to picking up Syd Bruskin in Gmunden and joining the task force of Major Ralph Pearson in Alt Aussee. As we drove up over the Pötschen Pass, it was difficult to keep our minds on the mission, so beautiful was the scenery. The road up followed a rushing mountain stream that cascaded merrily down the rocks in steep descent, its spray sparkling in the early morning sun. Above us and around us were snow-capped peaks, and on the green-covered Alps, brilliant displays of brightly colored mountain flowers. It was hard to realize that the sun that morning shone down on an Austria that had been at war until the previous day, and that my mission was to track down an Austrian native son who had been labeled by the press "the Gas Chamber and Atrocity Expert" of the Nazi Reich.

We left Bad Aussee and ascended the last four kilometers of mountain road into Alt Aussee at 8:30 a.m. into a town, an atmosphere and an experience I shall never forget. The town of Alt Aussee, a population [at that time] of 4,000 people, lay at the end of a winding road—the last village that can be reached by jeep in the ascent of the Dead Mountains. The town hugged the west shore of the deep, cold Alt Ausseer See [today Altausseer See]. Flanking the lake on the east was the Trisselwand peak, and on the north, the Loser Alm. Across to the south was the snow-capped summit of the Dachstein range.

To the Viennese, Alt Aussee was what Lake Tahoe was to Californians. And at that time, it was the center of the National

Dachstein Mountains. Photo credit: Wikimedia Commons, CC-BY-SA 3.0.

Redoubt. Three Gauleiters: Henlein, Jury, and Eigruber, had their summer homes there.

Prince Chlodwig [zu] Hohenlohe-Schillingsfurst, the largest landowner in the Salzkammergut region, lived there. Chlodwig's grandfather had been chancellor of Germany after Bismarck in the 1890s. Chlodwig was the third child of the eighth Prince of Hohenlohe-Schillingsfurst. He was born in Alt Aussee in 1897 and died in 1967. His family was in the Waldenburg-Schillingsfurst branch of Hohenlohe, originally from Franconia-Mayenne. Chlodwig's grandmother, Maria, was the one who had insisted that the chancellor buy land in Alt Aussee for hunting purposes. Chlodwig's relative, Prince Max Hohenlohe, was used by the SD in Spain and has been called the "most elegant figure in international espionage."

Prince Hohenloe at home in Alt Aussee. Photo from Matteson's self-published 1993 booklet titled "The Capture and Last Days of SS General Ernst Kaltenbrunner."

Prince Chlodwig had his own Nazi connections, as indicated by the fact that Kaltenbrunner and his mistress were housed in his guesthouse and that Adolf Eichmann and his family lived in another house on the lake owned by Hohenlohe. He also owned the building used by the local Nazis as their headquarters.

Prince Hohenlohe was the first person we encountered in Alt Aussee. He made obvious attempts to ingratiate himself. He secured living quarters for us in the Hotel Eibl and office quarters in one of his buildings down the street (ironically, the local Nazi Party headquarters). He invited us to tea and apologized for his poor hospitality by saying that the Nazis made him live in his barn. Actually, the accommodations were as comfortable as a modern New York apartment. He invited me to dinner, and as I signed his guest book I noticed four pages had been torn out.

Prince Hohenlohe had lived in New York City from 1928 until 1937. He had gone there to marry a prominent Philadelphian socialite, Mabel Taylor Cochran, divorced from Gifford Cochran, a carpet manufacturer. Chlodwig was later divorced in 1939 from Mabel Cochran. He was well known and well liked by New York's international social set, but later arrested by me for interrogation.

Eichmann

I established an informant net based on the persons listed on the CIC "white list" (list of anti-Nazis) and the most intelligent, trustworthy members of the Freedom Movement. This latter group was headed by Johann Brandauer, assistant Bürgermeister of Alt Aussee. Rumors were rife that Kaltenbrunner, Robert Ley—the Nazi labor leader, SS Kreisleiter [district leader] Stichnot of Gmunden, Gauleiter Eigruber, and Otto Skorzeny, together with strong groups of SS troops and high-ranking SS officers, were hiding out in the recesses of the Dead Mountains.

Adolph Eichmann. Photo from United States Holocaust Memorial Museum. Credit: Heritage Images

During the days and nights of 9–11 May, Syd and I worked 16 and 18 hours during 24-hour periods. Little did I know at that time that Adolf Eichmann, so prominent in the Holocaust, went out the other end of the village as I came in. Eichmann had been a long-time acquaintance of Ernst Kaltenbrunner. Eichmann was born in 1906 in Germany, and his family moved to Linz, Austria, in 1932; he joined the Austrian Nazi Party at the suggestion of Kaltenbrunner. When the Nazi Party was banned in Austria in May 1933, Eichmann fled to Germany and joined the Austrian Legion there. In 1934, he joined Himmler's security service. After 1935, he became the internal SD official responsible for handling issues related to the so-called Jewish question.

Beginning in 1938, Eichmann was in charge of Jewish emigration, and in 1939, he was transferred to Amt IV (Gestapo) in the Security Police Main Office, where he took over Referat IV B4 dealing with

Jewish affairs and evacuation. For the next six years, Eichmann's office was the headquarters for the implementation of the "Final Solution" as applied in Nazi Germany itself, the territory of Germany's Axis partners, and German-occupied Europe with the exceptions of occupied Poland, the occupied Soviet Union and occupied Serbia.

In the late summer of 1941, Eichmann visited Auschwitz in order to advise on methods of killing that could be applied in that facility. At the Wannsee Conference of 20 January 1942, he was present as Heydrich's assistant in keeping statistics on and coordinating final solution operations on behalf of the RSHA. By early May 1945, when he reported to Kaltenbrunner in Alt Aussee, Eichmann had moved his family to Alt Aussee to the See Villa, owned by Prince Hohenlohe. According to Prince Hohenlohe in 1960, when I came into Alt Aussee in early May 1945, Eichmann, on Kaltenbrunner's advice, went out the other end of the village up to the Blaa-Alm. But he surrendered to the Americans under a false name and was incarcerated as a prisoner of war in 1945. Fearing discovery, Eichmann escaped U.S. custody in 1946. From there, he found his way to South America, settling in Argentina in 1950.

Eichmann was tracked down and kidnapped by Israeli secret agents on 13 May 1960 in a suburb of Buenos Aires. Transported to Israel, placed on trial in Jerusalem on 11 April 1961, Eichmann was convicted on 12 December 1961 and sentenced to death three days later. After all appeals had been exhausted, he was hanged shortly after midnight on June 1, 1962.[24]

Skorzeny

Another highly publicized subordinate of Kaltenbrunner, who reported to Kaltenbrunner in Alt Aussee, was Hitler's favorite commando, Otto Skorzeny.

Skorzeny was born in Vienna in 1908. He became a Nazi in 1932. A protégé of Kaltenbrunner, whom he came to know at the time of the Anschluss in Vienna, he was transferred in April 1943 to Amt VI of the RSHA, where his task was to develop a school of warfare dealing with commando operations. In July 1943, he was ordered by Hitler to rescue Mussolini, a captive of the new Italian government. Skorzeny carried out this difficult assignment on 12 September 1943 with the use of glider troops. From the Abruzzi mountains on top of the Gran Sasso, the highest peak in central Italy, Mussolini was carried off by

Otto Skorzeny, with Kaltenbrunner (left) looking on, was greeted by Hitler after the rescue of Mussolini on 12 September 1943. Photo from Bridgeman Images, 1943, PNP1153875.
Credit: Peter Newark Military Pictures / Bridgeman Images

Skorzeny in a light Fieseler-Storch aircraft to Vienna.[25]

In 1943 and 1944, under Kaltenbrunner, Skorzeny engaged in numerous intelligence and sabotage operations on behalf of the SD. Later, in January 1945, he led a special unit consisting of 20–30 Englishspeaking Germans disguised as American soldiers in a [failed] behind-the-lines operation, the objective of which was to cause chaos behind the Allied lines and to kidnap Eisenhower—a rumor spread by some of Skorzeny's men.

In 1945, Skorzeny and his men were engaged in combat and sabotage on the Eastern and, after March, on the Western Front, including the destruction of a Rhine River bridge. Finally, in May 1945, he reported to Kaltenbrunner in Alt Aussee and disappeared into the Dachstein Mountains above Alt Aussee. He was eventually captured by American forces in Styria; tried as a war criminal two years later, Skorzeny was acquitted by an American tribunal at Dachau in 1947. He was rearrested by the Germans but escaped in 1948 to Madrid, from where he engaged in a number of intelligence operations and some neo-Nazi activity for various countries.

In 1951, Skorzeny opened an export-import business in Madrid under the protection of the Franco regime. In 1963, when I was on a speaking tour of Europe, I visited Madrid to speak to the Spanish Foreign Policy Association and to brief the government on arms control. From a *New York Times* article, I learned that Skorzeny was in Madrid, and so I called *The New York Times* correspondent and received Skorzeny's address and phone number.

I called Skorzeny and asked if I could see him. I told him about my background with his boss, Kaltenbrunner, in Alt Aussee, and Skorzeny agreed to see me. I told Skorzeny why I was in Madrid, and he told me he was a member of the board of the Spanish Foreign Policy Association and said he would be at the meeting that night. He came and I met him again, but questions were not allowed. Skorzeny died in Madrid in 1975.

The Kerry Villa: Kaltenbrunner's Headquarters

Our first important contact was with Albrecht Gaiswinkler, alias Georg Schumacher. Gaiswinkler was a native of Bad Aussee. Against his will, he had been drafted into the Wehrmacht. He had served in the Wehrmacht in France in 1944, then deserted, and brought four truckloads of German weapons and ammunition to the French Maquis [French Resistance fighters].

When the Third Army recaptured Alsace in November 1944, Gaiswinkler gave himself up to the Americans. The Americans turned him over to the British for use in the Aussee area, a territory allocated to the British for future occupation. The British trained him in sabotage, parachute jumping, and wireless transmission and flew him to Italy. From there, he was dropped, on 20 April 1945, into the Steiermark—mountainous Ausseerland with a mission of organizing the Freedom Movement and capturing the powerful Bad Aussee radio station.

Through Gaiswinkler, we were able to locate the headquarters of Nazi intelligence for the Redoubt area—the Kerry Villa—and get our hands on Wilhelm Waneck, chief of the Nazi Intelligence Net in southeastern Europe. Waneck and the Waneck Group were operating a wireless transmission station in the Kerry Villa located on a hill on the outskirts of Alt Aussee. By means of this wireless, Waneck kept in contact with the capitals of southeastern Europe and with the islands of Nazi resistance throughout the Redoubt area. As we were to learn later, Waneck was in contact with Kaltenbrunner until the day (10 May 1945) I arrested Waneck.

With Waneck in the Kerry Villa, when I arrested him (and others) on May 10th, was Dr. Werner Göttsch, leader of the so-called "Göttsch Group."[26] Göttsch was still a young man (about 35) who had earned his spurs in covert work for Heydrich and Himmler. His first job had been the organization of minority groups in the Sudetenland [border area of Czechoslovakia] for the purpose of staging revolts against Czech authority. In 1939, he was sent by Heydrich to Breslau to make preparations for creating disorder along the Polish border prior to the Nazi invasion in September. It was his efficient work in helping to provide a pretext for the Nazi's annexation of the Sudetenland and invasion of Poland that started World War II and which then earned him the promotion to chief of the Southeastern Europe Intelligence Net (chief of RSHA Amt VI-E) in 1939.

By the fall of 1939, Göttsch had organized and was operating a wireless transmission net in the Balkans. It was this net that Waneck later took over.

From 1939 to 1943, Göttsch had been a victim of TB [tuberculosis], and during this period became immersed in treatises on mysticism, political theory, astrology, and religion. His outlook on Nazism changed [and he began to secretly oppose it]. In 1943, Kaltenbrunner, at Göttsch's request, transferred him to Amt VII of the RSHA. Amt VII had been created as the research library of the RSHA with the purpose of developing the new Nazi world outlook—Weltanschauung—a published ideological and historical resource in the form of leaflets for members of the Nazi Party.[27]

Himmler took particular interest in Amt VII and had ordered Göttsch to make a study, at one point, of witchcraft in the Middle Ages. At another time, Himmler had ordered Göttsch to collect all books on occultism, astrology, and mysticism and transfer them to the Division of Ancestral Heritage in the SS Headquarters.[28] Many of these books we found in the Kerry Villa.

Waneck, Höttl, Göttsch, and other members of the so-called Austrian clique in the SD Foreign Intelligence Service who proposed to advise Kaltenbrunner in the last months of the war, sought to make contact with non-Nazi personalities in Austria in the hopes of establishing a negotiating partner to offer the Allies an "Austrian" inspired cease-fire in the West in anticipation of a future alliance of all non-Communist forces against the Soviet Union. This was the genesis of the "Free Austria Movement," also known as "Operation Herzog."[29]

Through his mistress Ursula Hegewald, Göttsch was introduced to Franz Popek and Rudolf Raab, leading Vienna socialists. Göttsch enlisted the support of other RSHA operatives: Kurt Auner, the former chief of the SD apparatus in Romania; Herbert Fehland, advisor to Waneck; Bruno Klaus, member of the elitist, conservative former ally to the Nazis, the Kameradschaftsbund (an organization of ethnic Germans in the interwar Czech lands) and the former chief of the SD apparatus in Bulgaria; Hans Boettig, radio operator from the SS Havelinstitut [cover name of RSHA signals center at Berlin-Wannsee];[30] Victor Zeischka, Nazi intelligence operator in Bulgaria; Rupert Mandi, Nazi intelligence operator in Hungary and considered one of the most clever and most dangerous agents of the Nazi intelligence; Dr. Wilhelm Höttl, deputy chief of the Nazi Southeastern Europe Intelligence Service; and Waneck.

Through Gaiswinkler's effective groundwork, I was able to arrest this group [see Appendix D], seal its headquarters at the Kerry Villa, and stop communication through the wireless transmission set. As we found out later, this put a complete stop to Kaltenbrunner's connection from the Austrian Alps to the outside world.

Hidden Art Treasure and Kaltenbrunner Sympathizers in Alt Aussee

The small mountain town of Alt Aussee, Austria, was a hotbed of fleeing Nazis who sought, for the most part, cover from the approaching American and Russian troops and time for themselves to collect their thoughts and prepare their anti-Nazi alibis. Among others, we arrested in Alt Aussee Dr. Gunther Altenburg, a former Nazi Reich plenipotentiary to Greece; General Erich Alt of the Luftwaffe; and Joseph Heider, who had been designated by Eigruber to blow up the Alt Aussee salt mines. These mines contained paintings from Belgium's Notre Dame Church in Bruges, Austria's St. Florian Monastery, and in Italy, the Abbey of Monte Cassino, among others. Also in the mines: *The Ghent Altarpiece*, the Michaelangelo statue of *Madonna and Child*, Caravaggio's *David and Goliath*, Vermeer's *The Art of Painting*, Bruegel's *Haymaking*, and over 6,000 other paintings, 137 pieces of sculpture, 122 tapestries, 1,600 cases of rare books, and over 500 other cases from all over Europe to be used in the "Great Hitler Museum" to be erected at Linz, Austria.[31]

We also arrested Dr. Hjalmar Mäe, chief of the Nazi puppet state in Estonia; Walter Riedel, Nazi chief of construction for the V-2 weapons at Peenemünde; Ernst Scarguras, secretary to the Nazi Foreign Office in Rome; Spiros Hadji Kyriakos, representative of the National Bank of Greece after the German occupation; William Knothe, general consul of the German Foreign Office; Dr. Carlos Wetzell, chief of the German Pharmaceutical Industry; and Dr. Bálint Hóman, Minister of Religion and Education in the Hungarian government between 1932 and 1942.

Gisela Von Westarp: Kaltenbrunner's Mistress

I must mention, finally, another group because they have a direct bearing on the Kaltenbrunner story. That is the group of Countess Gisela von Westarp, Iris Scheidler, and Dr. Rudolf Praxmarer, formerly Iris's husband. Gisela von Westarp was Kaltenbrunner's mistress. She came from an old-line Prussian military family. She had married, at the age of 17, Wehrmacht Officer [Paul] Wolf, who was killed in action in Africa. Inbred with Nazism and the principles of the Nazi Party organization for girls, the BDM (the "League of German Girls"), she took a job as secretary in Heinrich Himmler's headquarters in Berlin.

When Kaltenbrunner moved from Vienna to Berlin in early 1943 as chief of the RSHA, she became acquainted with him. At that time, she was 22 years old, a pretty blonde with blue eyes, a vivacious personality, and intelligent. On 23 March 1945, she gave birth to twins by Kaltenbrunner in what she described as a "cowshed" in Alt Aussee. Actually, it was Prince Hohenlohe's guesthouse that had been converted from a cowshed. In a letter that I obtained, written by her to her mother describing the event, she declared proudly that by producing twins for Kaltenbrunner, she "almost deserves the Mother's Cross." She goes on to point out that Mrs. Kaltenbrunner, in 12 years, had been able to produce only three children while she had already given birth to two in a year and a half. She had three children in all, for she had had a boy, Jens, by her former husband.

Iris Scheidler, 30 years old, the wife of Arthur Scheidler, Kaltenbrunner's adjutant and formerly Heydrich's adjutant, was an attractive brunette called the "Venus of Vienna." She has been referred to by people who knew her as the "first spy of the Nazi Government." She was the social type, seemingly more intent on having a good time than on espionage. She was a very good friend of many personages in the Hitler inner circle, especially of Heinrich Hoffmann, Hitler's photographer who had introduced Hitler to Eva Braun.

Others in Hitler's inner circle were Baldur von Schirach (also tried at Nuremberg), the Hitler youth leader and later Gauleiter of Vienna; Eva Braun, Hitler's mistress; and Hermann Fegelein, SS general and liaison officer between Hitler and Himmler, whose wife was Eva Braun's sister. Gisela was also a friend of these same people and others, including Dr. Karl Brandt, Hitler's personal physician, whom she told me proudly was godfather to one of the twins.

Countess Gisela von Westarp (left) and Iris Scheidler. Photo courtesy of Wisconsin Veterans Museum—from Matteson's WW2 scrapbook titled "Kaltenbrunner + World War II + Nuremberg Trial."

Dr. Praxmarer, the divorced husband of Iris, was formerly a prominent physician in Vienna. He had been a classmate and friend of Kaltenbrunner at the University of Graz. Praxmarer was the SS chief of the hospitals in Alt Aussee and the Ortskommandant (military leader of Alt Aussee). He was about 50 years old, apparently had a genial personality, and had a reputation for being a great sportsman. Though Iris and Praxmarer were divorced, they still had great affection for each other.

Kaltenbrunner's Intelligence Services

Kaltenbrunner, by order of Himmler, on 18 April 1945, became commander-in-chief of all unoccupied Southern Europe, which meant southern Germany, northern Italy, western Bohemia, and Austria. Himmler commanded the remaining forces remaining in Northern Europe and, as I learned later from Count Folke Bernadotte of Sweden, tried to use these as bargaining power in a surrender to the Western Allies.

Kaltenbrunner, upon assuming command of the forces in the southern regions, had already reorganized the Intelligence Services. [In May 1945,] I somehow received a copy of SHAEF's [Supreme Headquarters Allied Expeditionary Force – headquarters of General Dwight D. Eisenhower] classified document of April 1945 from the Counter Intelligence War Room in London, which had the best information yet available to me on the RSHA and the German Intelligence Service. This was an alarming document; it portrayed a scenario of resistance by the RSHA, including Skorzeny, which showed why Eisenhower and his chief of staff, Walter Bedell Smith, were genuinely worried about the Alpine Redoubt and the mysterious Werwolves.

The classified information indicated that Skorzeny's troops would be able to disappear into the Alpine Redoubt with their personnel and equipment in large enough numbers to continue resistance. They would be aided by other SS units experienced in partisan warfare. To these would be added thousands of non-German collaborators who had retreated with the German armies. Most of their military personnel had already been incorporated into Skorzeny's SS Jagdverband or into the SS Charlemagne division.[32] Like the Nazi leaders, they expected to be executed and so would resist to the end. The document went on to say that within Germany and Austria, the first phase would be terrorism—nighttime hit-and-run assaults on Allied troops and supplies. General sabotage should be expected. Skorzeny's units would also organize commando-type raids with the object of killing or assassinating key figures.

The document, based on all available intelligence, then outlined for the first time the organization of the RSHA related to the power struggle between Admiral Canaris's Abwehr, the intelligence arm of the German military, and Kaltenbrunner's RSHA, particularly Amt VI of the RSHA under Schellenberg. It stated that the struggle had come to a head in 1944 when Canaris was dismissed, and the Abwehr was dissolved and then recreated as the Military Office (Amt Mil.) of the RSHA. Thus, the defeat of the Abwehr was complete before Kaltenbrunner was assigned by Hitler the job of rooting out the conspirators for the 20 July 1944 plot against Hitler.

The classified document described the RSHA as having seven Amts or offices: Amts I and II – Administration; Amt III – Security and Intelligence within the Reich under Otto Ohlendorf (like our FBI); Amt IV—Secret State Police—Gestapo, under Heinrich Müller; Amt V – Kripo or Criminal Police under Arthur Nebe; Amt VI – Foreign Intelligence (similar to our CIA) under Schellenberg; Amt VII – Culture and Ideology, including Occultism, under Göttsch; and the Militärische Amt or former Abwehr under Colonel Georg Hansen until July 20, 1944.

Under Amt VI came Skorzeny. However, Skorzeny, an Austrian like Kaltenbrunner, assumed a certain independence as the terrorist and sabotage leader and often reported directly to Kaltenbrunner. Therefore, the three principal functions of the RSHA were: 1) internal security, including internal intelligence on moods of the population; 2) implementing Nazi population policy, including the annihilation of the Jews, Roma [also known as Gypsies], Soviet prisoners of war, Soviet leadership cadres, and crushing resistance of all kinds in German occupied territory; and 3) foreign intelligence, including sabotage. At that time (April 1945), there was little information on the RSHA's role in connection with the Einsatzkommandos (subgroup of the Einsatzgruppen) in the east, or even on Eichmann.

Amt III had its SD stations and agents throughout the so-called Greater German Reich [Germany, Austria, the Sudetenland, annexed regions of Slovenia and of Poland] and in every sphere of German life, including the Gestapo and civilian administration. Not even

Goebbels nor Göring could be certain who in their departments were RSHA agents. It was these agents who contributed to Heydrich's notorious file on all leaders of the German Reich, including Hitler, much like the files on various political leaders in the United States kept by the FBI's J. Edgar Hoover.

Amt IV (the Gestapo), as with Amt III, had regional and local police offices throughout the Reich, and the two agencies cooperated closely in identifying and arresting actual and potential opponents of the Nazi regime. The Gestapo frequently acted on the basis of Amt III reports in identifying opponents, though it also had its own network of undercover police officers and informants. Along with Amt V, the Reich Criminal Police Office, it had the authority to arrest and incarcerate persons in concentration camps for indefinite periods of time, and outside of judicial review. The Gestapo maintained a card index file on individuals suspected of actual or potential opposition, or who otherwise were deemed to represent a danger to the German Reich and its people.[33] According to the London War Room document, the power of the Gestapo within Germany was unlimited: "It makes arrests, tortures, and executes. It supervises concentration camps, censors telephones, telegraph, and mail, and may intervene whenever it chooses."

Amt V (the Kripo), under command of Arthur Nebe, was responsible for fighting crime in Germany, the annexed and occupied territories. It also managed the annihilation of the Roma population in occupied Europe and was deeply involved with the murder of persons with physical and intellectual disabilities residing in institutions in the Greater German Reich. The Criminal Police worked closely with the Gestapo.[34]

Amt VI (the foreign intelligence arm, SD Ausland), like the other offices of the RSHA, was divided into sections with letter designations. In the case of Amt VI, VI B covered Western Continental Europe and West Africa; VI C – Eastern Balkans, USSR, Near and Far East; VI D – United Kingdom, U.S., South America, and Scandinavia; VI E – Southeastern Europe; VI F – Technical Section (FAK—*Frontaufklaerungskommando* and FAT—*Frontaufklaerungstrupp*) units attached to operations crossing borders as well as involving stay-behind agents); VI G-Research; VI S-Sabotage (Skorzeny); VI Wi-Economic Intelligence; Z-Counterespionage.

Amt VI-E was largely Austrian under Waneck and Höttl, who often reported directly to Kaltenbrunner. VI-F supplied forged documents, secret inks, wireless, and sabotage equipment. Amt VI officers were attached undercover to each German embassy. For example, Nazi Ludwig Carl Moyzisch, of Operation Cicero (1950) fame in Ankara, Turkey, was one of them. Moyzisch wrote the book to explain his Ankara secret service work involving Elyesa Bazna (SD code name "Cicero"), valet for British ambassador Sir Hughe Knatchbull-Hugessen.

Kaltenbrunner placed Skorzeny in command of Groups VI-F and VI-S and Militärische Amt D (sabotage and insurrection in enemy territory), Group E (secret communications, especially wireless transmissions), and Group G (forged documents, invisible inks, Minox cameras).

Kaltenbrunner's Last Message to Hitler

However, press them as we did, we could secure no further information from the Göttsch-Waneck group about Kaltenbrunner's present whereabouts, other than he had been at Alt Aussee on May 3rd. It was through the Kerry Villa wireless station that Kaltenbrunner, up until the last week of April, had contact with Fegelein and through Fegelein with Himmler and Hitler. This wireless station was in contact with the station at Haid (near Linz) in Upper Austria, which was a station for the entire RSHA in communication with Kaltenbrunner and Himmler at the time.

Over this network, Kaltenbrunner sent his last radio message to Fegelein, a copy of which I later found at the Wildensee hut and that was to be used against Kaltenbrunner at Nuremberg as proof, despite his denial, that he personally attended to matters concerning the liquidation of Jews and political and concentration camp internees. It read: "Radio message to Gruppenführer Fegelein, Headquarters of the Führer through Sturmbannführer Sansoni, Berlin.—Please report to Reich's Führer SS [Himmler] and to the Führer that all arrangements against Jews, political and concentration camp internees in the Protectorate have been taken care of by me personally today. The situation itself there is one of calmness, fear of Soviet successes, and hope of an occupation by the Western enemies ... Kaltenbrunner."

Kaltenbrunner had been ordered by Himmler to wipe out all

concentration camps before the Allied occupation so as to remove any evidence of war crimes. By "taken care of," Kaltenbrunner meant the orders for their liquidation had been sent. [35]

The Göttsch-Waneck Plan for a Free Austria

One final word about the Göttsch-Waneck group I must insert here, for it pertains to a fantastic plan of this Free Austrian Movement that Kaltenbrunner and the Göttsch-Waneck-Höttl coterie were to use as their alibi at a later date. Since 1943, Göttsch and Waneck and their group had concluded that the Nazis would lose the war. Therefore, they reasoned that the best avenue to waging the "real war against the Bolsheviks" was a negotiated peace with the Western Allies and then a common front against Russia. The plan was to set up an independent anti-communist Austrian state in rebellion against the Nazi Reich that would have the support of the Anglo-Americans. For this, Göttsch had valuable contacts in Vienna—the Vienna socialists: Dr. Karl Doppler, Dr. Rafael Spann, Franz Popek, Rudolf Raab, Karl Renner, Dr. Karl Winkler, Professor Heinrich, Cardinal Theodor von Innitzer, and others.

Finding that Dr. Doppler, a Viennese freemason, had the same masonic degrees as President Roosevelt, the Austrian "group" in the RSHA considered sending him to the United States to seek an audience with Roosevelt and broach the plan. According to Waneck, among the men participating in the first consideration of this plan were Göttsch, Höttl, Professor Dorodiakiewich, Count Potocki, and Kajetan Mühlmann. Kaltenbrunner was later advised of it, and while he could not actively participate because of his high position, he gave silent assent.

In the second round of meetings, Dr. Spann, Professor Heinrich, Popek, and Dr. Winkler were brought in to continue the discussions. According to Göttsch, Winkler had contacts with America and England through Draža Mihailović, former leader of the Serb nationalist partisan organization, and Spann and Heinrich had an excellent contact with England through their friend, a "Major Christie," at the Travellers Club, London. An attempt to contact Major Christie by letter using the code words *"Vater der Schloss Kinder"* was unsuccessful.

In May 1944, Alfred Naujocks (another of the group brought into the SD by Heydrich) was sent with a letter for Christie, but no reply was received. Naujocks was able to get into Switzerland by false papers secured for him by Waneck. A second attempt provided by Mihailović to contact the U. S. Legation in Belgrade failed when Belgrade was occupied.

Höttl's Contacts with the Dulles Headquarters in Switzerland

Finally, in March 1945, Dr. Höttl contacted representatives of Allen Dulles, chief of the O.S.S. activities for Germany and Austria stationed in Bern, Switzerland. Höttl was accompanied to Switzerland by the Polish nobleman "Count Potocki" [likely Count Jerzy Józef Henryk Potocki]. Through Potocki and through Prince Alois Auersperg (who had been *persona non grata* to the Nazis since the 20 July 1944 attempt on Hitler's life), Höttl was able to contact Mr. Gero von Schulze-Gaevernitz, a German-born American and member of the American embassy at Bern, and through him to have contact with Dulles. Höttl also had contact with a "Mr. Leslie," who worked with an Allied commission in Bern.

Höttl learned at that time that the Americans did not want a strong Russian influence in Austria and that the Americans were interested, in particular, in Kaltenbrunner's attitude toward an independent anti-Communist Austrian state. This was an early indicator of the CIA's later use of Nazis against the USSR.[36]

Kaltenbrunner as Head of a New Austrian Government: His Alibi

With newly accumulated information, Höttl, Waneck, and Göttsch were able to urge Kaltenbrunner to set up a rival Austrian government, independent of Vienna, which was to be nationalistic, pro-Anglo-Saxon, and anti-Russian. The movement for an independent Austria received added impetus when the Western Allies refused in April to recognize the Russian-sponsored Vienna government. Kaltenbrunner then held two meetings with the following prominent members of the Free Austrian Group: Hermann Neubacher, Edmund Glaise-Horstenau, Dr. Mühlmann, Franz Hayler, Höttl, Göttsch, and

Waneck. A provisional cabinet was discussed, and Kaltenbrunner, with the anticipated support of the U.S., was to be prime minister.[37] In the meantime, Kaltenbrunner had been delegated by Himmler's full powers in the south and was in excellent position to put through this Austrian project, which had the code name "Herzog."

Höttl reported to Kaltenbrunner at Strobl on the results of his second trip to Switzerland, which occurred on 15 April 1945. According to later interrogations of Schellenberg and Martin Sandberger, Kaltenbrunner, [about] this time, had given up the idea of trying to continue the Nazi Intelligence Service (during the post-surrender period) as an underground net for the reason that it would have been an indication of defeatism not only to subordinates but to Himmler and Hitler. Therefore, realizing that it was not possible from a military standpoint to defend the National Redoubt, Kaltenbrunner decided (1) to divide the RSHA into north and south sections with a plan of maintaining a secret organization in occupied areas; and (2) to contact the Western Allies, push through the Austrian project, and with the intelligence nets of the RSHA and the remaining SS Redoubt divisions as bargaining forces, enter into a fighting alliance with the United States and Great Britain against the Russians.[38]

Despite the fact that Kaltenbrunner had tolerated but refused to join the Austrian project before the Nazi defeat seemed inevitable in April 1945, he was later to use his connection with it as his main alibi in his defense at Nuremberg. At that time, Dr. Höttl was able to testify to Kaltenbrunner's connection with, and interest in, the Free Austria project.

Alt Aussee, Austria
Line Drawing by Finette Magnuson
from an Oil Painting by Horst Jandl, a native of Alt Aussee

❶ Wildensee Hut
❷ Loser
❸ Kerry Villa
❹ 80th CIC Headquarters
❺ Altausseer See
❻ Trisselwand
❼ Eichmann Family in the See Haus
❽ Skorzeny hideout in the Dachstein
❾ Prince Hohenlohe's House

Alt Aussee, Austria, Places of Interest to CIC in 1945. Drawing by Finette Magnuson from an oil painting by the late Horst Jandl of Altaussee. Courtesy of Wisconsin Veterans Museum—from Matteson's WW2 scrapbook titled "Kaltenbrunner + World War II + Nuremberg Trial."

Wildensee Hideout where Kaltenbrunner and three other Nazis surrendered, 12 May 1945. Photo by Fredric Matteson, 1978.

CHAPTER TWO
Closing In

Kaltenbrunner's Last Meetings and Ascent to the Wildensee Hideout

Kaltenbrunner, in spring 1945, discussed the Austrian project with Field Marshal Kesselring, commander of Wehrmacht forces in the south who had replaced Field Marshal Gerd von Rundstedt after the failure of the Ardennes offensive, and Lieutenant General Winter—General Jodl's deputy—at Königssee.

But the sands were running out.

On 26 April 1945 at Strobl (where I had found Mrs. Kaltenbrunner on May 7th), Dr. Höttl reported to Kaltenbrunner, Glaise-Horstenau, Neubacher, Mühlmann, Waneck, and Göttsch on the result of his last visit to Dulles's people. "There were still some difficulties to be overcome," [said Höttl in *The Secret Front*,] "but at last on 29 April 1945, the capitulation [to Allied Forces] was signed at Caserta [Italy]. With this act, the fiction of an Alpine Redoubt could no longer be maintained—whether as the scene of a last stand or as a basis for bargaining."39

The reality at hand was that the war was coming to an unexpectedly rapid close. Kaltenbrunner could pursue the political way out no longer. Facing capture as the Russian and American troops closed in about him, he retired to Alt Aussee on May 3rd, after he bid a last farewell to his young mistress, Countess Gisela von Westarp.

On May 7th, accompanied by his SS guards, his adjutant Arthur Scheidler, and mountain guides Sebastian Raudaschl and Fritz Moser, he made the ascent to the Wildensee mountain hideout—Wildenseehütte or Wildensee hut (owned by Prince Hohenlohe) among the snowy crags of the Dead Mountains.

The First Tip on Kaltenbrunner's Mountain Hideout

On the morning of 11 May 1945, Mr. Johann Brandauer, deputy Bürgermeister (mayor) of Alt Aussee, and a member of the Austrian Freedom Movement, came to my office with the interesting information that the Alt Aussee forester, Fritz Moser, had seen SS General Kaltenbrunner, Scheidler, and two SS guards five days before in a cabin atop the Dead Mountains. Though the tip was five days old, it had the merit of coming from a reliable source, as Brandauer was one of our closest and most trustworthy co-workers. Furthermore, it was incumbent on me to act on such tips if we were to maintain working relations with the Freedom Movement.

I asked Brandauer to bring me immediately two trustworthy Austrians who knew the mountain trails and could guide me to the cabin. Brandauer complied by bringing not two, but four, Austrian mountain guides, all former German soldiers. They were Karl Moser, Johann Wimmer, Joseph Frosch, and Willie Pucher, all workers in the salt mine. Karl Moser later became mayor of Alt Aussee.

The Plan to Surprise Kaltenbrunner

We set the plan. According to the guides, it would take us five to six hours to reach the cabin. There would be 20 to 30 feet of snow in the area, and there would be no cover save drifts of snow for the last four kilometers up to the cabin. Therefore, we reasoned, we should leave at midnight so that we would arrive at the cabin under cover of darkness and at a time when the crust on the snow was still hard.

According to our plan, I was to dress in Austrian costume, lederhosen, Alpine jacket, and spiked shoes. My idea was that I approach the cabin alone and unarmed, posing as a passerby over the mountains on my way to Steyrling. This was not at all unreasonable at the time, for all transportation had been severed, and there were many deserters from the Wehrmacht, and many fleeing Nazis whose safest and most expedient mode of travel was by foot over the mountains. I was to approach alone for the simple reason that the Austrian guides were not willing to accompany me the last 500 yards.

I was to approach the cabin unarmed so as not to draw fire or arouse suspicion that I might be on a hostile mission.

Finally, I thought it would be an inducement to Kaltenbrunner, if we found him there, to have a note from Gisela urging him to come down and be taken into custody by the Americans rather than let the Russians capture and probably kill him. The Russians at that time had closed in to the Enns River, a few miles to the east of us, and there was great fear on the part of the civilians that they would soon occupy [Alt] Aussee.

That afternoon, May 11th, everything seemed to happen at once. The head of the task force, Military Government Officer Major Ralph Pearson, requested that he be informed of any developments regarding the whereabouts of General Winter, General Marshall Kesselring, and SS General Kaltenbrunner. Therefore, I sent word that we were going on a patrol that night on a lead we had on Kaltenbrunner, but I did not tell him where or how we were going. It was not required that CIC tell the troop commander all details of an operation for obvious reasons relating to the nature of CIC work. However, in line with his responsibility for the safety of the personnel within his area command, it was within Major Pearson's right to order that a U.S. military escort be given any U.S. mountain patrol in his area of responsibility.

Inasmuch as a military escort would spoil our plan if it were in evidence, we compromised, and it was agreed that I would have full authority to use the infantry squad in any manner I saw fit. Therefore, I arranged for the squad to follow the guides and myself and, after we reached the pass on the approach to the cabin, to keep under cover well to the rear. Their function was to offer withdrawing fire in case we ran into SS troops in our ascent. Because Kaltenbrunner was an SS general and in charge of the Redoubt area, it was logical to expect SS troops. Also, they, out of sight, were to cover me from within rifle range as I made the last leg of the journey to the cabin.

After the plan had been straightened out, I sent for Gisela. She was very reluctant to give any information but was extremely anxious to find out what information we had regarding Kaltenbrunner. I told her we had some leads and asked her to write me a note for Kaltenbrunner urging him to accompany the bearer into safe custody with the Americans. After a few moments thought, she complied.

Later on that afternoon, we were visited by several delegations from the Gisela-Iris group. Hans Unterkircher, the Viennese actor, was one; German film actress Lotte Koch and German actor Ernst von Klipstein [were] the others. Then came Praxmarer and Iris. We had received from our Austrian Freedom informants within the See Hotel-SS Hospital in Alt Aussee an accusation against Dr. Praxmarer signed by members of his own staff. It read in part:

> Until two days prior to the entry of the American Task Force in Alt Aussee, Praxmarer kept active association with the bloodhound Kaltenbrunner. He has not been afraid to shelter him in the hospital and provide him with medicines and food and weapons. Arms were loaded into a car at night to help Kaltenbrunner escape to the mountains. Praxmarer, prior to the arrival of the Americans, tried to force several of the patients into the *Kampfgruppe Kaltenbrunner* for the purpose of staging a last stand in the mountains. He also tried to get one hundred men from Georg (alias Gaiswinkler) for the same purpose. Under the pretext of angina pectoris, he took into the safety of his hospital the Kaltenbrunner Gestapo chief in Vienna, SS Brigadier General Huber.

It was here in the hospital we actually found and arrested Huber. I arrested Praxmarer several days later after receiving further proof of his complicity in the Kaltenbrunner affair.

As for Iris, what she was most concerned about was the safety of her husband, Arthur Scheidler. Although she was going to have a baby in 14 weeks, she insisted she be allowed to accompany any patrol that might go off into the mountains after her husband. She believed that if she were in evidence that there would be no shooting on the part of the Kaltenbrunner group. I told her it was not possible.

Never quite sure of what the machinations of these friends of Kaltenbrunner might be, I sent Syd Bruskin to their house—the Hohenlohe guest house—to keep an eye on them for the next 12 hours. Like so many of these Nazi Austrians, they had smiles on their faces but carried daggers in their walking sticks.

The Ascent to the Wildensee Hut

That night, May 11th, at 11:30 p.m., the patrol assembled in house #45 (my temporary office)—the former local Nazi Party headquarters—for final instructions prior to starting off. The infantry boys were a little dubious about the projected plan and were especially skeptical of using former German soldiers as guides. I can't say that I blamed them, for it was natural for all line troops who had had little association with civilians to regard all civilians as enemies. They wanted me to make it clear to the guides that if they made a single misstep, they would be "dead ducks." After all, they pointed out, they had come through the war alive and didn't want to get killed with peace and home in sight.

As we started off down the road at midnight, the infantry squad loaded with hand grenades and ammunition sounded to me, in the dead of night, like a company of tanks rolling through the streets. There could be no doubt in the minds of the village people, I thought, that a patrol was leaving. Would this alert the Nazi fanatics in the village to some ambush action? Past the See Hotel, where Praxmarer's SS hospital was quartered, past Fischerndorf along the [lake] Altausseersee [today Altausseer See], past the house where Eichmann's family was living, and then we started to climb, climb, climb.

Trees swept down by heavy snowslides blocked our path at first. Then we found the footbridge over the Stammen stream had been carried away by torrents swollen in the spring flood. Up through the timber, up past the timberline we went, winding our way in the dark, snakelike over the hairpin trail. Trees pushed down by snow slides and the infantry, loaded with weapons, were slowing us up. It became obvious that we were not keeping our schedule. Three of the infantry boys fell out along the way, exhausted by the climb in snow and the weight of their weapons.

At 5:00 a.m., we finally reached the pass, 30 feet deep in snow, from which we could see through glasses the Wildensee hut. There it was, just below the crest of the ridge, and from every indication, it appeared deserted. A dull glow by now was cast across the heavens to the east. The question that confronted me was whether I should proceed in full view down the snow-covered slope and up the ridge to the cabin or whether I should seek cover from the sides and take a more circuitous route to the cabin.

Everybody was thoroughly tired, for though the crust on the snow was hard, very often, one foot broke through to a depth of up to 18 inches. For that reason, and because the snow would soon be getting softer, I decided to take the most direct route. Also, to our surprise, we had seen no evidence of sentries.

A Lonely Climb to the Hideout and the First Encounter

At a ridge of snow approximately 500 yards from the cabin, we dropped what was left of the infantry squad. There, they assumed a prone position to cover our approach to the next ridge of snow. Here, I left the four Austrian guides.

Through glasses [binoculars], it was apparent to me that the west (to our left) side of the cabin had neither doors nor windows. So, to that side, I worked my way, taking advantage of any cover that presented itself. Imagining the cabin might be deserted, I laughed at myself for my precaution, but as I neared the cabin, I heard what sounded like a signal. But it turned out to be a bird, apparently as lost as I felt I was.

As I approached, I could see that the shutters were tightly closed; no smoke was coming from the chimney; there appeared to be no fresh foot tracks in the snow. Was it deserted? Was it a false lead? Or was it a "calm before the storm?"

Wildensee Hütte. Photo by Fredric Matteson, 1978.

Ernst Kaltenbrunner, 1938, Bundesarchiv, Bild 183-H03554. Sueddeutsche Zeitung Photo / Alamy Stock Photo

Etching by Altauseee artist Christl Kerry depicting returning route taken along Lake Altausseer See by Matteson and troops with captured Nazis on 12 May 1945. Purchased by Jane Matteson on 50th anniversary of Kaltenbrunner's capture.

CHAPTER THREE
Capture and Interrogation

I walked into the open area around the cabin and onto the porch. I knocked at the door. The cabin was a typical Alpine hut—three rooms, a wood shelter, and a porch that faced down the slope from the direction I had come. There was no response to my knock. I tried the door and found it locked. But at that moment, I heard someone inside the room to my left snoring a loud groan as he rolled over in his sleep. I knocked loudly on the shutter of the window.

The shutter opened, and there before me was a rough-looking man about 35, unshaven, his eyes swollen from sleep. "What do you want?" he asked in German. "I want to come in. I am cold," I replied in very American-sounding German. He shook his head and said I couldn't come in. So I decided to come straight to the point. I pulled from my pocket and handed him the note for Kaltenbrunner from Gisela von Westarp. He read it slowly and then indicated that he didn't know Kaltenbrunner nor Gisela, that he was merely a passerby on his way down to Bad Ischl. But at that same moment, he looked over my shoulder down the slope. I looked around. Coming up were the four guides, each with his rifle in a sling over his shoulder.

As I found out later, the four guides had concluded it was a false lead inasmuch as nothing had happened to me. Seeing them, my unwilling host quickly crossed the room and took from his trousers hanging beside his bed a revolver. I could see, then, a second person sitting up in bed. Neither of them fitted the Kaltenbrunner description. As I was to find out later, the first man was Zohrer, a driver and a member of Kaltenbrunner's SS protection unit, and the second, another SS guard.

Zohrer came toward me and slammed the shutter shut. I retreated to the protection of the cabin's blind side and motioned to my colleagues, including the infantry, to come up in a half circle around the front of the cabin. While they approached, Zohrer opened the door, came out on the porch, saw what was happening, and quickly reentered the cabin, slamming and bolting the door behind him.

With the men in position, we called out to the occupants to surrender and come out with their hands over their heads. There was no response. Apparently, counsel was being taken. So, after a few minutes, onto the porch we went and started to knock down the door, the paramount idea being to avoid shooting if possible. Thereupon, as if possessed of a similar idea, the door opened and out walked four men with their hands over their heads. They had decided to come peacefully. Perhaps Gisela's note had had its effect but, as I was to learn later, Kaltenbrunner, who was a cagey, calculating opportunist and a professional at getting himself out of tight situations, was depending on his alibi of resistance to Hitler and the setting up of an independent, anti-Communist Austrian state. He had a strong will to live and had no intention of dying a martyr for the Führer or a moribund National Socialism.[40]

We searched the four men and put them under guard. Inside the cabin, we found German Wehrmacht rifles, pistols, a large quantity of ammunition, machine pistols, and a machine gun, which was hidden in the recess of the chimney. Also, there was an empty case of champagne bottles, French candy, American tax-free cigarettes, some American and German money, and English counterfeit notes.

I interrogated each of the men. None of them admitted being either Kaltenbrunner or Scheidler. The two SS men readily admitted their identity as SS men but claimed no association with Kaltenbrunner.

From the description we had of Kaltenbrunner, it was difficult for Kaltenbrunner to conceal his identity. Furthermore, we found in the ashpan at the base of the chimney for the stove an assortment of items clearly and unmistakably identifying Kaltenbrunner. There was a picture of Kaltenbrunner, his wife, and children. I had seen his wife and children at Strobl a few days before. Here was a picture of the same woman, the same children, and a picture of the man who was now standing before me.

There was a copy of the radio message Kaltenbrunner had sent to Hitler through Fegelein via the radio technician Sansoni. There was Kaltenbrunner's identification card as chief of the SIPO and SD of the RSHA.[41] Finally, there were two metal identification discs; one was Kaltenbrunner's infamous Gestapo disc, which I had until 1973, with the words *Geheime Staatspolizei* and *No. 2* engraved.

Few Americans realize that the word *Gestapo* is an abbreviation of *Geheime Staatspolizei*, meaning Secret State Police. The *No. 2* indicated that Kaltenbrunner ranked behind Himmler—the No. 1—among the 50,000-odd Gestapo personnel.

Matteson holds in his hand Kaltenbrunner's No. 2 Gestapo badge and a small, confiscated espionage camera. Courtesy of Wisconsin Veterans Museum—from Matteson's WW2 scrapbook titled "Kaltenbrunner + World War II + Nuremberg Trial."

The other metal disc, marked also with a *No. 2*, was Kaltenbrunner's Kripo (Kriminalpolizei) identification. This latter disc, in June 1945, I gave to Thomas McMillen, the commanding officer of the 80th CIC detachment, who was later a federal district judge in the Chicago area. Tom returned it to me on 1 July 1979 after he had learned that I had lost the Gestapo badge No. 2 in a restaurant in New Delhi, India.

Captain McMillen (later Major McMillen) was considered by me to be the best commanding officer of any CIC detachment in the European Theater. Tom was a graduate of Princeton, Harvard Law School, and a was a Rhodes scholar. His father was a congressman from Illinois with a long and distinguished record.

Kaltenbrunner stood rigidly at attention as I interrogated him. He had papers identifying him as Dr. Unterwogen, an ex-Wehrmacht doctor. With him was a medical kit and all the other accessories a doctor might carry. Scheidler, likewise, had papers of another person. As Kaltenbrunner took pains to explain later, the papers were not "forged" but were authentic papers of deceased persons. Why he thought this explanation absolved him from any wrongdoing, I shall never know, but suffice it to say, it fell in line with other incidents that marked his personality.

While capable of murder (it is alleged but not verified that he shot the police president of Linz, and during his 10 years as "Little Himmler of Austria" that he shot for sport inmates at the Mauthausen concentration camp), Kaltenbrunner always tried to create the impression in other people that he was an Austrian gentleman and a good Catholic even though he despised the Catholic hierarchy.[42] But even then, he was trying to create a good initial impression by being earnest and cooperative.

Scheidler was the antithesis. He made no pretense at hiding his wrath. His eyes flashed furiously at me as we swung heavy packs on the four men for our trip down to the village.

Arrival Back in Alt Aussee

At 11:30 a.m. on May 12th, we arrived back in Alt Aussee. Apparently, word had circulated that a mountain patrol was returning, for gathering in the village street was a large group of civilians. As we passed Prince Hohenlohe, he remarked, "I see you have your man, Kaltenbrunner." At that moment, a very natural thing happened. Iris broke from the throng and ran up and embraced her man.[43] It was then that Kaltenbrunner and Scheidler dropped their masks, for they knew that there was no chance of their identities being concealed.

McMillen, Colonel Fleisher, and General Smythe of the 80th Infantry

Division all happened to arrive at Alt Aussee that day. McMillen and I interrogated Kaltenbrunner briefly before sending him on to 80th Division and 3rd Army Headquarters. During that interrogation, Kaltenbrunner stated that he had intended to come down from his mountain retreat after things had quieted down, and then with the aid of his underground organization, his independent Austria project, and his knowledge of Bolshevism, to come to terms with the Western Allies. As he stated during his interrogation, "If there is one man in Europe who knows Bolshevism, it is I." Kaltenbrunner also expressed surprise that we had encountered none of his guard patrols on our approach to the cabin.

We allowed Gisela and Iris one last tearful farewell and then sent Kaltenbrunner and Scheidler off to 80th Division and Third Army Headquarters. Here, as I found out later from the Third Army spot interrogation reports, Kaltenbrunner's interrogators characterized him as a "cagey, calculating politician with a veneer of Austrian charm."

The plan, which never materialized, was to have Kaltenbrunner talk with General Eisenhower and issue a statement calling on the underground to end all resistance. Kaltenbrunner, at the time of his initial interrogation, was very cooperative. He was engaged in establishing his alibi. He said, "Believing a military victory impossible and with Hitler's consent, I began to use in 1945, the Foreign Intelligence Service (Amt VI, RSHA) to counteract Ribbentrop's pernicious influence to find a political way out. Himmler, at this time, it was known to me, was engaged in conversations with Count Bernadotte in seeking through Sweden negotiated peace with the Western Allies. I had contact with the Americans and English in Switzerland."

Kaltenbrunner at Twelfth Army Group Headquarters

Kaltenbrunner's next stop on his way back through channels was the Twelfth Army Group Headquarters. About this time, I received from an officer at the Third Army Intelligence Center a letter written by Kaltenbrunner to his wife, Liesl, but obviously for American consumption. It read in part:

> My own destiny lies in the hands of God. I am glad that I never separated from him.... I cannot believe that I shall be held

responsible for the mistakes of our leaders, for in the short time of my activity, I have striven hard for a reasonable attitude, both internal and external. I was never discouraged by being slighted as an Austrian, but one ought to have paid more attention to my words. My dearest wife, you have had to renounce much in our marriage. We have no property worth mentioning. Perhaps the only resource for you will be my small stamp collection." (Note: Kaltenbrunner had at his disposal all the counterfeiting plants of the RSHA, a luxurious home at Wannsee, and an Aryanized villa in Vienna.)

"We have had to renounce much because of this stamp hobby of mine," he continued. "You, my dearest Lisi, will now have much grief as a result of my political activity, but was it not my duty to open the door to socialism and freedom as we imagined and desired them? Many a man was not worth your sacrifice, my dearest. Now I have written in a way almost as if I thought that my life was finished. But I have not given up hope that the truth will be found out and for a just legal decision."

I learned from the intermediate interrogation report on Kaltenbrunner, 28 June 1945—Twelfth Army Group Headquarters, that Kaltenbrunner professed to have a strong tie with Hitler but to have hated Bormann, Ribbentrop, and Himmler. Dr. Höttl, whom Kaltenbrunner at this point described as his principal subordinate, said, "Kaltenbrunner was fascinated by Hitler; he believed in him without reservation. Likewise, he thought the Führer was partial to him. Hitler was happy to strengthen him in that belief, seducing him into a state of subservience. Kaltenbrunner, for once, was not realistic. He believed he had a mission to serve Hitler with his entire RSHA."

Höttl's report continued, "Thus, in the fifth year of the war, he achieved unification of the German Intelligence Services under his leadership. Owing to this, Kaltenbrunner was charged with liquidating the plotters against Hitler on July 20, 1944. Here, he proceeded with a brutality and severity which struck all those who had known him as inconceivable. He came to believe that Hitler was the man sent by God. This developed into a mania."[44]

Kaltenbrunner at British Interrogation Center 020 Near London

Kaltenbrunner was sent back to the British Interrogation Center 020 outside of London. There, as I learned later at Nuremberg from both American and British Intelligence officers working on the Kaltenbrunner case, Kaltenbrunner was subjected to the third-degree treatment. He was placed naked under hot spotlights, given no rest, and only bread and water. Kaltenbrunner later said his treatment at Nuremberg compared to London was like the difference between day and night. This was at the time when the horrors of the concentration camps were being brought to light, and here was the first man apprehended who had played a significant and responsible part both in the extermination program and the concentration camp system.

Kaltenbrunner—the result of his being treated like the criminal that he was—became convinced that he was going to die no matter what alibi he might have. Henceforth, not only did he not cooperate in giving further information, but he refused to admit that he had any executive responsibility in the Nazi system. He refused to admit that he knew men who had been his closest associates; he refused to admit that he had ever been near a concentration camp; he refused to admit that he signed any protective custody orders incarcerating persons in concentration camps. In short, he denied any responsibility for Nazi crimes and any connection with persons responsible for such crimes. The task of the prosecution at Nuremberg was made ten times more difficult by this unfortunate development of the case.

The Final Interrogation of Gisela and Iris

At the end of October 1945, I was asked to interrogate Gisela von Westarp and Iris Scheidler once more in connection with the Nuremberg trial that was to start soon. Kaltenbrunner had refused to talk or to admit any responsibility of wrongdoing. So Lloyd Roach, a CIC agent from Texas who had been with me at the end in Alt Aussee, and I picked up Gisela at her mother's in [Bad] Hindelang and drove back to Alt Aussee, where Iris was with her newborn son, Peter. Iris was going slowly crazy and talked about suicide. Her baby was unwanted. Her husband was in prison. She and the other Nazis in Alt Aussee were hurting for food and fuel. Nazi Germany had been defeated. There was no way out.

Gisela, on the other hand, was less despondent. She was intent on contact with Kaltenbrunner, who had two children (twins) Ursula and Wolfgang by Kaltenbrunner, born in Prince Hohenlohe's guest house 12 March 1945. In my interrogation of Gisela, she said Ley, the labor leader, and Streicher, the Jew-baiter, were crazy; Ribbentrop, the foreign minister, was stupid; Himmler, the head of the SS, was sadistic; and Bormann, Hitler's secretary, was the devil incarnate. I showed her articles by Count Folke Bernadotte on his 1945 visit with Kaltenbrunner; she was visibly affected by the bad things Bernadotte had to say about Kaltenbrunner's influence and power. She and Iris had romantic ideas about Nazism and the Hitler court. They were apolitical in the sense of having little understanding or interest in matters political.

I asked her why most Nazis took a mistress. She said it was the rule, especially in the SS. Usually, a young SS man married a young woman in the BDM (Hitler's Girls' Organization) of the same rank. As the man rose to a higher and higher rank, he outgrew the woman, whose horizon was very often limited, and took on someone more sophisticated and usually younger. She said again that Frau Kaltenbrunner was too serious and coldly intelligent. Gisela said she had met Kaltenbrunner in Himmler's headquarters at Wannsee near Potsdam in the spring of 1943, shortly after he took over from Heydrich. She lived at the RSHA guest house, which was on a beautiful point on the lake.

Iris, on the other hand, was more interested in her former husband, Dr. Praxmarer, whom we had also arrested, than she was in her present husband, Arthur Scheidler. Dr. Praxmarer had been the one to outfit Kaltenbrunner with false papers of a Wermacht doctor and to provide him with a medical kit. As I learned later—in 1975, when Jane and I returned to Alt Aussee—Dr. Praxmarer had stayed at the house of Alois Raudaschl in Alt Aussee, the guide who took Kaltenbrunner up the mountain to his hideout. Iris, the complete opportunist, felt that Dr. Praxmarer would be a better associate in the present circumstance than Scheidler, who was connected to Kaltenbrunner.

After interrogating both Gisela and Iris, I left a memo with the area CIC giving the facts on Gisela and Iris as a basis for an arrest report.

I concluded that they might be potential security threats since they had the contacts and still retained their pro-Nazi sympathies, even though they were essentially nonpolitical. We left Gisela in Alt Aussee with the CIC under "house arrest" and dropped Iris off with the CIC in Salzburg on our return to Garmisch.

After leaving Iris with the Salzburg CIC, I checked in at the Marcus W. Orr POW camp [Glasenbach, Austria]; it held 8,000 POWs. I had heard some bad things about the POW camps, but here, I found no evidence of this. The POWs got one cup of ersatz coffee for breakfast, one bowl of soup made of cabbage and meat for lunch, and a hunk of bread and cheese for supper. Men who worked got squares of chocolate. They slept on boards on the floor. There was one latrine and six spigots of water for 150 men. The only clothes they had were the ones on their backs. Everything was clean, and there was no sickness.

Ernst Kaltenbrunner, Nuremberg, December 1945. Original photo by Erin Thompson, U.S. Army Intelligence Center; courtesy of U.S. Holocaust Memorial Museum. Artistic treatment of original photo by Kristin Mitchell of Little Creek Press, Mineral Point, Wisconsin.

CHAPTER FOUR
Testing Security

On November 2nd, I received orders from Third Army Headquarters to go to Nuremberg to set up a security plan and take charge of security for members of the International Military Tribunal and all dignitaries and ranking personnel at the trial in the Nuremberg-Fürth area. So I left the next day, taking CIC agents Lloyd Roach and David Marks with me. The request from Nuremberg to CIC headquarters in the European Theater was for, and I quote, "first-class intelligence operatives to be responsible for all dignitaries in Nuremberg, especially to guard against Nazi lone-wolf assassins." Lt. Colonel Edwin Van Valkenberg Sutherland [31 years old and among the first to start fighting the Germans in WWII] of the First Infantry Division was placed in charge of general security. The U.S. First Infantry Division was the division in the general Nuremberg area having responsibility for overall military security. Colonel Burton C. Andrus was chief of Internal Security and in charge of the 21 major Nazi war criminals in the cell block itself.

Kaltenbrunner was flown to Nuremberg for the trial in handcuffs. He was the only one of the major defendants thought to be dangerous enough to be treated in this manner. At Nuremberg, Colonel Andrus quickly released him from handcuffs and gave him the same treatment as Göring, Hess, and the others.

During the next days before the trial commenced, I had the opportunity to talk with Lieutenant Whitney Robson Harris, in charge of preparing the Kaltenbrunner brief for Justice Jackson, and with Lieutenant Colonel Smith Brookhart, who was in charge of the Kaltenbrunner interrogation. The gist of their characterization of Kaltenbrunner was that he was an intelligent gangster who had the blood of more persons on his hands than a thousand years could wash out. Still, though they knew this, they had to prove it.

I was given an office in the Palace of Justice, where the trial was to be held. I visited Justice Robert Jackson's assistant and found there were only 300 seats in the courtroom, of which 250 were for correspondents. Roach, Marks, and I were given complete access to all sessions of the trial. Colonel Sutherland was very cooperative and said I could use any military personnel I needed. My living quarters was a room in the Grand Hotel, the only hotel still standing. It was reserved only for people connected with the trial and was full of people of all nationalities, including a large number of Soviets, undoubtedly some NKVD [Soviet secret police organization].

In addition to being in charge of the War Crimes Trial Personnel Security Office, as it was called, I also was asked by Lt. Whitney Harris to assist in securing affidavits from concentration camp inmates regarding Kaltenbrunner's personal involvement in the camps. I was given the passes necessary for all parts of the Palace of Justice and the courtroom and was able to spend a great deal of time at the trial itself. I was allowed to wear any rank I saw fit to carry out an assignment, so I pinned on the gold oak leaves as a major, not wanting to upstage Lt. Colonel Sutherland and Colonel Andrus by assuming a higher rank. Often, I would wear only "U.S." on my collar. As a result, I can imagine very soon, everyone was thoroughly confused.

The first job was to draw up a security plan for the Nuremberg area, including the disposal of security troops, the guarding of visiting dignitaries, and the security of the area in the Palace of Justice that housed the 21 inmates. The courtroom itself, when I arrived on November 3rd, was only about half finished, and the trial was to start November 20th. Labor was short, so German prisoners were used, including even some SS. Consequently, the security was poor. Time bombs and plastic charges could very easily have been placed in the walls all over the Palace of Justice. With only two weeks to go before the trial started, the Americans were becoming concerned about Werwolves and lone-wolf assassins. Also, Robert Ley, one of the prisoners, had already succeeded in hanging himself by a towel tied to a pipe in his cell.

I submitted the security plan to the G-2 of the 3rd Army, Colonel Edward Fickett [of "Task Force Fickett" fame, otherwise known as General Patton's 6th Cavalry Group, which played a prominent role in the Battle of the Bulge] in person. After it was approved, I started to implement it. On November 9th, a week after we had arrived, I decided to test the security of the cellblock itself, which was Colonel Andrus's responsibility. Colonel Andrus was an old cavalry colonel who was said to be a friend of General Eisenhower.

So, to test the security system, I took along [CIC colleague] Lloyd Roach, and we proceeded to discover if it were possible to gain entrance to the Palace of Justice inner cellblock. To do this, we had to pass through four interior guard posts inside the Palace of Justice without the aid of Colonel Amen's Red Pass, without which no one was to be allowed to enter the inner cellblock. We had promoted Private Roach to a "captain" simply by procuring the captain's bars for him at the local PX military store. Together, we walked to Guard Post #1. We were surprised not to be stopped. What we were supposed to have was the red interrogation pass signed by Colonel Amen. On we went to Guard Post #2. Again, our officers' uniforms got us by.

Down the wooden corridor we went, past other guard posts, until we arrived at the iron grill gate leading into the cellblock itself. We had to pass through a fifth guard post to get into the individual defendant's cell.

A guard from inside moved aside the little "justice window" to see who we were and then slowly opened the heavy iron door. Again, we were not challenged. I started to walk down the cellblock when the voice of the captain of the guards called out, saying, "Sir, please sign the visitor book and indicate which prisoner you wish to see." So I signed the book and asked to see Kaltenbrunner. Since the suicide of Ley, a GI guard was now stationed at each cell door with orders to keep the prisoner under 24-hour observation. But Roach and I could have been anybody at all who was dressed in an American officer's uniform.

Kaltenbrunner, in accordance with procedure, had to stand tall when an officer entered. I was surprised by two things: once again, his size; and second, his appearance. While I had spent several hours with him in May at the time of his capture, I had forgotten how large he was—six feet, four inches in height and weighing 220 pounds. One somewhat exaggerated description, that Florence Miale and Michael Selzer (experts on psychological testing by Rorschach ink blots) in their book *The Nuremberg Mind: The Psychology of the Nazi Leaders* said, "He was almost seven feet tall and had a heavily scarred face—Kaltenbrunner looked like what he was, head of the Security Police (SIPO), the Security Service (SD), and the Reich Security Head Office (RSHA)." As such, they pointed out, he had under his authority the Gestapo, the extermination squads, and the concentration camps. Another more vivid description of Kaltenbrunner, which they referred to, was by one of Hitler's aides: "a tough, callous ox—looks like a big grizzly. Small brown eyes that move like a viper, all glittering, bad teeth, some missing, so he hisses." This, in my opinion, was somewhat exaggerated also.[45]

The second thing that impressed me as I stood there looking at Kaltenbrunner was his physical countenance. He looked like a man who knew he was about to die. He clearly showed the effects of what he had been through since I had last seen him May 12th. Little did I know then that he soon was to have a cerebral hemorrhage. As I indicated earlier, I had been told by one of the British personnel that Kaltenbrunner at Camp 020 had been given the third-degree treatment. He had been placed under a hot spotlight, was given no rest and only bread and little water. Later, in 1979, when I was at Oxford, I learned from [Hugh] Trevor-Roper that Camp 020 was under the supervision of "Tin-Eyed Stephens," a man with a monocle and riding whip who was known to be a master at psychological persuasion.

Kaltenbrunner gave no indication of wanting to remember me. It seemed as if he had mesmerized himself into a state of complete forgetfulness. That was ... until I mentioned the name Gisela. Then he nodded and asked several questions about her and the twins. During the few minutes we talked, his only interest was Gisela and the twins, not his wife and three other children. It was evident to him that his alibi (on the basis of which he had surrendered without a fight) had not worked. He had hoped to persuade General Eisenhower that he should be accepted as an adviser or even head an independent Austria. With his intelligence services, knowledge of the Soviet Union, with SS troops at his command in the National Redoubt area, and with Skorzeny's sabotage and werwolf brigade, his alibi was that he would join forces with the United States and the British in a final war against Russia. The contacts his SD man, Höttl, had with Allen Dulles's OSS [Office of Strategic Services] people in Switzerland were to be the basis of his position that he, against Hitler's wishes, had been trying to arrange a secret surrender of the Nazi Alpine Redoubt forces and thus an end to the war.

After this brief second encounter with Kaltenbrunner, "Captain" Roach and I left. Thinking it was a fluke and that security in the cellblock could not be that bad, we decided to try to repeat our entrance through the guard posts an hour later. Again, we were successful, and this time, I asked to see Reich Marshal Hermann Göring. Göring stood at attention when we entered. He appeared shorter and more trim than I had expected from his photographs. On a shelf by his cot, he had many pictures of his wife. I asked him how things went, and he said, "Good." I asked if he had seen his wife yet, and he said, "No." Both Kaltenbrunner and Göring seemed startled by the visit, for all the prisoners, except Hess, had recently been left alone. We exchanged a few more words then left quickly, not wishing to be caught by the prosecution interrogators invading their territory without the proper credentials: the red pass signed by Colonel Amen.

When I returned to my office, I wrote up and transmitted a report to Lt. Colonel Sutherland and Colonel Fickett. Then, within a few hours, all hell broke loose. I was sure it had not made Colonel Sutherland unhappy. He and Colonel Andrus were waging a silent jurisdictional battle. Colonel Andrus had been given special directives by USFET [U.S. Forces European Theater] that interfered with Colonel Sutherland's overall authority under the First Division of the Third Army for security of the entire area. Colonel Andrus had been given the security of the cellblock and courthouse, which were part of the Palace of Justice.

As soon as my report was read at Third Army Headquarters, the place exploded. Down came commanding General Lucian Truscott [one of only two generals to command a division, a corps, and a field army during the war and who took over command of the Third Army from General Patton on 8 October 1945] and the G-2. The result was that six officers and 20 men, including guards at the guard posts, were removed. I quickly became the most popular man living at the Grand Hotel, but the fact was that security had been lousy.

In the security plan for the Nuremberg-Fürth area, we had made

60 recommendations. The G-2 assured me all would be carried out. The name of my office was changed to "War Crimes Trial Personnel Security Office." It included security for Justice Jackson, chief counsel for the U.S., William Joseph "Wild Bill" Donovan of OSS fame; Francis Biddle, the former U.S. attorney general and the U.S. judge on the International Military Tribunal; his alternate, Judge John J. Parker; Lord Justice Geoffrey Lawrence of the United Kingdom, who was president of the court; Sir Hartley Shawcross, the UK chief prosecutor; Professor Henri Donnedieu de Vabres, the French judge; Francois de Menthon [leader in French Resistance], the French chief prosecutor; Major General Iona Nikitchenko, the Soviet chief prosecutor; his alternate, Lt. Col. Alexander F. Volchkov; General Roman A. Rudenko, the Soviet chief prosecutor, and his deputy, Colonel Y. V. Pokrovsky. In addition to these principals at the trial, there was a constant stream of dignitaries coming for a day or so to view the trial.

A week later, I tested the security of the cellblock again on orders of the First Army G-2. He wanted to see whether security had improved. This time, I was stopped at each guard post, but instead of showing the red interrogation pass signed by Colonel Amen, I showed my Counter Intelligence Corps badge. This was an impressive gold badge in a leather case. Again, Roach and I were allowed to pass through. Again, while security had improved, the guards were not literally following their orders.

On entering the inner cellblock for the third time, I asked to see Julius Streicher. Streicher was 60 years old. He had the lowest IQ of any prisoner—106. He had been one of the earliest and most fanatical supporters of Hitler. As editor of *Der Stürmer* [*The Attacker* –in English], the main anti-Semitic newspaper of Nazi propaganda, he very early led the fight against the Jews. He headed the lunatic fringe of the Nazi Party and was the most animal-like of the 22 defendants. During the trial, he fought with his lawyer and made wild, crazy statements.

On the day that I saw him, 16 November, Streicher was happy to see me—to see and talk with anyone. He impressed me as a short, bouncy extrovert. He was full of energy and looking forward to the trial. I asked him how he thought the trial would go—if he had any fears. He said, "Why should I have any? All I have to do is tell the truth, and they will release me. The others? They should all be shot." I asked him how prison life was. He said it was very good. His only complaint was that he hadn't seen his wife. He seemed particularly concerned about a hole in his trousers and said he needed to get from his wife a sewing kit or another pair of trousers. [Found guilty of crimes against humanity, Julius Streicher was hanged at Nuremberg on 16 October 1946, but like the others hung, he apparently did not immediately die.[46]]

The guards finally caught up with us this third time and quite correctly arrested us for illegal entry into the cellblock. Streicher pleaded with them to let us stay and talk. One of the prison officers said, "I don't know how you got in. You have no pass. So here you stay." When the word finally reached Colonel Andrus, he ordered our release. But again, there were reverberations up and down the Palace of Justice, for this was the third illegal entry in a week. Again, it was fuel for Colonel Sutherland's battle against divided responsibility. Each time, my report brought a reshuffling of the guards and the enforcement of more stringent security measures, and it was no wonder that those who were responsible for security became increasingly apprehensive about incidents marring the opening of the trial. The Russians, as our guests in the American zone for the period of the trial, were especially anxious that their security be attended to properly.

Lack of Security at the Trial

Many were the times that Roach or I came across groups of unguarded SS prisoners in the Palace of Justice halls conversing with German civilians who had access to the outside world and who were employed by our Office of Chief Counsel within the Palace of Justice. Our official CIC estimate indicated that there were still approximately 1,000 SS in the Nuremberg area who were at large and not accounted for; they presented a real security threat. In addition, there were a number of Gestapo and SD agents in Nuremberg who had not yet been arrested.

Another potential source of security trouble was the 45,000 disgruntled German civilians who had been expelled from their jobs by the military government for previous association with the Nazi Party. This had happened on 8 November 1945, 12 days before the trial was to begin. As late as 10 days before the trial commenced, there were unguarded open doors through which German civilians could gain access to the Palace of Justice and the courtroom without any pass at all required. Such people might have had as their purpose planting of time bombs, booby traps, or other similar devices. Unfortunately, a shortage of labor, which was necessary to finish the courtroom in the Palace of Justice on time, required the use of SS prisoners from nearby POW camps. They presented a distinct security threat, for redeployment had caused a woeful lack of American security guards.

On November 17th, I had a long talk with Colonel Y. V. Pokrovsky, the Soviet deputy prosecutor. At that time, with the Chief Soviet Prosecutor General Rudenko sick, he was the top Russian man. Pokrovsky's office was huge—much like the long office [Italian dictator] Mussolini had. On his desk was a telephone with a direct line to Moscow. His main concern was whether the U.S. was going to allow the USSR to have its own security people in the courtroom. It seemed to me that he couldn't make a move without telephoning Moscow. During our conversation, an American woman correspondent [possibly English writer Rebecca West, Tania Long of *The New York Times*, or Janet Flanner of *The New Yorker*] was able to break into the room.[47] She had one question she wanted answered: "Is it true that General Rudenko is ill and that the USSR has asked for a postponement?" General Pokrovsky didn't want to answer without calling Moscow, but finally, in embarrassment, he said yes, it was true.

As I left Pokrovsky's office, I ran into a half-drunk Russian officer in a shabby uniform, pressing a fistful of Allied marks into the hands of an American guard. He wanted the guard's wristwatch. That same night, as I stood talking with a fellow CIC man in the lobby of the Grand Hotel, a Russian soldier staggered in and fell at our feet in a pool of blood. He had been shot by a Nazi sniper who, like many others, was hiding out in the vast catacombs underneath the old city. It was virtually impossible to flush them out. Their practice was, like Werwolves, to come out at night. Their favorite target was Soviet personnel. The Nazis had a particular hatred for the Russians, and the Russians were well aware of it. Within a half an hour of this incident, I had a call to go at once to General Rudenko's villa.

When I arrived, a Soviet party was in progress, with vodka flowing freely. General Rudenko demanded to know how one of his men could have been shot—why the security wasn't better. While I was attempting to explain the difficulty, there was a loud explosion in the driveway. It sounded as if a dynamite charge had been set off. The immediate consequence was that several Soviet officers jumped through the window into the garden, whether in fright or anger, I don't know. This was the first time Soviet personnel had been in hostile territory outside of Mother Russia and the first time they were in a position of depending on someone else for security. I explained I wasn't in charge of general military security, only the security of dignitaries. I said I would report their concern to Colonel Sutherland. General Rudenko did not seem to be reassured by this, for the next day, he called me in and told me in detail what Moscow had recommended. He did it in a courteous manner but with no apparent thought of opposing Moscow's suggestions: a company of USSR soldiers was to be flown in from Berlin. Still, it was a source of wonderment to me that the acting Russian prosecutor could not take it on his own authority to render advice on the simple mechanics of security without referring the matter to Moscow for consideration and reply.

Nuremberg Trial courtroom. Kaltenbrunner seated fourth from a standing Göring. Photo given to Matteson by Commander Donovan of Justice Jackson's staff. Courtesy of Wisconsin Veterans Museum—from Matteson's WW2 scrapbook titled "Kaltenbrunner + World War II + Nuremberg Trial."

CHAPTER FIVE
War Crimes and the Trial of the Century

"The privilege of opening the first trial in history for crimes against the peace of the world imposes a grave responsibility. The wrongs which we seek to condemn and punish have been so calculated, so malignant, and so devastating, that civilization cannot tolerate their being ignored, because it cannot survive their being repeated.... Against their opponents, including Jews, Catholics, and free labor, the Nazis directed such a campaign of arrogance, brutality, and annihilation as the world has not witnessed since the pre-Christian ages."

—Justice Robert H. Jackson,
U.S. Chief Counsel, Nuremberg Trials

Opening of the Nuremberg Trials

The day that we all had been waiting for—20 November 1945—finally arrived. The trial of the 22 men who had cold-bloodedly plotted to conquer the world began. Actually, 21 men were to appear in the prisoner's dock, for Martin Bormann, not yet apprehended, was to be tried *in absentia*. The indictment had been served, and Ernst Kaltenbrunner was listed sixth (actually fifth, for Robert Ley had committed suicide.) Göring was first, then Hess, then Ribbentrop, Keitel, and Kaltenbrunner. In that order, they were to take their seats in the Nuremberg courtroom, opposite and facing the four judges and the four alternates of the United States, France, Great Britain, and Russia.

The great disappointment of the opening day of the trial was that Kaltenbrunner was not in the prisoner's dock. He had been stricken with a cerebral hemorrhage on November 18th. The pressure of keeping all of his lies straight, having no alcohol to relieve his anxieties about his future fate, and finding that his alibis wouldn't work was too much. Furthermore, his tension had increased as he found out that his professional ability of getting himself out of tight squeezes was of little avail in this case. In the meantime, I received a letter from Gisela von Westarp asking that she be called as a witness on behalf of Kaltenbrunner and stating she was writing me a long letter in German telling everything she knew about Kaltenbrunner. It never came, but I never expected it to come. She was not about to incriminate her man. Dr. Kurt Kauffmann of Wiesbaden, Kaltenbrunner's defense counsel, told me that Gisela was not going to be called as a defense witness because she was "not a political person."

It would be three weeks before Kaltenbrunner had his opportunity to plead, as he did: "I do not believe I have made myself guilty in the sense of the indictment...."

The indictment accused the defendant Kaltenbrunner of using his positions as general in the SS, general in the police, member of the Reichstag, "Little Himmler of Austria," and chief of the Gestapo, Kripo, and Intelligence Service of the Nazi Party "to promote the consolidation of control over Austria seized by the Nazi conspirators as set forth in Count 1 (in the indictment), and he authorized, directed, and participated in the war crimes set forth in Count 3 of the indictment and the crimes against humanity set forth in Count 4 of the indictment including particularly the crimes against humanity involved in a system of concentration camps."

I wrote [wife] Jane on November 21st, the day after the trial started:

> Yesterday was rather dull as they merely read the indictment and, as it has been read and published a thousand times (as Dr. Schacht said), "We can all quote it from memory." Hess looks and acts insane. He seems to be in a stupor most of the time. When he talks or moves, he does it in quick, jerky movements. He is very thin, and his eyes are black, sunken hollows. Twice, he had to leave the courtroom because of stomach cramps. When

he was asked whether he pleaded "guilty" or "not guilty," he stood up and yelled, "Nein." At one point, he got up and grabbed the microphone from his defense counsel. He also wanted to make a speech and seemed indignant when he was refused.

After the pleas of "not guilty" were entered, Jackson gave the opening statement for the prosecution. It was an excellent statement, but he made a lot of embarrassing mistakes in reading his manuscript. What should prove interesting are the movies that will be shown as proof of war crimes guilt and also, of course, the statement of the defendants. There are only a relatively few seats in our courtroom for people who are not press or participating in the trial, so I feel fortunate in being able to see the whole thing....

To be able to see the trial, a man named Tom Hodges from the Third Army had come down to take my job as head of security, so I was now free to attend each session. Tom was a lieutenant who had been a CIC Operations Officer in the Third Army. He was the nephew of Lieutenant General Courtney Hick Hodges, who had commanded the U.S. First Army. Tom, too, quickly donned the major leaf when he took over.

During this period, I talked with Robert Kempner [German lawyer in the Weimar Republic who sought to try Hitler for high treason and ban the Nazi Party; fled Germany in 1935],[48] chief of Jackson's staff, and his aide, Harriet Zetterberg, whom I had known at Carleton in 1935. I also talked at some length with Heinrich Hoffmann, Hitler's photographer, who was under "protective custody" at the trial and was assisting the prosecution in identifying defendants whose pictures were in his collection of photographs. I told him I had by accident come across his collection of photos at Winhöring in Count Karl Theodor's castle. He said that he had a farm near Winhöring and had given his collection to his nearby friend, Count Toringen, for safekeeping. He said this was the sole cache and that those were the photographs he was working from at Nuremberg. He then gave me several, including the one of Himmler, Kaltenbrunner, and Ziereis at Mauthausen concentration camp.

This photograph was one used by the U.S. prosecutor to prove that Kaltenbrunner had knowledge of Nazi concentration camps. In fact, Kaltenbrunner, it was shown, was the man who signed the orders for the incarceration. Hoffmann only had two original pictures of Kaltenbrunner, so I had made prints of each. One was the picture at the Mauthausen concentration camp, and the other was of Kaltenbrunner in his car. After Heydrich's assassination, I was told no one was permitted to take Kaltenbrunner's picture. His name and picture were removed from publication to preserve anonymity and avoid assassination. Hoffmann told me he had known Iris Scheidler well. His daughter was married to Baldur von Schirach, the Hitler youth leader who was one of the 22 on trial.

Our War Crimes Trial Personality Security Office was running full steam. I had brought in some German police types and translators—Stoeger, Soehner, Brink, Sitavitch. We had to arrange for a loan of 20 Criminal Police to be used as informants in the Nuremberg-Fürth area. I put Stoeger in charge of the Zirndorf-Dambach area and Brink in charge of the Kripo in the Erlenstegen area. Within the Grand Hotel, we had our people disguised as bellboys, cleaning women, and bar attendants, picking up information and conversation. While my major assignment was security, I gave Whitney Harris some limited assistance in obtaining affidavits from former concentration camp inmates on Kaltenbrunner's complicity in war crimes. Harris had been the head of the junior bar of California and later went to work with the U.N. on the codification of international law.

I attended each trial session through the nineteenth that ended 1 December. During this time, I met and talked to Gordon Dean, Jackson's public relations man; Whitney Harris, in charge of preparing the case against Kaltenbrunner; Colonel Brookhart, in charge of the interrogation concerning the Kaltenbrunner case; General Donovan; Major General Andrews, head of the First Division; Brigadier General Leroy Watson, the International Military Tribunal commander; some of the Soviet principals; many Soviet, French, and British trial and security personnel; many correspondents; and a number of others who visited the trial.

Kaltenbrunner's First Appearance at the Trial

Finally, on 10 December 1945, I was present to see Kaltenbrunner in the dock. Before the session started, I walked down beside him. He recognized me and requested to speak with me through his defense counsel. His counsel agreed. I asked Kaltenbrunner how it felt to be in court. He replied it was better than the hospital, which had been "very depressing." Again, he asked about Gisela. I thought he looked gaunt. He had lost weight, and his face was thin and hawk-like.

As the press release of the International Military Tribunal's public relations office stated: "Ernst Kaltenbrunner received a cool welcome from his codefendants when he made his initial appearance at the trial Monday afternoon. Entering the prisoner's dock just before the afternoon session began, no welcoming hands were proffered to greet him. When he offered to shake hands with some of the defendants, there was a noticeable reluctance on their part. Taking his seat in the dock between Wilhelm Keitel and Alfred Rosenberg, he tried to engage his neighbors in a conversation without much luck. Herman Göring was extremely sensitive that another defendant stole the

From left: Göring, Hess, Ribbentrop, Keitel, Kaltenbrunner, and Rosenberg. December 1945. Photo given to Matteson by Commander Donovan of Justice Jackson's staff. Courtesy of Wisconsin Veterans Museum—from Matteson's WW2 scrapbook titled "Kaltenbrunner + World War II + Nuremberg Trial."

Kaltenbrunner pleads not guilty, December 1945. Photo given to Matteson by Commander Donovan of Justice Jackson's staff. Courtesy of Wisconsin Veterans Museum—from Matteson's WW2 scrapbook titled "Kaltenbrunner + World War II + Nuremberg Trial."

Ernest Kaltenbrunner in the dock at the Nuremberg Trials. Credit: Encyclopædia Britannica

spotlight."

When he was approached by his own defense counsel, Kaltenbrunner held out his hand. His lawyer had, however, with studied casualness, locked his hands behind his back.

It was all too apparent that Kaltenbrunner's crimes lay heavily on him. Because of his deliberate falsifications, it had become increasingly difficult for him to keep the various strands of his story straight.

I walked down beside Kaltenbrunner during the intermission that same afternoon. He recognized me and motioned that he wanted to speak with me, but that was not permitted. I had received that day through the mail a note from Gisela addressed to Kaltenbrunner. It was a love note telling Kaltenbrunner that his heart must never grow cold, that she was thinking of him and would always love him.

"My Darling,

Even though I am presently able to write you only a couple of lines I want you to know that my thoughts are with you always. I love you so, Baerli, and nothing can change this. Please just know this and think about it so that your heart does not have to be so cold. Please sense my heartfelt and intimate embrace."

The closing (in cursive) is partly illegible, but reads in part:

"I will always remain Yours, E. Perhaps we'll see each other soon, please wish for that!"

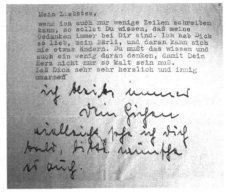

Gisela von Westarp's Final Note to Kaltenbrunner. Translation by Anthony Munson.

Perhaps Gisela thought a final visit would be allowed prior to Kaltenbrunner's execution.

I handed the note to Kaufmann, Kaltenbrunner's defense counsel. It happened that the AP correspondent Daniel De Luce was talking with Kaufmann at the time. De Luce took the note, wrote a story on it, and Kaltenbrunner, as far as I know, never found out that Gisela was keeping the home fires burning. Later that week, Kaltenbrunner was stricken with a recurrence of the cerebral hemorrhage. That was the last I saw of him, for I returned to the United States before he returned again to the dock in January 1946.

On 15 December, I left Nuremberg for home to follow the trial in the newspapers from there. I had been asked by Whitney Harris to sit with the prosecution when the SD, Gestapo, and SS were to be arraigned as criminal organizations on 19 and 20 December. But my transportation plans having been made, I left Nuremberg not knowing that Kaltenbrunner would have a relapse on 18 December and not return to the trial until much later.

As I left Nuremberg for the last time on 15 December, both Colonel Sutherland and Colonel Andrews expressed regret that I was leaving. Colonel Sutherland wrote a nice letter of commendation. Whitney Harris gave me his unrevised brief on Kaltenbrunner, and Commander Donovan, head of the photographic evidence on Jackson's staff, gave me some pictures of the courtroom with the defendants in the dock. I talked to the head of photography for the AP and told him the press was consistently carrying the wrong picture of Kaltenbrunner. The picture they carried was of a much older man who looked like H. V. Kaltenborn, the wartime radio announcer. A wire was sent out, correcting the mistake.

I arrived in Le Havre December 18 after a day-and-a-half drive with Roach from Frankfurt. The camp was Philip Morris, and I was assigned to stay in a winterized tent. It was on the top of a hill one and a half miles out of town, and the wind howled continuously. I wrote Jane from there on 19 December and ended the letter: "I can't believe that our period of separation is over (1½ years). I always look back to the day in June in New York when I left for Fort Dix, not knowing when or if I would ever see you again. And now to think it is all over!" That was my last letter home from Europe.

I left at 4:00 a.m. the morning of 23 December on a cross-channel ferry to Southampton. It was cold and very rough, and as usual, I got seasick. At Southampton, I was billeted in the C-19 staging area. It rained constantly. Finally, on 29 December 1945, we sailed on the *Queen Mary* with the 82nd Airborne for New York. The crossing was rough, and again I was seasick. There were 15 living in a stateroom built for two. We had two meals a day and a daily boat drill.

At 9:00 a.m. on 3 January 1946, there was the thrilling and heartwarming sight of passing the Statue of Liberty. We were greeted by shrieking whistles from tugs and other boats as we docked. From there, I went to Camp Kilmer, New Jersey, and from there, I was ordered to Camp McCoy, Wisconsin, for army discharge.

The Case Against Kaltenbrunner

On 2 January 1946, Lieutenant Commander Harris began the exposition of the prosecution case against Kaltenbrunner. I shall not attempt to detail what he said. I shall merely catalog the principal crimes for which Kaltenbrunner was held responsible.

The first crime for which he was responsible was the murder and mistreatment of civilians by so-called "action groups" in countries occupied by Hitler's forces. These action groups (Einsatzgruppen) from the RSHA came under Kaltenbrunner's general command and had the mission of exterminating all Jews, Communists, and other oppositionist elements to the rear of the advancing front. All gold teeth, gold bridgework, and gold fillings were removed an hour or two before they were murdered.[49] In some instances, the killers locked men, women, and children in barns, which were then set on fire.⁵⁰ In other instances, the women and children were herded into gas wagons (or as they were called, murder wagons) under the pretext of taking them for resettlement. The gas was turned on, and in 15 minutes, they would all be dead. However, as the testimony of the leaders of the action groups stated, another method of extermination was to have all the victims remove all outer garments, to align them in single file before an open ditch, and then fire a bullet into the back of each prisoner's neck. This made for convenience of the burial.

Ernst Kaltenbrunner, 1938, Bundesarchiv, Bild 183-H03554. Sueddeutsche Zeitung Photo / Alamy Stock Photo

As Otto Ohlendorf, chief of the Internal Intelligence (SD Inland) under Kaltenbrunner and leader of Einsatz Group D, testified: "I never permitted the shooting of individuals in Group D but ordered that several of the men should shoot at the same time in order to avoid direct, personal responsibility.⁵¹ The leaders, however, had to fire the last shot against those victims who were not immediately dead." (By way of a footnote, Jane and I saw Ohlendorf's wife, Kathie, in Göttingen [Germany] in 1979. She was spending the rest of her life trying to prove to the world that her man was "a good man who was only doing his duty.")

Einsatz [Deployment] Group A, headed by SS General Walter Stahlecker, proved most effective in this kind of shooting operation, according to documents found in RSHA files. In the first four months of the Russian campaign, this deployment group, based in the Baltic States and the approaches to Leningrad, along with other SS and police units as well as military personnel, murdered 135,000 persons and, in the next months, 230,000 persons. Eichmann, Kaltenbrunner's subordinate, estimated in a report that, all in all, two million Jews had been killed by Einsatzgruppen in the Russian campaign.⁵²

The second crime for which Kaltenbrunner was held accountable was the murder of prisoners of war who were considered by the Gestapo and SD to be racially or politically undesirable.

The third crime was the execution of escaped prisoners of war. Under Kaltenbrunner's order, named Kugel Erlass (Bullet Decree)—signed by Gestapo Chief Müller—escaped prisoners of war were sent to Mauthausen concentration camp to be shot.

The fourth crime was his commitment of persons to concentration camps for purposes of slave labor or extermination. Kaltenbrunner has been referred to as the originator of mass execution by gas.[53] While he was still "Little Himmler" of Austria, he had Mauthausen under his overall supervision. At this time, under the authority of the Inspectorate of Concentration Camps, a gas chamber was installed at Mauthausen and another at its subcamp Gusen. In all cases of persons committed to concentration camps during Kaltenbrunner's tenure as head of the RSHA, the protective custody order was signed by Kaltenbrunner or subordinates on his behalf.

Not only was Kaltenbrunner responsible for committing thousands of persons to concentration camps, he was also responsible for authorizing executions of prisoners upon the application of the Camp Commandant and the Security Police officer stationed at the camp. In a notable case concerning the American OSS Commission to Slovakia, which landed behind the German front in Slovakia in 1945, it was Kaltenbrunner who ordered Ziereis (commandant at Mauthausen) to execute them. It was Kaltenbrunner who ordered the execution of Joseph Morton, the American foreign correspondent.

The fifth crime for which Kaltenbrunner was responsible was the deportation of citizens from German-occupied areas into the Greater German Reich to be deployed as forced laborers and their murder and mistreatment in the Reich, in part through a system of so-called Labor Education Camps (Arbeitserziehungslager—AEL) in which forced laborers who violated the harsh labor discipline imposed upon them were incarcerated and which were run by the local Commander of Security Police and SD, who in turn reported to the RSHA.[54]

His sixth crime was his responsibility for executing captured commandos and paratroopers and for permitting civilians to lynch downed Allied fliers.

The seventh crime was the confinement and execution of persons in concentration camps for crimes allegedly committed by their relatives.

The eighth crime was the wholesale liquidation of concentration camp inmates who happened to be in the path of advancing enemy armies. In the Wildensee, I had found a Kaltenbrunner message that confirmed the intent of this alleged crime. There were to be no living witnesses to crimes ordered and sanctioned by Kaltenbrunner and Himmler within the concentration camps. A large part of the basis of this charge [which didn't materialize because of war's end chaos] was the testimony of Bertus Gerdes, who was chief of staff of the Gauleiter of Munich.[55]

On 20 November, the day the trial started, Gerdes voluntarily surrendered himself to us—the CIC in Nuremberg. Gerdes testified that in April 1945, he had received, through Gauleiter Geisler, orders from Kaltenbrunner to liquidate by poisoning concentration camp inmates at Dachau, Landsberg, and Mühldorf, or, in the case of those camps that had been hit by Allied bombing, to use the Luftwaffe. Under this latter directive, the Allies then could be blamed for the extermination of the inmates.

The ninth crime for which Kaltenbrunner was responsible was the persecution and extermination of the Jews. This was a fundamental purpose of Kaltenbrunner's security police and SD. So well did the Gestapo, Kripo, and SD carry out this function that six million Jews were exterminated out of a total European Jewish population (at that time) of nine million. Dr. Höttl testified on 25 November 1945 in Nuremberg that Eichmann had told him that "approximately four million Jews had been killed at the various extermination camps while an additional two million met death in other ways, a major part of which were shot by operational squads of security police during the campaign against Russia."[56]

Finally, the tenth crime for which Kaltenbrunner was responsible was persecution of the churches. This, again, was a fundamental function of the Gestapo, Kripo, and SD.

As the American prosecution stated, Kaltenbrunner had become so powerful toward the end that even Heinrich Himmler feared him and guided his actions to appease Kaltenbrunner. For example, in April 1945, when Himmler was asked to receive Swedish delegates representing the Jewish World Congress, he refused with this remark to Schellenberg: "How am I going to do that with Kaltenbrunner around? I should then be completely at his mercy."[57]

The Testimony Against Kaltenbrunner

The prosecution didn't get around to the Kaltenbrunner case again until 12 April, when he returned to the courtroom after a second cerebral hemorrhage. As *The New York Times* on 13 April 1946 reported: "American prosecutors produced more than a dozen new documents today linking Ernst Kaltenbrunner with some of the German's worst crimes, and the former Nazi security police chief, flushed and shaking with anger, cried out in reply that the documents were all 'lies and nonsense.' The color mounted in Kaltenbrunner's face as prosecutor Colonel John Amen of New York read affidavits from SS (Elite Guard) leaders showing that the German's security police who participated in the bloody 1943 extermination of the Warsaw ghetto had received their orders directly from Kaltenbrunner."[58]

On 13 April 1946, as reported in *The New York Times* of 14 April, the prosecution finally broke down Kaltenbrunner's obstinate claim that he knew nothing of the Nazi concentration camps and the Jewish extermination program and was interested only in intelligence. He admitted that he, like others, had received reports on this.

Another witness on 25 April (Maurice Lampe, a former inmate of Mauthausen) testified how, under Kaltenbrunner's orders, 47 U.S. and Dutch fliers had been stoned to death at Mauthausen the morning of 6 September 1944. Dressed only in their underwear and bare feet, they were each forced to carry 60 pounds of stone up 186 steps in the Mauthausen stone quarry. They were beaten and stoned all the way. If any survived, the load was increased, and they were stoned again until they died.[59]

On 25 April, Hans Bernd Gisevius, former Gestapo officer under Kaltenbrunner, also testified against Kaltenbrunner. Allen Dulles, later in 1966, described Gisevius as the link between himself and the July 20th anti-Hitler resistance group. *The New York Times*, on 26 April 1946, reported that Gisevius first met the U.S. OSS personnel in Switzerland in 1942. Throughout the war, he had sent information to the OSS in Switzerland and was the one who, on 13 July 1944 (a week before the event), advised the U.S. of the bomb plot against Hitler, which took place on 20 July 1944. As a witness, Gisevius, according to the *Times*, "denounced Kaltenbrunner, security police head, as 'even worse than that monster Heydrich' and said at luncheon meetings Kaltenbrunner and his Gestapo cohorts discussed in gruesome details their gas chambers and hideous crimes."⁶⁰

Likewise, in connection with the Kaltenbrunner case, it was established that Kaltenbrunner had a key role in the Nazis' plans for a last fanatical stand in the Redoubt and destruction of the concentration camps. General Eisenhower, as reported later (*New York Times*, 23 June 1946) said that even though Hitler had been cut off in Berlin, the Alpine Redoubt containing an area 240 x 80 miles consisting of western Austria, northern Italy, and part of southern Germany could have "still been the scene of a desperate stand by the fanatical elements of the armies south of the dividing line together with those that might retreat northwards out of Italy.... The conquest of the Redoubt area thus remained an important objective of the Allies despite the collapse of the rest of Germany." Kaltenbrunner had been placed in command of this area by Himmler's order in April 1945.

The Verdict and the Hanging of Kaltenbrunner

Finally, on 1 October 1946, the tribunal's verdict was reached. Kaltenbrunner was described that day by the AP as: "Toughest looking man in the dock.... He even denied his own signature." On the day before the verdict, as the 21 prisoners listened to the court's decision on their guilt that would determine the verdict, a *New York Times* story by Kathleen McLaughlin described Kaltenbrunner: "His facial contortions, convincing some of those present he was trying to smile but was about to weep instead, were so marked that the suspicion was generated that he might be about to suffer a recurrence of a cerebral hemorrhage that put him into the hospital for a time early in the trial."

Kaltenbrunner's defense, according to the AP story by Daniel De Luce, was centered on the unbelievable claim that he was a secret peace agent for the western Allies. "The chief of the Nazi security police, hulking Ernst Kaltenbrunner, was pictured by his attorney before the international military tribunal Monday as a secret peace agent who had been in contact with U.S. agents (Allen Dulles) since 1943. This description of Kaltenbrunner as a peace negotiator topped all defense outlines. But his claim of having combatted Nazi cruelties, interceding for Jews, and being ignorant of the worst aspects of concentration camps was matched by claims of Rosenberg, Frank, and Frick."

On 1 October 1946, the court found Kaltenbrunner guilty of war crimes and crimes against humanity but innocent of being involved in crimes against peace.[61] The sentence was death by hanging. Göring, Keitel, Jodl, Ribbentrop, Rosenberg, and von Neurath were found guilty on all four counts. However, the sentences differed because of differences in degree of the kind of crimes. For example, von Neurath was sentenced to only 15 years, although he was guilty on all four counts, whereas Kaltenbrunner was sentenced to hang though guilty on just two counts. Twelve, including the absent Martin Bormann, were sentenced to hang. Schacht, von Papen, and Fritsche were acquitted. Hess, Funk, and Raeder received life sentences. Göring, Ribbentrop, Keitel, Kaltenbrunner, Rosenberg, Frank, Frick, Streicher, Saukel, Jodl, Seyss-Inquart, and Bormann were the 12 sentenced to be hanged.[62]

Of all these, Kaltenbrunner was the only one sentenced to be hanged who attempted to plea either for clemency or for mitigation of his sentence. Even his defense counsel said he was guilty. On 2 October 1946, the American prosecutor in the Kaltenbrunner case, Whitney Harris, very thoughtfully wrote me saying, "You will be interested to learn that of all of the defendants who were sentenced, Kaltenbrunner was by far the most formal. He bowed to the tribunal when he entered the dock, and after having been told that he was to be executed by hanging, he again bowed to the tribunal and stepped back to the door." This was a different picture from the one *Newsweek's* Berlin Bureau (James P. O'Donnell and Toni Howard) gave of him on 1 October: "Kaltenbrunner—surly, defiant, and fresh. Wears a professional, almost Hollywood sneer, with his hard, scarred face as if chiseled from granite." Knowing Kaltenbrunner, I believe the Harris picture was the more accurate one.

In the tribunal's verdict of 1 October, reported verbatim in the 2 October 1946 *New York Times*, Kaltenbrunner was said to have been active in the takeover of Austria in 1938 by Hitler. But "The Anschluss, although it was an aggressive act, is not charged as an aggressive war." Consequently, Kaltenbrunner was found innocent of "crimes against peace" as leader of SS in Austria in 1938. However, as indicated earlier, there was plenty of written and oral evidence to convict him of "war crimes" and "crimes against humanity."

During the week before the hanging, which took place on October 16, defendants who were to be hanged were allowed to see their wives. Kaltenbrunner chose to see his mistress, Gisela von Westarp, not his wife. According to *Time* magazine of 21 October 1946, "Ernst Kaltenbrunner desperately tried to kiss his mistress (and mother of his two children) through the grill of the visitor's room." On the day before the hanging, according to Dana Schmidt of *The New York Times*, on 16 October 1946, Kaltenbrunner received communion and avoided conversation.

There was no report on letters he may have written. One letter that he wrote his wife toward the end of my stay at Nuremberg was given to me for delivery to her. It was sent to Strobl but may never have reached her. I have a copy (in English) of this letter, which I was going to give to Frau Kaltenbrunner in Linz in 1975, but she hung up the telephone when she heard my name. In the letter, Kaltenbrunner apologized to her for all of the trouble his political activity had caused her. He said the only property he had was his small stamp collection (which Iris Scheidler said had been "stolen"). In his letter, Kaltenbrunner said that "Iris" would know where it is. He referred to himself as a martyr and said it had been his duty to open the door to socialism and freedom.

The hangings began at 1:00 a.m., 16 October 1946, and were finished at 2:45 a.m. That night, at 10:45 p.m., a guard saw Göring "twitching on his cot." Aid was summoned, but it was too late. Two hours before he was to have been hanged, Göring committed suicide by biting a cyanide capsule. The glass fragments were found in his mouth. The brass container found in his cell was two inches long and a half-inch thick. The board investigation determined that he had the vial hidden on his body when he was captured. There was evidence that he carried it in his navel and also his alimentary canal.[63] With Göring's suicide, the first to be hanged was Ribbentrop, the Nazi foreign minister. He shouted, "God save Germany!" The second was Keitel, who called on God "to protect Germany." And the third was Kaltenbrunner, whose last words were "Good luck to Germany." All 11 were stoical. None collapsed. Some were defiant, others resigned.[64]

The executions were carried out in the prison gymnasium. Only two of the three gallows were used. There were tables for two German witnesses, eight correspondents, and the four generals on the Allied Commission. At one end was a black curtain behind which the bodies were laid. One photographer from the U.S. Army Signal Corps was allowed to take one picture of each dead man. The British voted against releasing the pictures, so no British publication reproduced them. *Life* magazine carried them in the United States. The bodies were cremated, and the ashes "dispersed secretly" so there would be no shrine for some future brand of Nazis. I heard later that they had been dumped into the river near Munich.

With the executions, the Nuremberg Trials ended, but they produced strident debates, particularly in the United States and the United Kingdom. In the United States, for example, Senator Taft of Ohio, in a speech at Kenyon College on 5 October 1946, said there was no existing international law that said making war was a crime. Therefore, the defendants were being judged by *ex post facto* law, and there shouldn't have been a trial before something called an "international court."[65] The Nazi leaders, instead, he said, should have been taken before a military tribunal and hanged, shot, or imprisoned as their military judges saw fit.

The opposing view was that the war was outlawed as an instrument of national policy by the Kellogg-Briand Pact that Germany had signed and by the Covenant of the League of Nations. Charges of crimes against humanity are covered by the Geneva Convention. Taft made the point that the Nazis had been tried by their enemies, then vanquished by the victors. But the head of the American Bar Association, Willis Smith, disagreeing with Taft, said that persons convicted of crimes were also enemies of society.

An enemy of society. At the very end, Kaltenbrunner not only destroyed RSHA documents, but he wanted to wipe out all concentration camps and the evidence that might be held against him. He tried to undercut SS General Karl Wolff in his secret surrender of northern Italy to Allen Dulles so that he might have more leverage through the surrender of his so-called Alpine Fortress in receiving better terms for himself. Finally, when this failed, and when he was confronted at Nuremberg with evidence of his tremendous guilt, he tried to escape the hangman's noose by denying everything—any responsibility for war crimes against humanity, denying he had ever set foot in a concentration camp, and denying even his signature on documents. He declared wildly that he barely knew Adolf Eichmann, although they had known each other for many years in Linz, Austria, and had collaborated in the extermination of Jews for years afterwards. Eichmann served under Kaltenbrunner in the RSHA, and it was to Kaltenbrunner at war's end that Eichmann came for his final instructions.[66]

1946 New York Times headlines from Matteson's WW2 scrapbook titled "Kaltenbrunner + World War II + Nuremberg Trial", courtesy of Wisconsin Veterans Museum.

CHAPTER SIX
Perspectives

Press Coverage

Condemned to death and then hanged on 16 October 1946 by verdict of the International Military Tribunal at Nuremberg, SS General Ernst Kaltenbrunner was a man whose name was (and still is) as little known to the American people as it was to the people of Germany until the Nuremberg Trials. Yet to the Nazis in power, his name became a symbol of terror. After the assassination in 1942 of Reinhard Heydrich, his predecessor, seldom did Kaltenbrunner's name appear in public print. So little was known about him that the American press in 1945 persisted in printing the wrong photograph. They published instead the photograph of H. V. Kaltenborn [1878-1965], the famous American radio announcer during the war. It is true that the nature of his work caused his personality to be shrouded in heavy cover. Almost never was he photographed in public.

The first press notice that I saw on the capture of Kaltenbrunner was a UP dispatch dated May 15, 1945, in the *Stars and Stripes* saying, "Gas Chamber Atrocity Boss Taken in Chalet." It reported: "General of Police Ernst Kaltenbrunner, Heinrich Himmler's ace atrocity expert, has been reported captured by a special agent of the 80th Division with the aid of Austrian patriots in a fortified chalet in the Tyrol.... Kaltenbrunner's capture places in the hands of the Allies the man charged with the responsibility for the ghastly German gas extermination program which is alleged to have snuffed out four million lives."⁶⁷

The RSHA and Heydrich

In order to understand Kaltenbrunner's role in the last two years of the Nazi Reich, one must understand the role of the RSHA, the Reichssicherheitshauptamt or Reich Main Security Office. In the best-seller *A Man Called Intrepid*, published in 1976, the author William Stevenson described (p. 189) Kaltenbrunner's predecessor as head of the RSHA, Reinhard Heydrich, as "that most sinister chief of the most vicious of Hitler's terrorist agencies. Heydrich's power as an opponent in the secret wars had been underestimated. He was the monster which outgrew the masters."⁶⁸

Jane and I, after some searching, finally caught up with Heydrich's wife, Lina, in 1979. She was leading a secluded life on the Island of Fehmarn in the Baltic. She was still defending her husband and the Nazis.

Until he died, Heydrich boasted that he had started World War II by the ruse of taking inmates from German concentration camps, dressing them in Polish uniforms, and having them attack a radio station. German forces, then, had the pretext they needed in world opinion for invading Poland on 1 September 1939. With this act, World War II began.⁶⁹

In another vital area, Heydrich was a major customer of the Enigma coding machines, which were mass produced on the Czech border near Poland. These cipher machines had been built to Heydrich's specifications in a factory in Berlin.

They were called Heydrich-Enigma, the machine for carrying top-secret signals to guide the massive Nazi war machine. As quoted in *A Man Called Intrepid* (p. 38): "Heydrich was in charge. His signature was to become, in secret warfare, greater than any rival within the Nazi camp."⁷⁰

In another major deception, Heydrich, in 1936, had 32 documents forged and planted to inflame Stalin's paranoid suspicions of the people around him. This resulted in the famous Moscow trials and the Red Army purges that followed. Thus, more than half of the Russian officer corps—35,000 men—were executed or banished, leaving the Soviets in no position at that time to fight a major war against Hitler.⁷¹ Heydrich, according to *A Man Called Intrepid* (p. 37), was "the architect" of this triumph in Nazi deception, and he was Intrepid's opposite number in the developing battle of wits.[72]

So monstrous were Heydrich's plans for mass extermination and so powerful in his RSHA that the British began plans in August 1941 to assassinate him. Two Czech agents, Josef Gabcik and Jan Kubris, were selected to kill Heydrich as he left his Hradčany castle in Prague on 27 May 1942.[73] Because they had been parachuted by the British into the area near the village of Lidice, 20 milesnorthwest of Prague, in June, Lidice was later burned to the ground, and all of the men killed and the women sent to concentration camps. (Those children "suitable" for adoption by German families were kidnapped and placed with different families.)[74] I visited Lidice in 1947 with Harold Stassen and Jan Masaryk, the foreign minister of Czechoslovakia. A little later, Masaryk committed suicide, or, as some say, was pushed from a window by Soviet agents.

Schellenberg and Kaltenbrunner

SS General Walter Schellenberg, head of foreign intelligence under Heydrich and then Kaltenbrunner, in his *Memoirs* (originally published in 1956), said of Heydrich (p. 30): "This man was the hidden pivot around which the Nazi regime revolved. The development of a whole nation was guided indirectly by his forceful character. He was far superior to all of his political colleagues and controlled them as he controlled the best intelligence machine of the SD.... He made Hitler dependent on him by fulfilling all his most insane schemes, thus making himself indispensable. He supplied Himmler with brilliant ideas so that he could shine in conference with Hitler, Hess, Bormann, and the general staff."

Schellenberg considered Kaltenbrunner to be his (Schellenberg's) most formidable opponent. He said, "My choice (for head of the RSHA) would have been almost anyone except the man whom Hitler finally selected, SS Obergruppenführer Ernst Kaltenbrunner." He went on to say that "Kaltenbrunner was a giant in stature, heavy in his movements—a real lumberjack. It was his square, heavy chin which expressed the character of the man. The thick neck, forming a straight line with the back of his head, increased the impression of his rough-hewn coarseness. His small, penetrating brown eyes were unpleasant; they looked at one fixedly, like the eyes of a viper seeking to petrify its prey. When one expected Kaltenbrunner to say something, his angular, wooden face would remain quite inexpressive; then, after several seconds of oppressive silence, he would bang the table and begin to speak. I always had the feeling that I was looking at the hands of an old gorilla. They were much too small, and the fingers were brown and discolored, for Kaltenbrunner smoked up to 100 cigarettes a day."[75]

Kaltenbrunner also drank heavily during the day. Dr. Felix Kersten, Himmler's physician, said, "I've seldom had such a tough, callous ox to examine as this fellow Kaltenbrunner. A block of wood would be more sensitive. He's coarse, hard-bitten, probably only capable of thinking when he's drunk. Naturally, he'll be the right man for Hitler."[76]

Schellenberg reported further on his relations with Kaltenbrunner (*Memoirs*, pp. 374-375). He said that Kaltenbrunner and he hated each other; that Heydrich disliked Kaltenbrunner, and Kaltenbrunner disliked Heydrich. Schellenberg was the only one of Kaltenbrunner's departmental chiefs who had direct access to Himmler and even Hitler. Schellenberger stated: "My having direct access to Himmler was the worst thorn in Kaltenbrunner's flesh. My limited interest in nicotine and alcohol was another thing which infuriated him— the more desperate the situation became towards the end of the war, the more Kaltenbrunner drank." At staff meetings, Kaltenbrunner "availed himself of the opportunity to attack me in the most sadistic manner." When Schellenberg complained to Himmler about this, Himmler warned Schellenberg not to react to it "because of Kaltenbrunner's relationship with Hitler."[77]

By the beginning of August 1944, Kaltenbrunner had finished the consolidation of the German military intelligence (the Abwehr) under Admiral Canaris into the RSHA. Kaltenbrunner, according to Schellenberg, had ordered Schellenberg to arrest Canaris after the July 20 plot (p. 409). Kaltenbrunner had already been placed in charge—by Hitler, not Himmler—of the investigation and the rooting out of all people involved in the 20 July 1944 plot against Hitler's life. In March 1945, again, according to Schellenberg, "Hitler and Kaltenbrunner jointly ordered the execution of Canaris" (p. 412).[78] In July 1944, two dispatch cases containing incriminating documents were discovered in a safe in one of Canaris's offices outside Berlin. Canaris had been involved with the opposition to Hitler since 1939 in peace negotiations centered on the Vatican (p. 400). One of the most important documents, however, the diary of the mysterious Admiral Canaris, was never found.[79]

Dr. Wilhelm Höttl and Kaltenbrunner

Dr. Wilhelm Höttl was deputy head of Kaltenbrunner's Central and Southeast Europe Intelligence Section under General Schellenberg. As indicatedearlier, I had arrested Dr. Höttl in Alt Aussee in May 1945. I was to talk with him again at length in 1956, 1960, 1975, and 1978. He was one of the brightest and mostarticulate of the people around Kaltenbrunner. He testified at length on Kaltenbrunner and the RSHA. Some of this testimony must be treated with skepticism. Still, he was one of the best sources of information. In a book titled *The Secret Front: The Inside Story of Nazi Political Espionage*, first published in Great Britain in 1953, he had some interesting things to say about Heydrich, Kaltenbrunner, the RSHA, and, particularly, the Alpine Redoubt and its relation to Allen Dulles's negotiations for the surrender of northern Italy.[80]

Höttl related how, in 1938, after Hitler's annexation of Austria, he was recruited by "the Secret Service"—the SD. He was a post-graduate in history at the University of Vienna, specializing in Southeast Europe questions. He climbed rapidly until 1944, when, in the course of his promotions, he came to know Heydrich, Kaltenbrunner, Schellenberg, and Himmler well. His description of Heydrich and the organization he created, using Himmler as a foil, compares well with that found in *A Man Called Intrepid*.

According to Höttl (in *The Secret Front*, pp. 32-33), Heydrich was "without doubt an outstanding personality and leading figure—not only of National Socialism but of the whole conception of the totalitarian state.[81] [Italian] Cesare Borgia [1475-1507, ex-cardinal obsessed with control/power and inspiration for Machiavelli's *The Prince*] is perhaps the closest historical analogy that can be drawn.[82] Both men were imbued with the same complete disregard for all ethical values, the same frigidity of heart, the same systematically calculated ambition, and even the same physical beauty of a fallen angel." He went on to say that Heydrich "was devoid even of the most elementary and instinctive moral sense. Not the State but power—personal power—was his god.... As a result, the man's whole life was an unbroken chain of murders—murders of people whom he disliked ... of opponents and of those whom he regarded as untrustworthy....

The light of human life had no value in Heydrich's eyes—his crimes were not the outcome of uncontrollable impulse but the devilish nihilism of an undoubtedly great mind."[83]

Höttl's summation of Heydrich was that Heydrich was the "most terrible of all the leaders of the Third Reich." A source of his power, according to Höttl, was detailed in the files he kept on the leaders of Nazi Germany, including Hitler himself. "The secret files, which Heydrich kept in his own hands, were among the most dreaded documents in the whole of the Third Reich. It was he who devised the scheme for the Final Solution of the Jewish Problem, and it was he who invented the horrible machinery by which, in an 'imperceptible manner,' millions of people were hounded to their deaths."[84]

Höttl's description of Himmler, who in position, but position only, was next to Hitler in power, is equally interesting. Himmler "in both mentality and appearance resembled some petty bank clerk." To the question of how Himmler achieved such prominence, Höttl said there was only one true answer. "Heydrich carried him to the top." Hitler eventually "realized that Himmler was nothing more than a puppet of Heydrich, and he began more and more to draw directly the latter to his side." Heydrich's aim was to topple Himmler and then, with his position of power consolidated, to replace Hitler as head of Nazi Germany. His premature death in 1942 prevented this.[85]

According to Höttl, "Kaltenbrunner [who officially succeeded Heydrich in January 1943] neither possessed the necessary personal drive and initiative to oust Himmler from his privileged position with the Führer, nor for a very long time did he evince the slightest desire to do so." Kaltenbrunner, according to Höttl, had been earlier a close collaborator of Heydrich as chief of the forbidden Austrian SS before 1938. Hitler and Kaltenbrunner were fellow Austrians and: "To the very end, Hitler's personality held an almost mesmeric fascination for him; he sincerely worshipped him." Only at the end did he see that Hitler was leading Germany to inevitable annihilation, and only then, likely motivated by his desire to stay alive, did he join a separate effort to secure peace through Höttl's contacts with Allen Dulles's office in Bern.

Still, Kaltenbrunner, according to Höttl, "had risen to become the second most powerful man in Germany" (p. 305). He had become so because of the unusual power with which Heydrich had endowed the office. Contributing to Kaltenbrunner's rise in power at the end was the fact that "Hitler realized more and more what a really insignificant person Himmler was."[86]

Dr. Höttl is also the source of some interesting information on Hitler's Alpine Redoubt. It was only after the Allies began to show concern about a last stand at the Alpine Redoubt area, which extended from Berchtesgaden to Alt Aussee, that Hitler ordered Gauleiter of the Tyrol, Franz Hofer, to proceed with plans for its construction in November 1944. Gauleiter Rainer of Carinthia [Austria] also started work on the fortification. The Allies' concern, according to Höttl, arose partly as a result of German propaganda and partly as a result of false plants by Schellenberg's Secret Service. This concern then became the basis for Kaltenbrunner and his agent Höttl to try to secure better terms for at least that part of Austria that was affected.

Höttl reported that the German Secret Service first became aware of Allen Dulles's presence in Bern, Switzerland, in the fall of 1944. He claimed (pp. 290-291) that Dulles's messages to Washington were picked up, deciphered, and passed to the Nazis by the Hungarian monitor service in Budapest, where Höttl was located, until he left for Alt Aussee to be near Kaltenbrunner. Kaltenbrunner, as indicated earlier, had been placed in command of western Austria and southern Germany by Himmler in March 1945, in the face of the Allied threat to split Germany. But, in April, when Himmler learned of Kaltenbrunner's efforts to contact Dulles, he left Kaltenbrunner only with western Austria. By this time, all of the German generals— Field Marshal Kesselring (Army Group South); General Rendulic, commander in chief of the Austro-Hungarian frontier; General Löhr on the Austro-Yugoslav frontier; and Field Marshal von Rundstedt— were in support of the Alpine Redoubt plan and using it as a bargaining tool with the Allies to get better terms.[87]

According to Höttl (p. 296), Kaltenbrunner realized that if SS General Karl Wolff (the senior SS and police officer in Italy and for years Himmler's chief of staff and close friend) was successful in arranging the surrender of southern Germany Army groups in northern Italy, that this would wreck Kaltenbrunner's plan to use the Alpine Redoubt as a bargaining piece. Kaltenbrunner, therefore, persuaded Himmler to tell Wolff to cease his talks with Dulles. Despite an order from Himmler, Wolff proceeded anyway. On 19 March 1945, Dulles, Wolff, U.S. General Lyman Lemnitzer, and U.K. General Airey reached complete agreement on the surrender of the forces of northern Italy.

Wolff then tried to get Himmler's agreement, but Himmler, fearing Hitler, left it to Kaltenbrunner, who then decided to take part in this [plan] himself.[88]

Kaltenbrunner arranged to meet Professor Burckhardt, president of the International Committee of the Red Cross, at the Austro-Swiss frontier near Feldkirch. At this time, from late March 1945, after his twins by his mistress Gisela were born, until his capture in May, Kaltenbrunner had been spending time in Alt Aussee in Prince Hohenlohe's guest house. Hitler had done nothing to discourage the idea of the Alpine Redoubt, and Nazi officials and Nazi puppet governors from Eastern Europe were moving in numbers to Alt Aussee (as the command post for the Alpine Redoubt) nestled between the 7,000-foot precipices of the Dachstein and Dead Mountains. It was all but invisible to aircraft, and two major demolitions would render the roads impassable for a very long time. It was here that Gauleiter Eigruber wanted Hitler to come, and it was here that he wanted, according to Höttl, to construct the great defensive Redoubt. It was here that Hitler's private papers were to be sent. Instead, at the end, these papers were destroyed in the Berlin bunker (Führerbunker) on Hitler's order.

It was also to Alt Aussee that Otto Skorzeny came to report to Kaltenbrunner and to make preparations for guerilla warfare. He wanted Kaltenbrunner to take refuge in a hut that he had prepared in the Dachstein and where he himself hid out until late May when he surrendered to an American general in Salzburg. It was also at Alt Aussee that Adolf Eichmann came to report to his boss Kaltenbrunner. Kaltenbrunner, knowing that Eichmann was likely a priority target pursued by the Allies, wanted nothing to do with him, so he told him to take off for Spain and reportedly gave him a large sum of money in gold and foreign currency. Eichmann didn't need the money, for he had brought "Jewish treasure" with him from Prague.

As I was to learn in 1960 from Prince Hohenlohe, and as indicated earlier, as I entered Alt Aussee on 9 May 1945, Eichmann and his men slipped out the other end to ascend to the Blaa Alm. His truck broke down, however, and, according to Höttl, large amounts of gold and other valuables were buried in the surrounding forest. As Höttl stated (p. 316), "Alt Aussee became a veritable second Klondyke."[89] All of the Balkan leaders brought with them gold and foreign currency, which they buried here and, if not arrested, returned later to retrieve.

German foreign office officials from Berlin started their trek to the Redoubt in April and buried gold around Alt Aussee.

Europe's priceless works of art were being transferred to the Alt Aussee salt mines starting in 1944. Gold and foreign currency were also dumped in nearby lakes—Altausseer See and Toplitzsee. RSHA officials were said to have buried the gold around Villa Kerry above Alt Aussee. Christl Kerry, the 85-year-old owner, pointed out these places to Jane and me in 1975. By strange happenstance, I was to be associated with the gold of Alt Aussee in September 1979 when I returned there. An article in the October 1979 *Salzkammergut Illustrierte* reported that I was back on a secret mission for CIA to track down the missing gold. With gold prices up to $400 and later $800 an ounce, this fantastic story was given more credence.

As Höttl reported, in 1949, Walter Schellenberg was finally sentenced by the Allies at the trial of German foreign service officials to six years' imprisonment. Through his Bernadotte connections, he first took refuge in Sweden. But Schellenberg was a sick man and, therefore, did not serve his sentence. He went to Switzerland, then (as indicated earlier) to Spain, and finally to Italy, where he died in the summer of 1952 as he was writing his memoirs. They have since been published.

Kaltenbrunner, according to Höttl (p. 320), left Alt Aussee with his adjutant [Arthur Scheidler] and two SS men on 7 May for his hiding place in Prince Hohenlohe's *Jagdhaus* in the Dead Mountains.

Höttl said the false papers Kaltenbrunner carried were ridiculous—an army pay book in the name of a medical officer. Höttl said the mountains were still under heavy snow at that time of year, and no

Wildensee Hut. Photos by Fredric Matteson, 1978.

progress could be made without skis. It was true there was heavy snow, but progress could be made without skis, as I found out if one went up at night into the early morning before the sun melted the heavy crust. Höttl inaccurately reported that "over a hundred men led by a guide who had betrayed him rushed the hut" and "out staggered a man half asleep who after the briefest interrogation admitted that he was indeed Kaltenbrunner."[90]

I didn't read this account by Dr. Höttl until 1977, but it explained the reason for Höttl twice asking me (1956 and 1975) if I would send my account of the capture of Kaltenbrunner. He knew he didn't have the correct account, and this may be equally true of other parts of his book. In fact, on 27 April 1955, he wrote Major Ralph Pearson a letter saying, "It was very important for me to hear from you about the arrest of Kaltenbrunner which happened in May 1945. I will consider correcting my version in my *Secret Front*. My opinion and basis for it came not only from the German press at that time, but also it was presented before the Nuremberg trial, and Dr. Kaltenbrunner did not deny it. On the basis of your explanation, I will take your representation as the correct one."[91] I later sent Höttl my account written for CIA's *Studies in Intelligence* in 1959.[92]

★ ★ ★

At the end of the war, Kaltenbrunner was, according to Dr. Höttl's book, "the second most powerful man in Germany."[93] Höttl could say this because, in the end, Himmler and Göring had been disowned by Hitler because Kaltenbrunner's influence with Hitler, by everybody's account, had increased enormously since July 1944, with his ruthless rooting out of the Hitler opposition; because, like Hitler, he was an Austrian; because he controlled the Heydrich-created monstrously powerful RSHA; and, finally, because in the end, he was placed in charge of the Alpine Redoubt, where the Nazis' last stand was to take place. Having done so well in his competition for power, Kaltenbrunner had inevitably a certain confidence in his ability to survive any situation.

Höttl ended his book by saying, "It seems strange as I look out over this peaceful lake [at Alt Aussee] and mountains that this placid Alpine resort was eight years ago refuge to half of the 'wanted' men of Europe and the hiding place of Hitler's loot and stolen property of Europe's oppressed peoples."⁹⁴ To a certain degree, this was a fair description.

Allen Dulles and Kaltenbrunner: "Operation Sunrise"

In 1966 (after he retired), Allen Dulles invited me for dinner, and we discussed the possibility of a book on Kaltenbrunner and the RSHA. He wrote a letter to his publisher and sent him a short account of the CIA publication.

Dulles's book [The] Secret Surrender, published in 1966, sheds further light on what Kaltenbrunner's and his agent Höttl's roles were in negotiations for the final surrender of the Nazi forces in northern Italy. The code name for that operation was "Operation Sunrise." Dulles reported that the first contact with his office in Bern by the Kaltenbrunner people was at the end of February 1945. He stated (p. 50) that an Austrian agent had been "sent by Kaltenbrunner himself, chief of the RSHA and the most powerful man in the SS after Himmler. The Austrian had been acquainted with Wilhelm Höttl, one of Kaltenbrunner's intelligence officials in Austria, and through him had met Kaltenbrunner. Kaltenbrunner wanted him to tell us that he and Himmler were anxious to end the war and were contemplating liquidating the warmongers within the Nazi Party, especially Martin Bormann."⁹⁵

What was important, Dulles said, in this new opening was that there was a "powerful person who did not intend to go along with Hitler, Bormann, and the diehards in the plan to hold out in an Alpine Redoubt." Dulles recognized that Kaltenbrunner was trying to maneuver himself into a favorable position as peacemaker, "perhaps even under the illusion that the Allies would allow this group to take the lead."⁹⁶ This certainly dovetailed with what Kaltenbrunner told me the day of his capture on 12 May. Kaltenbrunner was hoping, in his surrender of the Alpine Redoubt and the forces there, that the Allies would put him in as chief adviser or even prime minister of a free Austria that would join with the West in a final war to wipe Bolshevism off the face of the earth.

SS General Karl Wolff had been sent by Himmler on 9 September 1943 to take charge of northern Italy from Naples to the Brenner Pass and to be the adviser to Mussolini. Kaltenbrunner had sent SS General Wilhelm Harster [commander of the Security Police—SIPO and SD] with Wolff. As stated earlier, Wolff had previously been chief of Himmler's personal staff and liaison between Himmler and Hitler, and Himmler and Ribbentrop. I had been told that Wolff had been married to a countess at first. I was led to believe that this was Gisela von Westarp. This would have been previous to her becoming Kaltenbrunner's mistress and producing twins by him in March 1945. This seemed to fit with the fact that Kaltenbrunner had first met Gisela at Himmler's headquarters in the spring of 1943 after Kaltenbrunner had succeeded to Heydrich's position. In 1979, however, Jane and I learned from Gisela in Munich that the "Wolff" mentioned was a Nazi war correspondent, not General Wolff.

According to Dulles, Kaltenbrunner had a strong dislike for General Wolff.[97] On 9 March 1945, Kaltenbrunner ordered Wolff to meet him in Innsbruck. He had become aware of Wolff's dealings with Dulles. Wolff was afraid that Kaltenbrunner would arrest him, so he didn't go. Wolff was then summoned to Berlin on 23 March to see Himmler and Kaltenbrunner. Dulles stated (p. 132) that Himmler and Kaltenbrunner "came close to wrecking 'Operation Sunrise,'" which was the code name for the secret surrender of northern Italy.[98] Kaltenbrunner saw the surrender of northern Italy as undermining his plan to surrender the Alpine Redoubt. A prior surrender of the North Italy German forces would remove much of the leverage Kaltenbrunner hoped to obtain from his own deal with the West.

Wolff was a close friend of Himmler's, so in Bern, on 9 March 1945, instead of arresting Wolff for treason in his contacts with Dulles and [German economist and assistant to Dulles in Europe] Gero von Schulze-Gaevernitz, Himmler simply reprimanded him for bypassing Kaltenbrunner and Schellenberg. He instructed him to meet with Kaltenbrunner and others in a castle near Hof in northern Bavaria, which was the relocation center of the RSHA headquarters. Wolff then boldly suggested that Kaltenbrunner and himself meet with Hitler on the subject of negotiation with Dulles. Himmler and Kaltenbrunner, fearing Hitler's anger, vetoed this idea. Himmler then compromised with Kaltenbrunner and ordered Wolff to keep the door open to Dulles but not to go to Switzerland again. Himmler already had his own line open to the West through Count Bernadotte.[99]

Dulles reported that on 13 April 1945, Höttl arrived in Bern to see Dulles with a message from Kaltenbrunner. Dulles, knowing Wolff's meeting with Kaltenbrunner and Himmler in Berlin three weeks earlier, feared that this was an attempt by Kaltenbrunner to undercut Wolff. So he refused to see Höttl, but he did want to hear Höttl's message. He asked an aide—I believe it may have been [future CIA operative] Tracy Barnes—to see Höttl in Zurich. Only Barnes, Dulles, Schulze-Gaevernitz, and one other aide knew of "Operation Sunrise." The Höttl message from Kaltenbrunner to Dulles (p. 152) was that Kaltenbrunner "wanted to help the Western Allies by doing everything possible to prevent the establishment of the Alpine Redoubt."[100]

On 15 April, only two weeks before Hitler's suicide, Wolff was again ordered to meet Himmler and Kaltenbrunner in Berlin on 17 April. He flew to Berlin and was driven to Hohenlychen, 100 kilometers north of Berlin, where Himmler and Kaltenbrunner were waiting. Again, Wolff suggested they see Hitler. On 18 April, Kaltenbrunner and Wolff drove to Berlin, where they first met with SS General Hermann Fegelein. Fegelein was married to Eva Braun's sister and had succeeded Wolff as liaison between Himmler and Hitler. Fegelein and Kaltenbrunner then attended a briefing for Hitler, and afterward, Wolff was called in to meet with Hitler, Kaltenbrunner, and Fegelein. Kaltenbrunner had already told Hitler of Wolff's conversation with Dulles, thinking that Hitler would order Wolff's arrest. But Wolff reminded Hitler that on 6 February, in a meeting with Hitler and Ribbentrop, Wolff had told him of the opening to Dulles, and Hitler had not said "No." Hitler then broke off the conversation and told Wolff to see him later that day. Hitler was by now (April 18) a mental and physical wreck.

At 5:00 p.m. on 18 April, Hitler resumed meeting with Wolff, Kaltenbrunner, and Fegelein. [Ten days later, he had Fegelein shot for treason, thinking that Fegelein was trying to escape to freedom.] He spoke of the USSR's great losses and how he would establish three strongholds—one in the center under him, one in the north, presumably under Himmler, and one in the south in the Alpine Redoubt, presumably under Kaltenbrunner. The strategy was to have the USSR and the U.S. collide in open areas between three strongholds, not stopping at the line agreed at Yalta. At this point, Hitler would step in on one side or the other.

According to Dulles (p. 179), Hitler then ordered Wolff back to Italy and told him to get better terms from Dulles.[101] On 29 April, Dulles received two pieces of information from his OSS sources: First, Kaltenbrunner was desperately trying to stop the surrender of northern Italy so he could make his own peace deal; and second,

Kaltenbrunner would arrest General Wolff and his envoys. This had been confirmed by Höttl, who, entering Zurich on forged papers, said that Kaltenbrunner wanted to come to the Austrian-Swiss border at Feldkirch and discuss the whole matter. Höttl reported that General Vietinghoff, in charge of northern Italy, Field Marshal Kesselring in the west, General Rendulic in the south, General Loehr on the Balkan-Adriatic front, and the Gauleiters of Austria (Hofer, Jury, Eigruber) were in agreement with Kaltenbrunner's plan.

To Dulles, it was obvious that Kaltenbrunner was trying to invalidate Operation Sunrise and the surrender of Vietinghoff's forces. At the same time, Höttl was promising that Kaltenbrunner would deliver all of Austria, including theAlpine Redoubt. According to Dulles (pp. 22-23), Kaltenbrunner, an Austrian, was "one of the most wanted men on the list of war criminals." Dulles wrote: "It is difficult to conceive, then and now, how he could have imagined that the Allies would deal with him, would believe his transparent lies and claims, or would entertain the idea of a separate surrender with Austria, which for some years had been an integral part of the Greater German Reich."[102]

Count Folke Bernadotte's Contacts with Kaltenbrunner

Schellenberg also reported how Count Folke Bernadotte of Sweden was in contact with Himmler not only to arrange for the release of Scandinavian concentration camp inmates but also to bring an early peace with Western Allies.[103] [Schellenberg:] "Himmler was afraid that if Kaltenbrunner found out, he would immediately report the matter to Hitler...." Schellenberg then tried to argue Himmler into assassinating Hitler and taking over command since Hitler would never surrender, and this meant the needless destruction of all of Germany.

Himmler indicated this was impossible, but he did agree to have Count Bernadotte take the Western Allies an offer of surrender. The Allies' answer was they didn't want to negotiate with Himmler. In the meantime, Kaltenbrunner, having been informed of Schellenberg's contacts with Bernadotte, ordered Schellenberg dismissed and, in his place, put Wilhelm Waneck as chief of all foreign political activities of Amt VI of the RSHA. At the same time, he placed Otto Skorzeny in charge of the foreign military intelligence activities. As indicated earlier, I had arrested Waneck in Alt Aussee in May 1945, but Skorzeny, who was hiding out in the Dachstein mountains across from Alt Aussee, escaped. I later interviewed Skorzeny in Madrid in 1963 when I was on a European speaking tour for the State Department explaining Kennedy's new U.S. disarmament policy.

Count Folke Bernadotte, in his book *The Curtain Falls: Last Days of the Third Reich* described in his own words his mission at the end of the war as representative of the Swedish Red Cross. The mission was to get Himmler and Kaltenbrunner to agree on the release of Swedish and Norwegian and Danish concentration camp inmates and Swedish women married to Germans.[104] In June 1946, Bernadotte was the honored guest at the traditional Scandinavian "Svenskarnas Dag" festival in Minneapolis. I had the honor of introducing him to an audience of 10,000 people in Powderhorn Park. In 1947, Harold Stassen and I visited his wife, Countess Bernadotte, at their palace "Dragongarden" outside of Stockholm. On 17 September 1948, Count Bernadotte, acting as UN mediator in the Middle East, was assassinated by terrorists in Jerusalem.

In his book, Bernadotte describes SS General Kaltenbrunner as "my opponent"—as one who "was trying to wreck my agreement with Himmler: for the evacuation of Scandinavian inmates to Sweden." Bernadotte, in a letter to me dated 24 October 1946 from Stockholm, said, "I have never met as hard a man as Kaltenbrunner, whose whole expression gave an impression that you met a cruel man without any heart and without any wish to help the many suffering people who at that time were prisoners in the German concentration camps." Schellenberg told Bernadotte that Kaltenbrunner, "possessor of great influence over Hitler, was furious at the concessions Himmler had granted me, and Kaltenbrunner was a very dangerous man."[105]

In his assessment of the leaders of the Third Reich, Bernadotte, in his book, described Kaltenbrunner as "one of the most evil spirits among the little group of men and women who guided Germany's destiny in those days." He went on to say, "These four—the two sisters Braun, Kaltenbrunner, and Fegelein—were among the most dangerous in the circle surrounding Hitler. In the final phase, Kaltenbrunner spent several hours every day with the Führer and did all he could to work him [Hitler] up to continue the course upon which he had embarked so long ago." [106]

In his *Memoirs* (pp. 241-242), Schellenberg gave a vivid portrayal of the physical layout of his office as head of Amt VI of the RSHA under

Kaltenbrunner. "Microphones were hidden everywhere, in the walls, under the desk, even in one of the lamps so that every conversation and every sound was automatically recorded. The windows of the room were covered with wire mesh. There was an electrically charged safety device that was switched on at night and formed part of a system of photoelectric cells that sounded an alarm if anyone approached the windows, doors, safe, or, in fact, tried to get close to any part of my offices. Within 30 seconds, a squadron of armed guards would have surrounded the entire area.

"My desk was like a small fortress. Two automatic guns were built into it, which could spray the whole room with bullets. These guns pointed at the visitor and followed his or her progress towards my desk. All I had to do in an emergency was to press another button, and a siren would summon the guards to surround the building and block every exit.... Whenever I was on missions abroad, I was under standing orders to have an artificial tooth inserted which contained enough poison to kill me within 30 seconds if I were captured by an enemy. To make doubly sure, I wore a signet ring in which, under a large blue stone, a gold capsule was hidden containing cyanide."[107]

One of the most interesting aspects of the intelligence game—played by all countries the world over—is what and whom is to be believed. With intelligence officers adept at forgeries, planting stories, and using double agents, it is no wonder that much good intelligence is never believed or acted on. A classic case is Operation Cicero in which Pierre, the valet to the British ambassador to Turkey, was copying documents from the ambassador's safe and selling them for huge sums (of counterfeit British pound notes) to C. L. Moyzisch, the Schellenberg and Kaltenbrunner agent in Ankara. The ambassador usually took sleeping pills, and after he had fallen asleep, the valet would remain in the room to clean his master's suit. He would take the key to the safe, open it, and using a strong light and Leica camera Moyzisch had given him, take photographs.

One of the films, for example, contained a report on the conference Eden, Molotov, and Hull held in Moscow in 1943. Another concerned "Overlord," the code name for the Allied invasion of France. Others were reports on the heads of government conferences in Cairo in November 1943 and at Teheran in early December 1943. But Kaltenbrunner, Ribbentrop, and Hitler were never sure the documents were not a plant, and therefore, the intelligence was not acted on.

Operation Bernhard: The Printing of False Money

One of the operations of the RSHA to which Schellenberg refers was Operation Bernhard. Wilhelm Höttl, in his book *Hitler's Paper Weapon*, described the operation in greater detail. Höttl had a responsibility for this, working out of Schellenberg's Amt VI of the RSHA. As indicated earlier, I had arrested Höttl on 16 May 1945 in Alt Aussee. Because the foreign currency and gold reserves of the Nazi Reich had become strained, the RSHA began to forge British pound notes, bank notes, and Russian rubles for its own foreign intelligence purposes. It took two years to imitate the greaseproof paper, and two paper mills, one in Rhineland and one in Sudetenland [parts of northern, southern, and western former Czechoslovakia], were devoted solely to this task. The highly complicated process of engraving could be started only after 160 main identifying marks had been determined. Professors of mathematics worked out the system of British bank note registration numbers so that the German output was always 100 to 200 notes ahead of the Bank of England. The forgeries were so perfect that even the Swiss and British bank cashiers could not detect them.

Counterfeit Bank of England Five Pound Note, 9 March 1938. From Robert E. Matteson's WW2 archival collection. Courtesy of Wisconsin Veterans Museum.

One plan was to send bombers over Britain that would drop the forged bank notes by the ton, thus disrupting the entire British economic system. Because Britain was too well defended and because of a scarcity of fuel, that part of the plan was never carried out. However, millions of dollars of pound notes got into circulation through the use of forgeries to pay for operations abroad. One famous example was the payment of the valet to the British ambassador, Hughe Knatchbull-Hugessen, in Turkey for secret documents taken from the ambassador's safe. This was the famous Operation Cicero [mentioned previously] that later became the basis for a successful movie called *Five Fingers*. It was Kaltenbrunner's subordinate man in Ankara, C-2 Moyzisch, who was the RSHA contact with the valet called Pierre.

Kaltenbrunner's Personality

G. M. Gilbert, the American prison psychologist at the Nuremberg trials, in his book *Nuremberg Diary*, reported that while Kaltenbrunner had above average intelligence, as did all the Nazi leaders except Streicher, he ranked next to lowest in IQ. Hjalmar Schacht had the highest, 143, and Streicher the lowest, 106. Kaltenbrunner had 113. Those at the top after Schacht were Seyss-Inquart, 141; Göring, 138; and Doenitz, 138. Those at the bottom third, above Streicher and Kaltenbrunner, were Sauckel, 118; and Rudolph Hess, 120. Albert Speer, 128; Field Marshal Keitel, 129; and von Ribbentrop, 129, were in the middle range.[108]

One of the better books on the Nuremberg trial is Eugene Davidson's *The Trial of the Germans [Nuremberg: 1945-1946]*. His research covered a period of seven years. His description of Kaltenbrunner was "A giant of a man, heavy set with a thick neck that went up like a block from his shoulders to his head, with piercing brown eyes, a deep scar that rose from the left of his mouth to his nose, and bad teeth with some missing. Kaltenbrunner looked like what he was—a killer" And: "Toward the end of the war, even Himmler said he had to watch out for Kaltenbrunner. Kaltenbrunner would use any weapon to advance himself, and anyone might be his Victim.... He was a gangster filled with hatred and resentment and plans for improving his own condition."[109]

People have asked me what manner of man Kaltenbrunner was. I am not a psychiatrist, and I cannot give an exact answer. His mistress,

Gisela von Westarp, has told me that Kaltenbrunner, as a person, was kind and courteous and that he couldn't tolerate an unthinking person. She said he was the type who could compose poems and fairy tales for children. Dr. Höttl, who perhaps knew Kaltenbrunner as well as anyone, told me that Kaltenbrunner was a typical Nazi leader, though his manners were better, his outlook wider, and his personal integrity less compromised.

Those were his friends.

His enemies, for example, Schellenberg, who occupied an important post under him, have said that he lacked any spark of humanity and that, like Hitler and Heydrich, he only believed in his star. Gisevius, the Gestapo double agent, described Kaltenbrunner as a monster worse than Heydrich. Certainly, if we judge him by the cold facts of documentary proof, we must conclude that, according to our ethics, he was amoral. He, like all other Hitler fanatics, was detached from human laws, and the abnormality of his environment became a law for him. Persons became nothing more than numbers. The infinity of the power lodged in his hands became a breeder of madness, and, as in all such people, the picture of Kaltenbrunner changed rapidly.

At the end, Kaltenbrunner could, with equanimity, annul apparent reason and order the wholesale slaughter of all concentration camp inmates. But likely due to the late stages of the war, with the Allies advancing, the camps under Kaltenbrunner were neither evacuated nor scenes of last-minute massacres. Afraid of the picture he had created, he tried, however, in the last days and in his final defense plea, to erase his role by denying responsibility for anything that happened in concentration camps.

To the consternation of the prosecution at the Nuremberg trial, documents with Kaltenbrunner's signature were few. Still, Kaltenbrunner will be long remembered by those who know—his undeniable connection with the Nazi police state, the concentration camps, the extermination of six million Jews, and the foreign and internal spy system of the Nazi Reich.

There is no doubt that Kaltenbrunner was an intelligent but primitive man who, under different circumstances in a different job, might have used his better-than-average abilities to less horrible ends. That is the most that one might say for him. But one fact is certain, as Justice Jackson has already said, "His personal capacity for evil is forever gone though his sinister influence may lurk in the world long after. He wrote his name in blood—a name to be remembered as a symbol for cruelty, degradation, and death."

Speculation on Why Kaltenbrunner Surrendered

It is interesting to speculate now that I have more background on Kaltenbrunner, as to why he chose not to shoot it out in the early morning of 12 May 1945 at the Wildensee hut on top of the Dead Mountains. He had the weapons and the strategic location from which to prevent or delay his capture. I was unarmed and the only one close to the cabin. The others would have had to approach across an open area that had relatively little to no cover. Kaltenbrunner's men not only had rifles and machine pistols but a machine gun. The Kaltenbrunner force could see their opposition when they moved, but the opposition could not see them. Also, as Kaltenbrunner indicated at Nuremberg, he must have realized that his chances of surviving after his capture were slim.

Why, then, did he surrender? So far as I know, he was not asked that question. But several things are clear. First, he had some hope that the Western Allies would accept his story that he had been trying to negotiate a separate peace since 1943 with the idea of setting up an anti-Communist government in Austria. Second, he believed that he could convince the Western Allies that he was involved only with intelligence and not with the Gestapo and concentration camps—that he was not a Heydrich and that Mueller and Eichmann, in reality, reported to Himmler. Third, in shooting it out, he might get killed and thus lose any chance of future survival and of satisfying his curiosity about what would happen next. Fourth, as Iris Scheidler pointed out to me in 1975, Kaltenbrunner was basically a coward. She described how, in March, on a trip to Salzburg with her, he had flung himself into a ditch at the first sound of an airplane above them. Fifth, he had read the note from Gisela von Westarp pleading with him to give up and surrender to the Americans before the Russians got him. And, finally, Kaltenbrunner, all his life, had been engaged in the conspiracies and jungle warfare of survival in competition with men like Mueller, Heydrich, Himmler, and Bormann, and he had survived.

Postscript: Away, Into the Mountains

In Alt Aussee on Sunday in late May or early June, when the mountain air was still cool and the mountain flowers in full bloom, the men would walk around the lake, Alt Aussersee, wearing Alpine hats festooned with a feather or a soft, short brush rising up at the back. They wore lederhosen, dark green stockings up to the knee, polished dark brown oxfords, green jackets, white shirts, and green neckties. The women wore dirndls, each with bright-colored skirts, white puffs at the shoulder, and bright-colored bodices. It was a beautiful sight with the flowers spilling out from the rocks, the snow-capped Dachstein in the background, the Loser and Trisselwand towering above, and the deep, cold, steel-blue waters of the lake in the foreground.

In the ensuing years—1956, 1960, 1975, 1978, and twice in 1979—Jane and I returned to Alt Aussee, to this lake and its surrounding mountains. Of all the places in the world that we have been outside of the United States, this is our favorite place.

On a Sunday morning in late October 1945, in order to get some exercise and get away from the desk [office stationed near Füssen, Germany], I crossed the Lech into Austria and started walking up the Achsel to the Musauer Alm. As I wrote Jane, "It was a beautiful day—warm sun, clear blue sky, red leaves, and snow on the mountain peaks. The first hour was straight up, then a long walk through pines along a ridge, then up again to the alm. I ate a sandwich I had brought with me and then started climbing to the Otto-Mayr-Hütte. From then on, I was above the timberline. I kept going until I had climbed the peak in front of me, Scharf Schrofen. The paths were covered with snow, so I went on a straight line up as best I could.

"Finally, after crawling along a sharp escarpment, I reached the top; the sun was sinking lower and lower. I could see for miles in every direction … huge billowing clouds surrounding the peaks all around me…. When I got back, I took a hot bath, drank some mulled wine, and went to bed. I had never felt so physically tired for a long time."

Bob Matteson in the Austrian Alps, 10 October 1945. Photo from Matteson's WW2 scrapbook titled "Kaltenbrunner + World War II + Nuremberg Trial." Courtesy of Wisconsin Veterans Museum.

Counterclockwise: photo by Heinrich Hoffmann of Kaltenbrunner - with Kaltenbrunner's signature; Gisela Von Westarp and Iris Scheidler; Matteson interviewed by Press; printed Extract of Award of Silver Star; Defendants at Nuremberg Trial; Chart showing Kaltenbrunner's importance in the German police state. Courtesy of Wisconsin Veterans Museum—from Matteson's WW2 scrapbook titled "Kaltenbrunner + World War II + Nuremberg Trial."

CHAPTER SEVEN
Coda

"Social scientists noted that the economic and political instability in Germany after World War I was crucial for Hitler's rise. But it took writers, philosophers, and historians to explain how authoritarians like Hitler harnessed societal instability into their own service."

—Heather Cox Richardson,
Democracy Awakening: Notes on the State of America.[110]

"Abundant evidence, too, lies before us in our time that the hostility [of racism] can be proof against reason and the standards of morality that are otherwise firmly rooted in the society and that it can erupt into slaughter."

—Eugene Davidson, The Trial of the Germans

Final Thoughts on the War

What were my thoughts regarding World War II? I had plenty of time to think about this as I moved from Le Havre to Southampton to New York City to Camp McCoy and home. Although World War II officially ended 2 September 1945, on V-J Day, the war ended for me 6 January 1946, when I was given an honorable discharge at Camp McCoy.

Because of the Kaltenbrunner capture, I was interviewed extensively by the public relations people at the discharge center. This became a press release for the Twin City newspapers and other newspapers featuring the Kaltenbrunner story.

When I arrived by train in St. Paul on Monday night, 7 January, Jane and I were finally reunited. Next day, in the *St. Paul Pioneer Press*, there was a picture of Jane meeting me at the station. I was given terminal leave until 26 January and put in the Army Reserve. It wasn't until 1 April 1953 that I was finally and officially discharged from the Army of the United States. I had been awarded the Combat Infantry Badge, the European Theater Ribbon with four bronze stars, the Silver Star, the American Theater Ribbon, the Victory Medal, and a battlefield commission. But more rewarding than any of these was the fact that the Allies had won instead of Hitler and Tojo, and the fact that I was one of the more fortunate ones to return home safely.

In Germany, I had been impressed in 1937 by some of the "good things" Hitler had done to improve economic conditions for the German people. There was a certain justification even—as seen from Germany's viewpoint—in why they felt the Versailles Treaty to be a humiliation. But with the annexation of Austria and the Munich agreement to dismember Czechoslovakia in 1938, and the annexation of Czechoslovakia and invasion of Poland in 1939, any dispassionate feeling I had about Hitler had disappeared. It wasn't until later that I learned of the concentration camps and the unbelievable war crimes. It became crystal clear from his actions that [Hitler's autobiographical, racist manifesto] *Mein Kampf* was his program.[111] In rapid succession followed the invasion of the lowlands and the occupation of France in 1940. And then, in 1941, came the invasion of Russia and the Japanese attack on Pearl Harbor.

The toughest physical part of the war for me, oddly enough, was desert maneuvers in Arizona in the winter of 1944. I had come out of several weeks in the hospital at Camp Callan, [La Jolla] California, where I was recovering from an infected leg wound [after scaling a cliff], and joined the 80th Division near Yuma, Arizona, the middle of February. The 80th had already been through tough maneuvers south of Murfreesboro, Tennessee, and at Camp Phillips, [Salina] Kansas. In November 1943, they had moved to the California-Arizona maneuver area near Yuma for their final hardening. They had been there three months when I joined them—a tough, callous bunch by then.

The European Theater of actual war was a picnic by comparison, for we were largely mechanized and had none of the long foot marches we experienced in the desert. When I was transferred into CIC to track down Nazis, plus the excitement of the front lines—this was high adventure. We always had plenty of food, clothing, and ammunition. The only time we were short of anything was the dash across France when we ran low on gasoline; it was nothing like World War I with its stalemated trench warfare in the mud and rain.

What is to be learned from this terrible episode—the Second World War—in world history? It can be said without exaggeration that the 20th century has been one of the bloodiest periods in all annals. Two world wars and a Vietnam War have left a legacy of death and destruction that may be said not to be equaled by all the wars of ancient and medieval history. Not even the days of Genghis Kahn and Attila the Hun have witnessed such slaughter, such cruelties, such wholesale deportations of people into slavery as have taken place in the 20th century. As someone pointed out, the Terror of Torquemada in the fifteenth century pales before the Nazi and Soviet inquisitions. If posterity is to survive, then we must eliminate the conditions creating the conditions and causes and prevent a recurrence of these events. This is the task of meaningful foreign policy.

But this task is not accomplished by merely the stating of it. The 20th century is evidence that with the products of the technological revolution, the task appears to have become more difficult than at any time since the rise of nation-states. But strong, clear-sighted women and statesmen provide hope, and as Henry Stimson pointed out in 1947, the Nuremberg Trials were another step on the path upward and marked "a landmark in the history of international law." Yet, hopes of successful international law or more remote, effective world government and general disarmament cannot be counted on for an early solution of the problem at hand. So long as there exists in the world a nation as powerful and power-minded as the Soviet Union [today, Russia], effective international law cannot be a reality, and the Eisenhower and Kennedy goal of "general and complete disarmament," in which I played a role as director of the White House Disarmament Staff, is but a distant dream.

The will and the power do not currently exist conjointly to bring nations before international law and have them obey it or to enforce general disarmament. We must accept the fact as it is—that the Soviet Union [Russia] will not coexist in true peace with other states of this world until a radical evolution or revolution has taken place within the USSR [Russia]. One of the great tasks of our foreign policy, in this long "balance of terror" period in endeavoring to provide the world with security, is to help educate the people of the so-called "free world" to the true nature of such potential antagonists so that they are ready and equipped to deal with them.

It is with this in mind that I now look back at SS General Ernst Kaltenbrunner and his RSHA—the security police and intelligence apparatus of the Nazi police state. For the instruction on the Soviet [Russian] power system, we can look to the parallel system in Nazi Germany, about which we have quite extensive information. I hope in this book that a description of the Nazi Reich Main Security Office (the RSHA) and its head, SS General Dr. Ernst Kaltenbrunner, has thrownsome light, particularly on existing totalitarian systems. This might assist us to understand and counteract more intelligently the principal power—the USSR [Russia]—that in the last part of the 20th century [and now well into the 21st century] still threatens world security.

As Justice Robert Jackson, the United States prosecutor at the Nuremberg Trials, said in his opening statement, these police-state leaders, these prisoners "represent sinister influences that will lurk in the world long after their bodies have returned to dust. We will show them to be living symbols of racial hatreds, of terrorism and violence, and of the arrogance and cruelty of power. They are symbols of fierce nationalisms and of militarism, of intrigue and war-making which have embroiled Europe generation after generation, crushing its manhood, destroying its homes, and impoverishing its life."[112] Later [in Jackson's closing statement], pointing to Kaltenbrunner, he said, "Kaltenbrunner, the grand inquisitor, took up the bloody mantle of Heydrich to stifle opposition and terrorize compliance and buttressed power of National Socialism on a foundation of guiltless corpses.... Where, for example, shall we find the hand that ran the concentration camps if it is not the hand of Kaltenbrunner?"[113]

No one I knew ever claimed that the 22 major war criminals did not get a fair trial. The fact that three (Schacht, von Papen, Fritzsche) were acquitted, and seven were given various sentences rather than hanging is some evidence of this. One of the greatest contributions of the trial was the conclusion that orders of the government or of a superior officer do not free men from responsibility for a crime. Criminal acts were committed by individuals, not by nations, and law, to be effective, must be applied to individuals. This even applies to military personnel. The Nazis were given the kind of trial that they themselves never gave to any man. Finally, one of the greatest achievements was getting the USSR [Russia] and 22 other nations to agree in London on 8 August 1945 that aggressive war is a crime against international society and that to exterminate, enslave, or deport civilian populations on political, racial or religious grounds, is also an international crime.

The Silver Star

On 5 June 1945, in a ceremony at the division headquarters in Vöcklabruck [Austria], I was awarded the Silver Star for the capture of Kaltenbrunner. Besides the G-2 staff and Captain McMillen's CIC, there was the G-3 staff headed by Major Coe Kerr. Colonel Richard Fleischer, the Division G-2, read the citation and pinned the decoration on me. He shook my hand, I saluted, and the audience clapped. The citation was in General Order-140, dated 29 May 1945. It read:

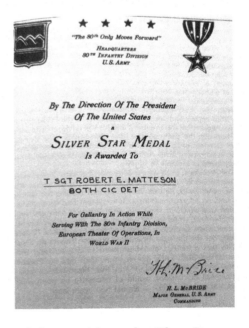

Award of Silver Star: By direction of the president, the Silver Star Medal is awarded to the following named personnel: Robert E. Matteson for gallantry in action in Austria 12 May 1945 in connection with military operations against an enemy of the United States. On 12 May 1945, after learning of the hideout of Gestapo Chief Kaltenbrunner and SS guards, Special Agent Matteson organized and led a patrol at night over the dangerous glacial trails to their mountain retreat. Dressed in Austrian clothes, Special Agent Matteson approached the cabin alone and unarmed, and after repeatedly knocking on the door, aroused the occupants, who were prepared to fight until they observed the patrol approaching. Breaking down the door, Special Agent Matteson and his men captured Kaltenbrunner, his aide Arthur Scheidler, two SS guards, and found two machine pistols, four rifles, two pistols, and a sub-machine gun with a large supply of ammunition. Special Agent Matteson's careful planning and fearless execution of a dangerous mission against an armed enemy of the most vicious and desperate type are a credit to himself and to the Armed Forces of the United States.[114]

The Silver Star Medal came in a nice case. It was a large gold star with a small silver star in the center and suspended from a red, white, and blue ribbon.

Photo by Fredric Matteson.

APPENDIX A

Excerpts from the *Last Valhalla of the Nazis* by Geoffrey Bocca[115]

The road up to the ski resort of Alt Aussee in the Austrian Tyrol is winding, but wide and dramatic.[116] The ascent begins at Salzburg, leads through dreamy Tyrolean villages, and sweeps past cold, black lakes into and out of tall forests of birch and pine and along by the foot of sheer peaks which are snow-capped all the year round. Alt Aussee is a town of rustic inns, fine restaurants, and magnificent ski tows. This is the Austrian Tyrol of today.... Alt Aussee was crowded 18 years ago with the SS, with Gestapo agents, with leaders of the collapsing Third Reich. It was then known as the Alpenfestung—the Alpine Fortress—or Hitler's Redoubt. Here, the German Army planned a last stand against the Allies. By flashing missiles down from the peaks like the thunderbolts of the old German gods, they would shatter their enemies and gain a 12th-hour victory against all odds.

Today, the great Hitler Redoubt has passed into legend, and the truth about it remains one of World War II's least-known stories.... The anxiety it caused Churchill and Eisenhower increased as the war progressed and percolated down to every fighting soldier.

The Nazi who conceived the idea of the Hitler Redoubt was Heinrich Himmler. Without consulting the Führer, who was totally consumed with stopping the Russians, Himmler gave the job of fortifying a sector of the Austrian Alps forty miles square to Dr. Ernst Kaltenbrunner, the scarfaced 6' 4" head of the Security Police and Intelligence or SD....

By the fall of 1944, whole industries had been moved to the Tyrol from the cities in the north to escape from Anglo-American bombers and the Russian hordes advancing from the east. Dr. Meindl, head of the Steyr Works, the largest of all Austrian munition factories, told Kaltenbrunner that he could move his entire plant without loss of production into caves, into the mountains—if Kaltenbrunner could provide the needed caves.

"We will provide them," said Kaltenbrunner, and he moved the whole population of Oranienburg concentration camp to a new camp which he established at Ebensee in the Austrian Alps about ten miles north of Alt Aussee. These slave laborers were set to blasting holes in the rock.

Kaltenbrunner, by the end of 1944, had reported to Himmler that the Alpenfestung was practicable. Arms and missiles would be produced in the caves, and the missiles would be tested on remote Lake Toplitz in the mountains where the German navy had already established an experimental station.... In the greatest natural fortress in Europe, almost bomb-proof, with neutral Switzerland at their backs, the Wehrmacht might hold out forever.... It would all be paid for in counterfeit English notes.

The manufacture of these notes, $600 million worth of them, is one of the more extraordinary stories of the war.... The notes were superb, almost faultless specimens which defied every test. Their manufacture—it was called Operation Bernhard—was the idea of Reinhard Heydrich, predecessor of Kaltenbrunner....

The presence of Lake Toplitz was another advantage Kaltenbrunner found in the Redoubt area. It is a beautiful but eerie three-mile stretch of water accessible only on foot.... Lake Toplitz has a distinct air of menace. Black rocks rise sheer around it so that no breezes riffle the water, and its surface is like polished ebony....

A [German] military HQ had been set up in Salzburg, [the] gateway to the Redoubt area. Roadblocks had been established across all access routes into the region. Plans for resistance were drawn up by Otto Skorzeny....

So, as soon as the Allies were over the Rhine, the SS headed pell-mell for the Tyrol. So did the staff of the German Foreign Office, which quit Berlin in a long convoy on April 20. So did all of the heads of the various Nazi satellite states which Hitler had created during the great era of conquest.... All the long lines of vehicles converged on Alt Aussee.... The fugitives included Ante Pavelic of Croatia, who, with Hitler's blessing, had ordered the massacre of a half million Serbs; Mihailov, leader of the Macedonian fascists; and the slimy Monsignor Tiso of Slovakia....

In charge of the Alpenfestung, Himmler (who had elected to stay in the north, and Hitler, who elected to stay in the bunker in Berlin) left its builder, Ernst Kaltenbrunner, who had made his headquarters in a pleasant chalet. His own plan was to disappear and lie low until Himmler and Eisenhower had sorted out everything in a friendly manner....

How much treasure found its way to the Alpenfestung can only be guessed. Apart from the counterfeit money with a face value of about $400 million (a third of the original $600 million printed having been spent), there was real folding money and gold and silver. Kaltenbrunner had control of all funds for SS espionage and the Gestapo, a fortune built on gold removed from the teeth of millions of concentration camp victims....

[As the Allies drew near] Kaltenbrunner decided that it was time for him to make his planned temporary withdrawal from civilization.... Kaltenbrunner then set out for his hiding place, a mountain refuge called the Wildensee hut, 10 miles up the mountains, a whole day's walk.... Informers in Alt Aussee promptly told the Americans [CIC] Kaltenbrunner's whereabouts. They went up to the hut and brought him down....

So, the Alpenfestung fell without a struggle. The Werwolves never materialized, but the area has a Nazi legacy which persists to this day. At the end of the war, it held the densest concentration of Nazi war criminals in all of Europe.... The investigators scarcely skimmed the surface, and even after men like Eichmann and Skorzeny were caught, they simply walked out of their camp to freedom.

APPENDIX B

Testimony of Ernst Kaltenbrunner,
12 October, 9–10 November 1945[117]

12 October 1945

Colonel Brookhart to the Witness Through the Interpreter:

Q: You are the same Ernst Kaltenbrunner that has appeared here before, and do you understand that you are still under oath?

A: Yes.

Q: I asked you once before about the title Reich Security Commissioner. Was that not a title held by Heydrich, to which you succeeded?

A: I am not familiar with the title of Reich Security Commissioner. It was not in use in my time.

Q: Wasn't that term used to refer to the position you held?

A: No, it was not.

Q: I want to turn now to the matter of action taken to evacuate Jews from Hungary and ask you what you had to do with the formation of that policy and the carrying it into effect.

A: Nothing in both respects; I had nothing to do with that.

Q: The record shows that the action in Hungary was carried out under [Otto] Winkelmann [SS Police Leader—later SS General—who likely aided Eichmann in deportation of over 400,000 Hungarian Jews to Auschwitz and other camps; post-war, American authorities denied an extradition request by Hungary, and he never stood trial for alleged crimes].[118] Do you know him?

A: Yes, I know Winkelmann.

Q: What was his position in Hungary?

A: He was Hitler's representative.

Q: What did you talk to Winkelmann about when you visited him in Budapest during the month of March 1944?

A: I made a trip to Hungary to be present and to try to contribute to the setting up of a democratic regime in Hungary.

Q: You were also there to help set up the political police, were you not?

A: No, this was not my mission.

Q: Did you have any dealings with the local police officials?

A: No.

Q: Other witnesses say you did.

A: No, I had nothing to do with them.

Q: How many times did you visit Hungary during the months following the 20th of March, 1944?

A: Once, just then.

Q: Other witnesses say that you have visited it two or more times during that month.

A: Definitely not.

Q: At that time, was there any activity in rounding up Jews in Hungary and shipping them to Germany?

A: Then, definitely not. Not at the time I was there.

Q: Did you know Ladislaus Endre [Hungarian Nazi directly responsible—reportedly unlike Winkelmann—for deporting to death camps over 400,000 Hungarian Jews],[119] the Government Commissioner and State Secretary for Jewish matters?

A: No.

Q: Did you ever have anything to do with the program of moving, first into one section of the country and then into another, under the supervision of Endre, for the purposes of rounding up Jews to ship them to Germany?

A: I never had any assignment in connection with this.

Q: Whether you had any assignment or not, did you have anything to do with it?

A: No, never.

Q: You didn't initiate any action on your account?

A: My mission in Hungary was entirely political, and I had nothing to do with this question. I was to investigate the possibility of setting up a democratic government under [Miklos] Horthy [head of Hungary's government during the War, anti-Semite, who aligned himself with Hitler because of his antipathy toward Russia].[120] This was exactly my personal mission. The order to do this had come to [Edmund] Veesenmayer.[121] I was only supposed to support him and to assist him. [Veesenmayer was an SS subordinate under Kaltenbrunner; he was tried and convicted in 1949, sentenced to 20 years imprisonment but only served two—for his role as a Holocaust perpetrator.]

Q: What did you have to do with the activities of Winkelmann and Eichmann during that period?

A: Nothing, because Winkelmann worked directly with Himmler.

Q: Let us turn to a meeting in which you did have something to do; that was in December 1944 in Berlin, between the 10th and 12th of December, to which [Gabor] Vajna, the Minister of Interior, came to you after having seen Himmler and [Gottlob] Berger [chief of the SS Main Office; post-war, convicted as a war criminal and spent six and a half years in prison]. Do you recall that?

A: Yes, he came to me. [Vajna, as Hungary's Interior Minister, worked closely with Veesenmayer to deport 76,000 Hungarian Jews to Third Reich officials. Vajna was tried and hung in Budapest in 1946 for crimes against humanity.][122]

Q: What was said at that meeting?

A: He requested me to assist him in accommodating parts of the Hungarian police in Germany because they had sought refuge in Germany. He had discussed the matter with Himmler, and Himmler had designated Berger, who arranged matters in this connection. Berger generally was Himmler's deputy.

Q: Did you get any prior information from Berger or Himmler before Vajna came to call on you?

A: No.

Q: What was the program that was under discussion?

A: The visit of Vajna with me was essentially a courtesy call.

Q: That's not how we get the story. I wish you would refresh your memory a little about the set-up of the five commands of gendarmerie that was proposed, about which you were particularly assigned the task of going forward with.

A: This was not mine, but Berger's assignment. Besides, I didn't have to arrange for the accommodation of gendarmerie divisions because this did not fall under the competence of the Security Police. It was a matter concerning the Order Police. In stating this, I am for a moment following your theory that I had something to do with the Security Police, but I had nothing to do with the latter, either. My concern was Intelligence.

Q: Well, I of course don't want to force any admissions from you as to what your responsibility would be, but I do want to cite to you some facts about that meeting and what took place and see whether you will concede that they took place. In the first place, Vajna came to Berlin to discuss the organizational set-up, as I referred to it, of these five police divisions. He first saw Himmler and Berger. He was then referred to you and had a meeting alone with you. Is that right so far?

A: No. I am convinced that he came to see me first and then went to see Himmler and Berger, and I definitely did not undertake to accommodate those five divisions.

Q: When he came to see you, what did he ask you about the Jews and how they were being treated in Germany?

A: Nothing.

Q: You do recall, don't you, that he expressed some concerns about the reports that had reached Hungary, that Jews were being maltreated and killed in Germany?

A: Nothing. Not a word did he tell me about this.

Q: And you reassured him, saying that Jews were being well-treated in Germany and that it was because of their work that the output of the Jaeger program, the construction of pursuit planes, had risen 40% since the Jews had begun working there?

A: Not a word was said about this. This is perfectly impossible because it would have been illogical at the time when Vajna came to Berlin to find shelter for his police, who had fled Hungary, to discuss the Jewish question. This question would have been a concern of Vajna's perhaps a year before or so, but not now when the front in Hungary had collapsed, and all they were concerned with was how to find the place to rest their bodies. Like all Hungarians, he came to see me and to pay a courtesy call, to have a glass of cognac and to establish as many contacts in Germany as he could. He could have discussed this question any day with Winkelmann, who may have—I don't know that he was—been completely informed by Himmler, at least about conditions in Hungary.

Q: Aren't you confusing the facts a little by referring to the police who fled, when actually it was a question of organizing these police divisions to screen the populace who had fled, and it was expected in the screening to pick up all the Jews because they would have a yellow card of identification?

A: Not a word was said about this; not a thing. We didn't even discuss the territories because it was Berger's function as the representative of Himmler, who in this respect was the Minister of the Interior. As such, he was the one to designate the districts and areas where the streams of fleeing populace would be directed.

Q: I don't recall mentioning territories in my question. Why do you bring up that subject?

A: Because you are speaking of populace.

Q: That has nothing to do with territories. That indicates to me that you do recall that he did come to talk about territories, which were, to you, the various police divisions.

A: No, certainly not. Ask Berger or Vajna. I made it very clear to him that we would not be concerned with the sheltering of these gendarmerie because they were not of the Security Police or of the Intelligence Service, and besides, he did not insist in the matter because he said himself that this had been discussed with Himmler and Berger.

Q: Wouldn't the true fact be that you said that a restoration office would be established immediately and that the transport of the Jews would be arranged by a railway if possible, and further, that Winkelmann would have general charge but that your man Eichmann would be on hand to see that the program was carried through?

A: May the lightning strike me if a word of this was said.

Q: You definitely referred to Eichmann as "my man"; isn't that true?

A: I definitely did not call him that, nor have I ever mentioned him in my conversation to Vajna. It was also extremely improbable that Vajna would come to me with these matters since he had daily contact with Winkelmann. At least he had the possibility of access to Winkelmann; whether he availed himself of it or not, I don't know.

Q: Let's stick to facts and not possibilities. I am talking about the meeting in Berlin and what was said there. The record indicates that it was as I have related it to you; that you had used the expression "my man" referring to Eichmann and that you insisted on an immediate and energetic delivery of the Jews.

A: I have already told you, but I believe you have not put it on the record that I did not mention Eichmann with a single word.

[Three days later, on 15 October 1945, Lt. Colonel Smith Brookhart interrogated both Kaltenbrunner and Gabor Vajna together in Nuremberg. Here is what transpired during part of that interrogation]:

Q: (To Gabor Vajna) State again what Kaltenbrunner said about Eichmann.

A: He said, "He is our man. He belongs to us." And he told me that I should support him in his activities in Budapest.

Q: Is there any question in your mind as to Kaltenbrunner's saying that? You are sure that is what he said?

A: That is what I can remember. I tried to find out from all these posts, even as to questions regarding mistreatment of Jews, and I have always received the same answer.

Q: But before we leave Eichmann, you have said, under oath, before that, you were certain that Kaltenbrunner referred to Eichmann as "my man," or "our man," and I want you to say again that you are sure that was what was said, if that is true.

A: I am quite clear in my conscience that this is what he said, "This is my," or "our man."

Ernst Kaltenbrunner: I think what the witness said up to now was: "He was of the opinion."

Q: (to Ernst Kaltenbrunner) There will be no questions from you to Vajna or remarks addressed by you to Vajna, but you will be given an opportunity to state your version....

Q: (To Gabor Vajna) Did you understand from your conference with Kaltenbrunner that Eichmann was the special representative of his office?

A: I had this impression. I had the impression that Eichmann was in very close contact with him.

Q: Did you understand him to be a specialist on Jewish matters?

A: Yes. I knew that Eichmann was a special referent for Jewish questions.

[Continuing with 12 October 1945 interrogation of Ernst Kaltenbrunner:]

Q: Yes, everything you have said has gone on the record as clearly as we are able to interpret what you said. I want you to understand this. There is no disposition to misrepresent anything or omit anything. We don't work that way. Thereafter, Eichmann went to see Vajna in Hungary several times and always reminded him of the fact that he had your backing and that he was also Winkelmann's personal or local adjutant in Jewish matters.

A: No, definitely not.

Q: In substance, you have denied practically all of the conversation attributed to you by Vajna in the course of your meeting in Berlin on December 10th or 12th, 1944.

A: Vajna could only have obtained any results in what he was after in Berlin from Himmler or Berger.

Q: I will come now to another meeting. Did you know a Hauptscharführer Blank?

A: No.

Q: One of the older SS men supervisors of arrests for Dachau?

A: No, definitely not.

Q: A man described as being well trained in killing?

A: No, definitely not.

Q: Do you recall before Anschluss [annexation of Austria into the German Reich, 13 March 1938] when you received an order from either Himmler or Hitler to bring about the disappearance of certain political personalities in Austria?

A: I have never received any such order; besides, if such orders would have been issued, they would have been given to

Heydrich, who was then Himmler's right-hand man, and never to Kaltenbrunner. A man like [Arthur] Seyss-Inquart [Austrian Nazi politician who worked in Poland and the Netherlands and was responsible for the deportation and murder of Dutch Jews; hung at Nuremberg 16 October 1946] can confirm that I never enjoyed this measure of confidence in those days.[123] Heydrich objected jealously that instructions to complete tasks were given to member[s] of the local government in Austria bypassing his office in Berlin.

Q: Regardless of all that, the story goes on that Kaltenbrunner and Blank discussed the best manner to dispose of these people, it being desired that they be killed in Germany, and decided that they would kidnap the persons, bring them in a car to a lake in Bavaria, where they were to be shot and sunk in the lake. Blank first proposed that the corpses be spoiled to make their features unrecognizable, which you said was unnecessary, and the result was that thereafter, the corpses, having ultimately come to the surface and being identified, caused a scandal that was well known.

A: This mad and absolutely untrue report is beyond me. Who is supposed to be involved in it?

Q: You, Ernst Kaltenbrunner.

A: Yes, but who is supposed to have been murdered? Somebody must have heard about it.

Q: That's all you have to say about it?

A: I don't know this Blank, and I never had any such conversation in my life.

Q: Did you know a Dr. Wehrner, Kriminalrat Wehrner?

A: No. A man of a similar name was adjutant to Wolff.

Q: You have no recollection of the disposition of Dr. Wehrner towards Blank?

A: No. Besides, I don't know whether this Wehrner who was with Wolff had the title of Doctor. I don't think so; therefore, it probably is a different person.

Q: Did you know a Herr Morgen? [Dr. Konrad Morgen was an SS judge investigating crimes committed by officers in concentration camps and was able to bring 800 cases of corruption and achieve 200 sentences, including two death sentences. He once tried to arrest Eichmann, but the warrant was dismissed.][124]

A: No.

Q: Inspector of concentration camps?

A: No, definitely not.

Q: Maybe it will help to refresh your recollection if I recall to you a few of the facts that occurred late in the autumn of 1943 as set forth in the report of Morgen, following the visit to Lublin. You do recall the time when several thousand Jews were slain in Lublin in one day?

A: No.

Q: And that their bodies were thereafter burned, there being so many that it caused a light dust to lie over the whole town and penetrate the air like smoke?

A: These three stories are such fabrications, especially inasmuch as my person is concerned!

Q: It was during the period in which you were chief of the Reich Security Police.

A: As I said, these stories are pure inventions, and besides, your idea that I had anything to do with it in my official capacity is erroneous. As for the killing of Austrian officials in 1943 by a certain Blank, that does not make sense.

Q: No, that was after the Anschluss, but I have passed on from that unless there is something more you wish to say.

A: Before the Anschluss, no members of the Austrian government were slain, and I am also convinced it was not done later on.

Q: I don't believe they were identified as members of the Austrian government, merely personalities in Austria.

A: That is not known to me either.

Q: Referring again to the Lublin murders, the result of this mass execution could not have escaped your attention, because as reported by Morgen after his inspection, it resulted in losing much of the available labor supply. There were no more people to work machines and in the handcraft shops. The factories were left with a tremendous stock of raw material, and the people in charge said that the order of the execution came as a complete surprise.

A: I never saw any such report, and I never heard about them.

Q: The local SS Oberführer [Erich] Muhsfeldt [headed the crematoria at Auschwitz, Majdanek, and Flossenbürg; in one incident, he was known to have shot 80 Jewish prisoners in the back of the neck prior to cremation; was present at Operation Harvest Festival at Majdanek: the largest single-day Holocaust massacre—43,000—in November 1943; convicted of crimes against humanity in Poland and hung 24 January 1948][125] who was formerly a confectioner, at Zuckerbäcker in the neighborhood of Kassel [in Germany], was in immediate charge of the butchery at Lublin [in Poland], and he told Morgen that he took credit for killing 20,000 by his own hand. Was he known to you?

A: No.

Q: A man of those attainments would certainly be pretty well known throughout the service, would he not?

A: He definitely did not belong to my staff.

Q: You say that you received no reports of the effects of this mass extermination because of the loss of manpower.

A: Definitely not. Even if this report were true, it is obvious that such a report would not have been addressed to me, but it would have been addressed to a person concerned with manpower questions. For instance, [Oswald] Pohl [administrator of Nazi concentration camps; arrested by British troops while disguised as a farmhand in May 1946; convicted by an American military tribunal in November 1947 of crimes against humanity; hung 7 June 1951],[126] chief of the concentration camps, or to

Himmler, because Pohl carried on production right inside the concentration camps. He was interested in manpower questions. If I had ever received a report like this, I would immediately have taken it to Himmler or to Hitler, and I would have declared to them that things couldn't be done this way.

Q: The message that came, ordering the mass execution, read in the following terms: "By the order of the RFSS, the Jewish company in the camp Poniatowa [in Poland] is to be carried to its final conclusion."

A: I have never seen any such order.

Q: I will read you the description that Morgen gave as to what took place: "The proceeding was always the same. The night before the execution came the order to build very hastily shelters in zig-zag against air-raids. In the early morning came troops, and the execution began in these trenches. The prisoners had to leave their work and [go to] the neighborhood of the trenches. When their time came, they had to undress and naked pass through the trench one after one in an infinite line. Coming to the first deaths (Interrogator: I think, meaning 'dead one'), the victim had to lie down on the dead body and then was killed by a shot from a gun in the neck. This went on so long until the trench was filled, and the last person was dead. Then the trenches were closed.

"The naked men had their own trenches, and the women theirs. Children were with their mothers. Nobody of the victims had been ill-treated before executions. All passed in a methodical, silent way. The troops formed only a cordon and had nothing to do with it. There had been a few German police, and the most were Ukrainian. On each place, there were only two or three killers who were placed above the trench. Behind them were two or three other men who spent all their time [changing] empty magazines. So the executions were going very quick, and the responsibility was only in the hands of very few men."

Here is a second sentence: "It was the old, tried system." Do you agree that it was an old tried system?

A: I am not familiar with the method.

Q: Further on, this report of Morgen's states that extermination had been so complete that there was at last nobody left to burn the cadavers, and it was only with great difficulty that they rounded up enough Russian prisoners of war to do the burying. Did you know SS Sturmbannführer [Georg] Wippern, in command at Lublin? [Wippern—never brought to trial—was responsible for processing and forwarding to Berlin and Krakow the currency, bullion, pearls, diamonds, gems, and other valuables taken from concentration camp victims.][127]

A: No.

Q: What became of all the money, jewelry, and gold of the dead prisoners out of these camps?

A: I don't know.

Q: Didn't you ever receive any report as to what was done with these valuables?

A: No.

Q: You disclaim any knowledge of this incident that took place in the autumn of 1943 at Lublin?

A: Yes. It is impossible that this report had been sent to me. I would have been to see Himmler or Hitler on the very first day, on the very same day.

Q: When Morgen made inquiries into the reasons for the mass executions, he was told by the local Sturmbannführer that this was top secret (Geheime Reichssache) but that it had been ordered by Himmler himself after a personal report by Dr. Kaltenbrunner. How do you account for that?

A: Absolutely impossible.

Q: What report did you make on the camp at Lublin, or camps holding Jewish inmates elsewhere, that contained any recommendation which would lead to extermination of these people?

A: I never in my life made any such recommendations.

Q: That's all you have to say about it, is it?

A: Yes. Please ask Dr. Morgen where he has it from that I have ever made such reports or recommendations.

Q: Let me ask you about one more situation before we close today. Do you know Dr. Karl Brunner?

A: No.

Q: Did you ever visit Hohenlychen Hospital?[128] [Known as Hohenlychen Sanitorium, which operated north of Berlin from 1902 to 1945, SS doctors trained and lived there, with the most notorious being Dr. Karl Gebhardt, medical superintendent and consulting surgeon of the Waffen-SS and Himmler's personal physician. Gebhardt performed medical and surgical experiments on Auschwitz and Ravensbrück inmates, breaking legs and treating purposely infected patients who developed gangrene and sepsis with sulfonamide, which was known to be an ineffective treatment. He also experimented with transplanting limbs to wounded German soldiers on the Eastern Front. Found guilty of war crimes and crimes against humanity at the Nuremberg Military Tribunals, which followed the original Nuremberg Trials, Gebhardt was hung on 2 June 1948.]

A: Yes.

Q: When?

A: The last time I was at Hohenlychen was when [General] Wolff was there.

Q: What was the occasion?

A: There were the negotiations that Wolff had carried on in Italy and Switzerland and on which he had reported to Himmler.

Q: Why was that meeting held at the hospital?

A: Because Himmler was there.

Q: Is that the only time you have visited Hohenlychen?

A: I must have been there about three times. I was there on the occasion of Himmler's sickness.

Q: Do you remember Dr. Gebhardt?

A: Yes.

Q: What was his position?

A: He was the owner and chief physician there.

Q: Don't you recall a meeting with Dr. Karl Brunner, who was a bone and surgical specialist? He was also a lieutenant colonel in the Waffen-SS.

A: No.

Q: He recalls you.

A: Perhaps you can show me a picture of him. Maybe I have seen him, but I am sure that I haven't had anything to talk to him about.

Q: Do you remember Dr. Rosenthal? [Ravensbrück camp survivor Olha Froliak-Eliashevska, arrested as a political activist on 11 December 1943, in her memoir wrote: "The Ravensbrück camp infirmary, known as the Revier, was often simply a way station to death, the places where doctors and nurses carried out terrifying experiments and eventually killed the sick, the weak, and the so-called 'idiots.' ... They were called 'Die Kaninchen' (The Rabbits), women prisoners who were used as human guinea pigs for brutal experimental surgeries performed on the bones, muscles, and nerves of the lower limbs, mostly on the shanks, and sometimes on the thighs." Among the participating SS doctors: Dr. Rolf Rosenthal, who was tried by a British Military Tribunal and hung for his crimes on 5 March 1947.][129]

A: No.

Q: What did you learn were the principal activities along the experimental line at Hohenlychen?

A: Nothing. To me, Hohenlychen was a hospital in which SS men who had been wounded in battle found a cure.

Q: Didn't you go in and visit the vivisection section?

A: I didn't even know there was one there.

Q: Weren't you familiar with experiments carried on by several of these doctors at Hohenlychen, where they used human beings for their guinea pigs?

A: No, this is perfectly impossible.

Q: Removed bones, did various things to the skin, injected poisons, and various other types of highly harmful material into the body to see what the results would be?

A: This is perfectly impossible. This was a public hospital.

Q: You didn't see any of the inmates from Ravensbrück [concentration camp for women] that were brought over to the hospital and operated on or experimented on by this staff?

A: I never knew that women were also in the hospital. I only saw wounded soldiers.

Q: Did you ever visit Ravensbrück?

A: No, never.

Q: Do you know what experiments went on over there?

A: No, there is not a person in this world that can claim that I have ever been to Ravensbrück.

Q: Whether you have been there or not, perhaps it would be reasonable to assume that you had, through your intelligence services, received information as to what went on there.

A: Permit me, but why would this be possible? It is most unlikely that I, as chief of the Intelligence Service, should have agents among the inmates of concentration camps of Pohl, and if anybody would make a report about the results, it would go to Himmler and not to me.

Q: You reported on all affairs of German life. Here were thousands of women at Ravensbrück whose health and whose possible contribution to the Reich welfare would be of interest to you.

A: I have already said, and put it down in a statement, that the concentration camps had either been taken over or organized by Himmler, and they were under Pohl, and anything that happened there could only be reported to Himmler by Pohl, as I have also said. All I could report about was what may have been said outside these camps about them. To give you another example, I would never report to Hitler, "You have dined today with a certain lady." The only thing I could possibly report to him was it is rumored that "You have dined today with a lady."

Q: Well, people who were on the staff at Ravensbrück and Hohenlychen say that Kaltenbrunner knew about the vivisection experiments performed on inmates there.

A: I can't imagine that you don't have many members of the staff or of the inmates of Ravensbrück in your hands, so please ask any of them if I have ever been there a single time. These are imputations made on the basis of the assumption that the functions of the head of the RSHA now were the same as at Heydrich's time.

Q: Let me point to another fact that may be a little further evidence of your interest in Hohenlychen. Is it not true that children of high-ranking Nazis were born at the hospital; for instance, two children of Himmler's by his secretary?

A: I never heard of women being in the hospital. May I explain this? Gebhardt was a well-known surgeon who specialized in certain bone operations, such as the Meniskusriss. He had performed an operation on the king of Belgium, for instance. He was famous in this specialty throughout Europe, and I have never seen anybody but soldiers in this hospital.

Q: And you don't know anything about illegitimate children of Nazi officials being born there?

A: I knew that Himmler had some, but I didn't know that they had been born there.

Q: Where were the children of Gisela von [Westarp]-Wolf born?

A: They were born at Alt Aussee on the 12th of March, 1945.

Q: Those are alleged to be twins, boy and girl, of whom you, Ernst, are the father?

A: Yes.

Q: But still, you don't know anything about the illegitimate children of other high-ranking Nazis?

A: No, I didn't take any interest in this.

Q: That will be all today.

9 November 1945

Q: There is another matter about which I would like to ask you. When you were appointed as Deputy Reich Führer SS for Austria, in the closing phases of the war, what were the orders that Hitler gave you with regard to inmates of concentration camps?

A: The question itself contains an incorrectness.

Q: All right. Correct it.

A: I have never been charged with dealing with concentration camps, neither by Himmler nor by Hitler. I have on one single occasion used a certain authority, which was issued to me by Himmler for quite different reasons. That was on the 19th of April. That was to give a certain order to the concentration camp at Mauthausen.

Q: What was there?

A: I don't know whether I have included that in my statement in London or here, but in any case, it has always been glossed over. I had dictated a letter in the presence of several witnesses and dispatched it to Mauthausen with an officer. It prohibited any ill-treatment or killing of inmates under any circumstances, and it included all outside camps of camps. I further ordered that the camp was to be surrendered to whatever enemy would first approach the camp in an orderly and proper condition. This order or instruction was, as I heard later on, entirely contradictory to a previous order which had been given by Himmler or Hitler.

Q: Can't you say which?

A: I don't know because I did not visit Berlin after the 18th of April.

Q: You were aware of the order that concentration camps should be evacuated or the inmates should be liquidated, were you not?

A: No.

Q: What was the order that you mentioned?

A: According to what an American officer told me during an interrogation at Bamberg [Germany], an order signed by Himmler himself was found at the concentration camp of Dachau, according to which it had been ordered that thousands of inmates—it either mentioned five thousand or fifty thousand, I cannot recollect which—were to be liquidated.

Q: Was this the order that you were referring to when you had that note written? It reads: "Radio message to Gruppenführer Fegelein, Headquarters of the Führer, through Sturmbannführer Sansoni, Berlin. I beg you to report to the RF (meaning Reichsführer SS) and submit to the Führer that all arrangements against Jews, political and concentration camp prisoners in the protectorate have been completed by me personally today. The situation there is quiet. Fear of Soviet successes and hope of an occupation by the Western enemies."

Signed "Kaltenbrunner"

A: This could be easily explained.

Q: This is No. 259-PS.

A: To my knowledge, this radio message was never passed through, nor was it composed by me. This handwriting is unknown to me. It may possibly be that of my adjutant Scheidler, but the whole affair is connected with my journey, which I made from Berlin into Austria with the aim to bring about the second discussion with the representatives of the Red Cross at Innsbruck. This discussion took place on the 24th of April.

I had a personal meeting with the representative of the Red Cross, Burckhardt, at Feldkirch on the Swiss frontier as early as the 12th of March. With reference to that discussion, I wish to expressly refer to my statement in London....

Q: Who wrote this message?

A: I cannot tell you.

Q: It was found among your papers.

A: Yes, I know. I know the papers; I had it shown to me in London. It is possible that it is the handwriting of my adjutant Scheidler.

Q: Did you dictate the message?

A: No.

Q: Who is Sansoni in Berlin?

A: He was a signals officer.

Q: How do you account for this message being among your papers?

A: All these messages, which were found with the three arrested persons, were put into one envelope which had "Kaltenbrunner" written on it. And the officer in London ascertained himself that these papers referred to me but belonged to the people who accompanied me and were arrested together with me. A large number of photographs, notebooks, and hotel bills were found among those papers, which clearly could not belong to me, but in spite of that, they were all put into an envelope with my name on it. I, therefore, assume that this is a draft of a radio message compiled by Scheidler, which was not dispatched, however. Otherwise, it would have either been destroyed or endorsed "send on such and such a date and time."

Q: Do you concede that this message was prepared on the basis of something said by you to your adjutant?

A: No. But the man stood next to me when I was talking to the commandant at Theresienstadt [concentration camp in the Czech Republic],[130] and he must have gathered the contents of my conversation and composed this message, and, presumably, he intended to show it to me and ask me whether I agreed with it.

10 November 1945

Q: Referring again to the draft of a message found among your papers (259-PS), just what did you do that caused this message to be written?

A: It is not correct that it was among my papers. It was among papers of people who were arrested at the same time. I assume that it originates from the papers of Scheidler.

Q: Why did you assume that?

A: I believe it to be his handwriting.

Q: Are you familiar with Scheidler's handwriting?

A: I don't know it exactly.

Q: He served as your adjutant for a long time, did he not?

A: He was administrative chief.

Q: Examine the writing closely and see whether you believe that to be Scheidler's handwriting.

A: I would have no possibility of comparing this handwriting; there is not much sense in examining it. At first sight, I would say it is his handwriting.

Q: On what possible basis could Scheidler have written this, except on your direction?

A: It doesn't have to be on my direction. He could have gotten it together on the basis of discussions with me—on the basis of discussion not with me, but discussions between me and the commander, witnessing our discussion.

Q: Did you have such discussions to the effect, as stated in this message?

A: This is not a correct interpretation of the contents of my discussion; that I stated yesterday.

Q: Do you think someone made this up?

A: On every trip, reports have been made.

Q: What do you mean by that?

A: Whenever I made a trip, I would send reports to my superior officers or to third persons.

Q: Did you usually report by radio, through the Reichsführer SS to the Führer, in this matter?

A: No, that was not the ordinary way.

Q: What was the ordinary way?

A: My reports had a larger distribution list.

Q: By the time this message was composed, which was in the closing days of the war, your regular channels were no longer open to you, isn't that right?

A: That may be true, if this was a radio message. I do not think it is possible for me to prepare, at the same time, my defense counsel and the prosecution.

Q: Do you mean you want at this time to be with your counsel?

A: I would like to talk with my defense counsel about this piece of writing before I make statements here. Apparently, my statements yesterday were not believed here because I was interrogated on it yesterday.

Q: Well, you recall that we interrupted your interrogation to permit you to talk to counsel. We had not completed. However, it is your privilege to talk to your counsel, and I would not impinge on that.

A: Now, I do not have any consultation with my lawyer at the moment.

Q: Well, I am not going to ask you any more questions about this document until you have had a chance to see him.

A: Has my defense counsel received a copy of this?

Q: That I do not know. Documents have been made available to counsel freely, as far as I know.

A: I have seen my defense lawyer for the first time this morning.

Q: Well, that is something over which I have no control. Let me turn to another subject. When did you first have knowledge as to the order issued by Hitler, dated 18 October 1942, dealing with the treatment of commandos and airborne troops?

A: I do not know that order at all.

Q: Never heard of it?

A: No.

Q: [I'll] show you a photostatic copy of the original order (498-PS) and ask you to examine it, particularly to examine the signature, and tell us what you know about it.

(witness examines document)

A: The signature I identify as that of Adolf Hitler.

Q: Others have already identified it too. It seems to be well known. What else can you say about the order?

A: The order itself has not been known to me, but I read something in the German press about this addition to the order of the armed forces, but I do not recall very much what provisions were made from the German side. I recall mainly the propagandistic evaluation of the brutal measures of the enemy.

Q: Well, if you will let yourself reflect, you will remember that is a basic order that was referred to right down through the war as the standard treatment for those kind of prisoners and that it was carried into practice.

A: I do not know that it was executed. I had nothing to do with the treatment of war prisoners.

Q: If that is true, how do you explain your letter of 23 January 1945, which makes reference to the earlier order of 18 October 1942 (535-PS)?

(witness examines document)

A: This letter cannot have originated with me.

Q: Isn't that your signature?

A: Yes, it certainly resembles my signature. I cannot recall that I ever signed such a letter.

Q: Well, the letter speaks for itself. It is not very old; it is only from January 1945. You have a pretty good memory on other matters. Think a little longer on it and tell us how it came up.

A: It certainly originated with Amt IV, and I myself had never been in written communication with an office of the armed forces. Therefore, I do not believe that I signed this letter. Maybe a rubber stamp was used.

Q: Maybe anything. Why don't you tell us what you know about it instead of being so evasive?

A: I am not giving evasive answers. I just don't know anything about it.

Q: You don't know anything about the Führer's order of 18 October 1942?

A: No. That which I have been shown before, no.

Q: You don't know anything about your conference with Warlimont [deputy chief of the Operations Staff, German Armed Forces High Command] on June 4, 1944?

A: No. About this, I was interrogated by you in the other room before.

Q: That is correct, and you denied the authenticity of the minutes, which were made by Warlimont, and it was on the same subject as this letter.

A: Yes.

Q: And now you say that this letter, although signed by you, was never seen by you and never known to you?

A: No, I never signed it.

Q: How do you expect any reasonable man to believe you in the face of this written evidence?

A: That I don't know. I hope that I will be believed because I will be able to prove in various other matters that I am telling the truth.

Q: I will prove in another matter that you have not been telling the truth.

A: I hope I will also be able to prove that Mr. Warlimont was not always used to telling the truth.

Q: Let me refer to another little matter, which has been the subject of considerable questioning. In your interrogation in London and here, both before other officers and myself, you have denied ever having visited a concentration camp, isn't that right?

A: Yes.

Q: Well now, in anticipation of what you can expect the prosecution to show, I will tell you that a very well-known Gauleiter from Austria has testified and given an affidavit that he visited Mauthausen, in company with you and Himmler, in 1942.

A: I can imagine why Gauleiter Eigruber said so.

Q: I didn't say it was Eigruber.

A: In his Gau [territory], the only concentration camp in Austria was located.

Q: That has nothing to do with the statement of facts that I have just made. The point is, you visited the camp, which you consistently deny.

A: I have never visited it, neither with Himmler nor with Eigruber.

Q: Another witness will testify that you not only visited the camp, but you were seen going to the observation point, where the gas chamber was operated while a gas operation was in progress, in which human beings were gassed to death, and you were seen leaving that same point.

A: I want to die on the spot if that is correct.

Q: Don't you recall who had charge of the military administration in prisoner-of-war camps?

A: No.

Q: Do you know General Berger of the SS?

A: Yes, I know him.

Q: You will recall General Berger had the administration of prisoner-of-war camps under the SS from 1 October 1944 to the end.

A: I think that is incorrect because the prisoner-of-war camps were not put under the SS, but Himmler, as chief of the German Replacement Army, was put in charge of all matters concerning war prisoners.

Q: And in turn, General Berger of the SS, acting as Himmler's deputy by direct order of Hitler, was put in charge of the PW camps?

A: It is correct that Berger was the general deputy of Himmler because he was chief of the SS Chief Office. That such an order was signed by Hitler is unknown to me. But I know that Berger repeatedly represented Himmler in questions of war prisoners.

Q: How did that come to your attention?

A: One discussed such matters.

Q: Well, tell us about the procedure where, when prisoners escaped from prisoner-of-war camps, they were turned over to the Secret Police and what was done with them thereafter.

A: They were not turned over to the Gestapo but were given back to the War Prisoners' Office.

Q: You remember the case of the 80 British flyers who escaped from Stalag Luft 3, that took place in March 1944?

A: That case is unknown to me.

Q: Don't you remember what Hitler said should be done to these men?

A: No.

Q: Then some of the army officials said that they could not violate the Geneva Convention?

A: No.

Q: But your police reported to General Keitel that 50 of them had already been shot?

A: No.

Q: Don't you remember the reports you got from the camp commander at Görlitz?

A: No.

Q: I am sure that was an important enough event to come to your attention. They took them outside the camp to shoot them and then cremated them later.

A: You tell me things I do not know.

Q: General Westhoff attempted to find out from the Gestapo what had happened to these men.

A: If he had negotiations with the Gestapo, he did not negotiate with me.

Q: Are you sure?

A: Yes.

Q: You deny knowledge of these 80 British flyers, British prisoners, having been captured and turned over to the State Police? What do you say about the general proposition that the escaped prisoners were turned over to the Gestapo?

A: Such cases are not known to me, and in my case, it is incorrect. I would like to call your attention to the following fact. You talk now as if always war prisoners, who escaped and were recaptured, would be turned over to the Secret State Police. At another point, you believe Herr Warlimont when this man says they were turned over to the SD. There is a discrepancy.

Q: You said that meeting never took place?

A: I only said now you believe Mr. Warlimont when he says—

Q: What I believe has no bearing on my question to you, wherein I state a fact, as I am about to state, that over 600 American prisoners were found in a Gestapo concentration camp.

A: That I do not know. That only should have been done on order from Himmler to the Gestapo. I had nothing to do with such orders.

Q: Well, let us go back to the subject we took up earlier before we get on [to] the question of veracity. I showed you your letter of 23 January 1945, which makes reference to the earlier Hitler Order of 18 October 1942 as to how commandos were to be dealt with. Let me show you some other documents.

The first two documents (540-PS) appear to be a draft, followed by the letter that was signed. Those two are dated 30 January 1945, and the second is dated 8 February 1945.

(witness examines documents)

Colonel Brookhart: I will read this paragraph into the record.

"On recommendation of the chief of the Security Police and the Security Service (SD), the letter of 28 September 1944 is corrected as follows:

"The Führer's Order on the elimination of terrorists and saboteurs in the occupied territories, of 30 July 1944, as well as 18 August 1944 (No. OKW/WEST/Qu2/Verw.1 009169/44g/Kdes) refers only to non-German civilian persons in the occupied territories.

"For the treatment of commandos the Führer's Order of 18 October 1942 (OKW/WEST/Qu 2/Verw.Nr 003830/42 g.Kdes) is still valid.

"By direction—"

To which there is a reply, which contains this last paragraph:

"However, since the Security Service (SD) does not agree to this, a difference of opinion in this case appears to be immaterial. Earliest decision is requested since answer to SS General Doctor Kaltenbrunner is to be sent as soon as possible."

Q: Now, do these communications serve to refresh your recollection any?

A: No.

Q: You still deny knowledge of the letter of 23 January 1945?

A: I do not recall the letter.

Q: And you deny knowledge of any subsequent action taken by the commander of the Southeast ... ? And they even revised the draft, which is the first copy, to include the sentence referring to you in the signed copy, showing that he had knowledge of your letter and the action that was to be expected.

A: From that, it can only be seen that the armed forces intended to write a letter to me. Whether rightly or wrongly and whether I was the right authority to write to is open to question. In any case, the armed forces wanted to get in touch with the Gestapo, as can be seen from this exchange of letters, and I am convinced that an officer of the Gestapo, namely that one mentioned on top of the letter, has written this document (pointing to 535-PS).

Q: Well, this is the letter that you know nothing about, but that nevertheless established just how you accomplished your desires by writing to the Supreme Command of the Armed Forces. That is very clear.

A: But I deny that I have written this letter.

Q: No, you just didn't know about it, but now you deny it?

A: I not only did not know the Hitler Order, but I also did not know this letter.

Q: But you acknowledge your signature?

A: I did not say that this is my signature; I only said that it resembles my signature, and I also said it is possible that a rubber stamp bearing my signature was used. I cannot recall a letter of such contents signed by myself.

Q: Would it be any more convincing to you if you saw the original letter, signed in ink?

A: I could be more convinced, but it would still not prove that I signed in ink.

Q: There was only one Dr. Kaltenbrunner on 23 January 1945 who was chief of the Sicherheitpolizei [Security Police]?

A: But maybe this certain Ernst Kaltenbrunner was not in Berlin just at the time.

Q: Just answer my question first. Is that true?

A: Certainly.

Q: And you were the man?

A: No, I did not have the function which you imply this man had.

Q: I do not imply anything. I ask you if you are the man who held this position?

A: No.

Q: You are not the man?

A: There was no other Ernst Kaltenbrunner who was chief of the Security Police. But this Ernst Kaltenbrunner, who sits opposite you and whom you call chief of the Security Police and SD on January 23, did not write this letter. (To the interpreter) I did not say this. I said this Ernst Kaltenbrunner, who sits opposite you, did not have the function of chief of Security Police and SD on January 23, 1945.

Q: What was your function at that time?

A: As I described to you frequently, I was in charge of the Intelligence Service.

Q: You had a sub-chief who was in charge of that by the name of Ohlendorf?

A: His reports were used, too, of course.

Q: You testified that your principal interest was in his department.

A: Yes, because he was in charge of all internal German areas, and for that reason, apart from foreign political reports, every report would contain part of his findings.

Q: The testimony of other witnesses, who served many years in the RSHA, is that you were, in fact, the chief of the RSHA and that you exercised and executed control throughout the organization as you would have been expected to do.

A: That testimony is incorrect.

Q: And further, that during the period between Heydrich's death and your appointment to the chief of RSHA, Amt chiefs did deal directly with Himmler and that thereafter, everything cleared through you, with a few exceptions.

A: That testimony is also incorrect....

Jane and Robert Matteson's wedding day, 21 June 1940.*

*Dear family friend, Mary Griggs, generously gave the newlyweds four acres of land at the end of Burgundy Point on northern Wisconsin's Lake Namekagon, where they built a summer cabin. Burgundy Point is later where they lived until 1988, when they moved back to St. Paul, Minnesota, for the their final years.

APPENDIX C
War Letters, July 1944 – October 1945

13 July 1944

Dearest Janie,

We are somewhere in England, as you have guessed already perhaps. More than that I am not allowed to say. Censorship over here is very strict, and consequently the letter is deprived of much I would like to talk to you about. Your letters have arrived, all seven of them, dating back to July 5th, and on the average, they have taken 9 days, which isn't bad at all. The V-mail [Victory Mail—allegedly expeditious mail service for overseas soldiers] isn't any better, I understand, and much less satisfactory.[131] None of our incoming mail, of course, is censored, as your letters arrive untouched.

Our work has become decidedly more interesting, for everything we handle is fairly hot, whereas before it had little current interest. I wish I could say more, for it very definitely would be of interest. I probably won't have an opportunity to see any of the people we know over here, as transportation and distances and free time are all obstacles.

We do have every evening off usually, and as daylight lasts until midnight, we seldom go to bed before 11:30. There are wonderful little local pubs around, and bitters and mild and stout ale are the fare.

It is not giving away anything to say that we occupy an old estate replete with the accoutrements of Ivanhoe forests, streams, lake, and beautiful walks. We occupy huts and eat in the cowshed, and the officers eat and sleep in the mansion, but it isn't as bad as it sounds, for there is really little difference. The food is the best yet and though, as you can read in the newspapers, the weather has been cold and rainy, it hasn't been uncomfortable....

14 July 1944

Dearest Janie,

I took a beautiful walk this evening around a lake, much the same as Tennyson lyricized about. It was a still, transparent evening. There was the kind of calm that I suppose one finds hovering over only the (censored) that is duplicated nowhere else in the world. The countryside is lush from heavy rains and continual dew. I used to think that English countryside was beautiful only because it was English and not because it was really beautiful. But now, after looking at it with dispassionate eyes, I am convinced otherwise.

A forest bordered the lake, and of course it reminded me of the kind Robin Hood and Allen-a-Dale used to rollick through in hunt of the king's deer and the noblemen's money. What I think I love most about the landscape, though, is the rolling hills and dales.

Captain Kerr has bought himself a bicycle, and I think I might, as you can get them for about nine pounds or cheaper. Speaking of pounds, the monetary system is much easier to grasp than I remembered. But [it] is impossible to spend much money. You can't buy much besides beer, or lager as they call it, or ale. After one or two, I have usually had enough as it is lukewarm.

You would love the old train I rode on the other night. I only went about 15 miles, but it took forever. We rattled along, and everybody was very conversational. In lots of [ways] I think I like the English coaches better than the American.

25 July 1944

Dearest Janie,

I received your V-mail today, and it took 9 days, which is a little worse than the average time it takes an airmail. It usually takes the latter about 7 days....

The news from the fronts continues to be unbelievably good, and maybe it will all be over here before, as Churchill said, we have a right to expect it. Things are going almost as well in the Pacific, and so my prediction of June 1945 sounds pessimistic even. At least I hope so. The news of the attempt on Hitler's life and the resulting disorder gave a terrific lift to the morale of everyone here, as you can well imagine.

I borrowed a bicycle the other night and pedaled off into the countryside again. I followed a beautiful lane for miles, went thru a forest, and around a lake, stopping at out-of-way pubs as I went. At one point, I stopped at an old church. Nobody was around. Very few houses were even near. I went inside, and it was everything you would [want] a church to be.

So I just sat there for awhile....

As yet, no promotions have been handed out to anyone over here. So we're all in the same rank we were before we left. Rank, as I have said, has lost its meaning, and everyone has become concerned with getting the job done. The job I have calls for a sergeant's rating, as you know, but it looks like it will have to wait until they start thinking in those terms again.

I forgot to tell you that when we arrived here, the people greeted us with waving flags, the V sign, and whatever they were doing, they stopped to come to the window and wave. I was surprised as I thought they were used to this sort of thing by now. Children follow us around asking us for gum and candy wherever we go. "Have you any gum, chum?" I have been tremendously impressed with the manner in which we're treated over here. We get the best movies, wonderful recreation equipment, and good food....

10 p.m. 27 July 1944

Dearest Janie,

I'm sitting outside under some huge trees with my wash boiling in a huge cauldron. It's the quickest and easiest way to do it, for I can read and write at the same time....

I was given the promotion to sergeant yesterday and, at the same time, a little speech by the boss. One of the officers came over right away and started painting the other stripe on. The boss said nice things and pointed out that a promotion thru the ranks from private to sergeant in 2 months was almost unheard of. Last night in celebration, 4 of us took a jeep into another beautiful town a little farther away. The boss and another officer came along. They all got more excited about it than I d[id], but it's nice of them. The news that Rommel had been killed just came over the radio. It sounds a little far-fetched, but I hope it's true.

15 August 1944

Dearest Janie,

A lot has happened since I last wrote you.

We are now somewhere in France. I can't tell you where. But if you follow the papers, you should know. If not, we have a poor public relations officer. Mentioning a historic church is no good, as that is crossed out [by the censors]. We weren't even allowed to say the children in our part of England wore wooden shoes, as that was supposed to give away where we were. Yet everywhere we went, the English children wore wooden shoes.

We are now allowed to say we have been in Glasgow, Edinburgh, Chester, Manchester, Northwich, Liverpool, Macclesfield, and Southampton. We were near Chester for the greater part of the time. I loved it all.

So now we are in France, and we have covered a lot of ground, seen many villagers, and drunk a lot of wine and cider. I am permitted to say that we have (and I mean [me] and a few others) have been among the first to enter quite a few villages, and that the reception was tremendous. They throw flowers, give you wine and cider and wonderful peasant bread, wave the tricolor, and sing "La Marseillaise." It's heartwarming, inspiring, and gives a feeling of a great bond.

But it isn't all that way.

Our G-2 is a swell guy. Today, we went down to a small lake and went swimming, and it was the first time since with you in La Jolla in Jan. I then had a chance to talk to a French couple with five children whose place was on the lake. As it was, I struggled through, and we understood each other. They lived in a town that was bombed by Americans, as have so many others. Their house, with all their belongings, was burned. They realized it was a part of war, but still, they had, on further questioning over a bottle of wine, a strong feeling against the Americans for it.

I was interested in finding out also how cynical they are about life, politics especially. But can they be blamed? They dislike leaders: Stalin, Hitler, Churchill, Roosevelt, de Gaulle, Petain, all [political] leaders. They have been disillusioned obviously by 2 wars and France's present plight. She is so poor, so divided, so beaten. But the spirit is still there. I loved the English, but I love the French more. I love the country.

The church plays a far greater part than I ever dreamt. Crucifixes are at the entrance to every lane leading into the farms and houses. The church is always the dominant building, huge spires, and rich-sounding bells. Like in The Bell for Adano. The houses are of poor construction, handmade of fieldstone. But there's a personality that you don't get in our machine-like, money-conscious Middle West.

Two days ago, two of us were in a small village of about Northfield's [Minnesota, USA] size, a driver and myself. I had accompanied the Major on a patrol mission and had an hour before I was to meet him again. I started handing out candy from my K. ration and was soon besieged by about 100 children and others. They gave me six bottles of wine and a loaf of bread, and one bottle of precious champagne. I conversed poorly for a while. A French gal pinned a small tricolor on me and, the only time, gave me a French greeting on both cheeks. It was a wonderful experience.... Being in Headquarters and being frontline troops, we have all we can eat and more. From the French, for a chocolate bar, we get a dozen fresh eggs, but alas, no milk, whenever we want them.

I have been getting enough sleep despite aerial activity at times, and the weather has been perfect: starlit nights, no clouds, warm breezes, and no rain at all. I hope it continues. The dust is bad on the road, though. We have pills [to] purify our water with. The French want chocolate and cigarettes like mad. They haven't had any bonbons for five years....

20 August 1944

Dearest Janie,

Believe it or not, we are in the midst of battle, but still there is now and then a pause that permits time out for a letter. We are always close to the line as fluid as it has become. We are moving around a lot, as you can see by the papers. I have had some exciting experiences. Yesterday we were visiting at 4 a.m.... right at the Front when we were strafed by a group of Focke-Wulfs [single seat, single engine German fighter plane]. Bullets flew all around us, but none hit. I dove behind a shock of grain....

So far the weather has been ideal, and it has been like a canoe trip, sleeping out under the stars, cooking over open fires, and washing out of lakes and streams. We pick up wine, bread, and eggs as we go, trading our cigarettes and chocolate and biscuits. The French are ravenous for them. Physically, it hasn't been nearly as bad as [desert training] maneuvers, mostly because we have been so well supplied, the weather, and because we have them on the run....

We are now sitting around waiting for a new mission to be given us. I can't see how the Germans can take so many losses and continue. But they're smart and fight as [if] they [have] nothing to lose....

The concussion from the big guns is terrific. It makes the tents shimmy. The flies aren't bad, but the bees are legion. You should see the cities devastated by the war. But the saddest sight is to see the refugees streaming back to their rubbled houses. They use carts with 2 big wheels and usually drawn by donkeys. The other day, the Germans issued an order to shoot every civilian in the town we were storming. As a result, we saw countless numbers of old and young streaming out of the town. A lot of them were crippled and had to be pushed on bicycles. But everybody seems to have plenty of food, which is contrary to what I believed previously. Also, the Germans treated the vast majority with indifference, but there have been many examples of brutality. I have been getting the story from our counter-intelligence, civil affairs, and interrogators' people as it has come out. The captured documents are especially interesting. But more I can't say.

10 October 1944

My dearest,

Things have been moving fast and furiously. The reports you read in the NY Times and Time magazine are very accurate, and your suppositions about us are on the nose. God, how I wish I could open up and tell you about a few thousand incidents as they happen because I know I'll forget half of it by the time I see you.

We live in buildings—an old factory—for a while now ... which is luxury compared to a foxhole. I have been up to see my friends of rifle-company days quite often. Life is tough. I have experienced enough of it without wanting it as a steady diet. So don't worry. I am cured now, whatever happens, from the desire for asking for a foxhole and mud, and hours on end of waiting and waiting in breathless anxiety for the thing to end, or the one that has your number on it.

My heart goes out to the uncomplaining doughboy who is holding the line day after day, trudging along with a base plate that gets heavier with every step. I shall never forget the looks on their faces in the early hours before the attacks. They seem to act as if they are the forgotten, and despite [war correspondent] Ernie Pyle's work, I think they are. Nothing is too good for them.

You know, it's a funny thing how adaptable one becomes to anything. Human life seemed so sacred once that it was with a feeling of great awe that I thought of death. But now that human beings are as expendable as tanks or jeeps or paper cups, that awe has lessened. A corpse is no longer a curiosity.

I am wondering if you have taken any snapshots of [daughter] Daidie and yourself. I'd love to have some if you have. I remember once saying something about it being better not to have them, but it is the opposite.... I was amazed to hear about D's independence and her great feat of bicycle riding. I eat up every word in your letters, so never fear it palls.

You ask about my boss, the colonel. He was the purchaser for the Philadelphia Gimbels' stores. He is a man of moods, and depending on his mood, his popularity rises or falls with the men in the Section. He likes to see what is going on—on all fronts, and is very fair about taking us along. Nobody but myself and another are interested in going, so we usually accompany him on his trips. In part, we are taken along as protection methinks....

I wish I could describe to you the day at the front yesterday. I visited several towns that were just liberated and explored the underground fortifications the Nazis had dug in some of the surrounding hills. For quite a while, I visited with some of the boys in a large foxhole.

I miss you and think of you constantly. Your letters are the happiest things that happen all day, and you are wonderful to write as often as you do. Please kiss Daidie for me and give my love to Mom and Pop.

All my love,

Bob

P.S. The Nazis no longer say they will win; instead, they say they must win. Der Führer has performed miracles in the past, so they believe he will in the future. Whatever happens, I believe, like so many others, that it will be a slow disintegration at first that will accelerate rapidly. It will snowball. But I know that barring some unheard of, fantastic, Wellesian weapon, the end is near. They are definitely at the end of their rope in every sense of the word. Those are general statements that I can't substantiate to you now, but they are statements anyone can make, as you well know.

My work in another week will change to counter-intelligence. I requested the change, and it should be fascinating now that we are approaching Germany....

15 October 1944

Dearest Janie,

Your letters continue to arrive in good time, usually from 9 to 12 days. Mine, I fear, take a bit longer, and perhaps it would be better if I used V-mail....

I think I told you in a letter of about a week ago that I had broached the subject of a transfer to Major Kerr ... and ... the opportunity of getting into more the kind of work my background suited me for. Major Kerr talked to both Major Bell, the CO of Civil Affairs, and Captain McMillen, the CO of counter-intelligence. Capt. McMillen ... was able to take me, and beginning two days ago, I am on special duty with CIC, which is called Counter Intelligence Corps. The name itself implies the function, and more than that, I'm told I can't say. The work is very interesting and of an independent nature. It takes some time, several weeks, before the transfer from G-2 proper to CIC is processed, and during that time, I am merely on special duty. If it happens that the War Department turns down the transfer at some later date for some reason, I will be neither fish nor fowl....

We are living in a little French town with a French family that cooks for us near the front. The meals are much better this way than before, for the French cuisine can't be touched.... Also, we have a roof over our head but no bed. I sleep on the floor in the dining room, and somehow it is a good deal warmer than the tent was. The French family is priceless. But not only the family lives here now. The town crier and his drum have moved in, a couple of other families who have lost their homes, and a couple of soldier-officers of the last war who wear their uniforms and medals very proudly.

For a while, we all slept in the basement, which was just a long tunnel as a means of protection. And that was a sight. Papa, Mama, and two children all piled into one bed, which was basically squeezed into the basement. The other families piled on top of each other at one end, and we at the other. The risks of shelling weren't bad compared to that, so I moved up a floor and now have room to stretch out across a whole room.

Today for dinner we had turkey, salad, Mirabelle, which is similar to a liqueur, wine, potatoes, cake, and bread.

The leaves are turning red and gold over here, and it is very beautiful. The colors aren't as vivid as they are in Minnesota, but still it makes it seem like the autumn we're accustomed to. You would love our village. The main street is a perpetual morass of mud in which pigs, cows, ducks, and geese wander up and down. The geese are a resplendent white in contrast to the mud. They are being fattened for the Christmas feast, they tell us.

Today, I talked to one of the boys I knew back in my old rifle company [soon after enlisting]. I am very lucky I didn't stay with them [due to a climbing accident, as they were wiped out].

You would love, too, the French people we live with. They are so polite, so kind, and so generous. I can't get over the wonderful faces we see every day in these little villages.... They are all so refined looking in contrast to the broken-down hovels they seem to live in.

Please give my love to Mom and Pop. Tell me how long my letters take to [reach] you. I hope you will send some snapshots if you have them. Kiss Daidie for me. I can't believe she is almost 3 now.

Take care.

All my love,

Bob

24 December 1944

My dearest darling,

Almost everybody has lost a son, a brother, or a husband, and everywhere you go in villages and cities, you see the black veil, the black stripe, etc....

We see quite a bit of the IPWs, otherwise known as Interrogators of Prisoners of War [PW]. Tonight we joined them and the Civil Affairs people for a bottle of rum. While we were there, the German PWs made a request to sing Xmas carols. The night was painfully beautiful—a bright moon, stars, a snow sheen over everything, the trees covered with frost; all was quiet except for an occasional out-going shell; then quite suddenly, upon the midnight clear, there came from down below in the barn the glorious song of old—in German, of course, but the same melodies and harmony. At least the war, and even Nazism, hasn't stamped out the universal Christmas spirit.

I miss you and love you and never more than at times like this.

Bob

14 February 1945

My dearest darling,

Call it imagination, but I definitely remember during the 1st war certain things that stand out quite sharply in my mind. One was waving a bunch of small silk flags, one of them German, and having it snatched from me by a person passing by the house [in St. Paul, Minnesota] on the street. Another was [my father] coasting down the high bridge to save gas on Sunday drives—[also] going to the Grand Ave grocery and being told we would have to get along on less sugar. It seems funny now to look back on it, for coupled with boys' stories about the Huns [nomadic 4th- to 6th-century people from Central Asia and Eastern Europe who threatened the Roman Empire], my mind had conjured up a super-man of a villain. I can imagine that Daidie now—for her life in this war parallels ours in the last—is forming some of the same general impressions. Knowing her at 3, you can see it isn't impossible for a small child to have imprinted certain experiences. But now, as we see the Germans as PWs and sometimes as civilians, there is little awe or little real hatred. There is nothing unusual about most of them. They are simple, plain people.... To be sure, there are arrogant ones born and bred in the military caste who are bastards and others not so born but [are] imitators who are worse for having none of the virtues and all of the defects of the virtues.

But this kind of a war is so impersonal, so much a war of machines, of precision bombing and long-range artillery duels that there is little feeling of real hatred. A sort of propaganda-hatred is induced by month-to-month rumors, movies, literature, etc., but I doubt there's much real hatred. Even when someone close to you is killed by legitimate warfare—if any warfare is legitimate—you feel sorrow, fear, but not hatred. It's different, I suppose, when someone close is killed by illegal warfare—such as the shooting of prisoners, or by gas, or shooting a man on a truce mission. For even in as uncivilized a thing as war, ethics play a part. If a friend is killed by a shell or bullet or bomb, your only feeling is that the other guy on the other end is only doing his part—the part he has been trained to do. But still, you can loathe the system and the leaders that made that shot or shell possible. That, to me, is the main reason why what we are doing in CIC is fundamental, for we aim at the Party and the worst tools of the Party—the agents and para-military units. It is much more satisfying to be aiming at them than at some infantryman you have no feeling against, and who 99 of 100 times is not recognizable for his acts but is executing orders. For them, war is an organized bore....

All my love always,

Bob

15 February 1945

My dearest darling,

The guns are rumbling along the entire front tonight. There are great flashings of light against the dark sky. The concussion from the explosion shakes the windows and makes the cellophane (we substitute for panes of glass) flap. But it is a beautiful night, a new moon and millions of stars.

Today we had our first foretaste of real spring. The sky was clear, not a breath of air, a hot sun, and sultry from the evaporation of dampness from the ground. The snow had covered the scars left by war, and now they are revealed again like bones in an opened grave. But hot fires of green are burning. The grass has not the stale late-March color of Minnesota but a freshness all its own. And it gives me spring fever. How I would like to lie down and bask in the sun again. But it seems you can never relax even when you're not doing anything.

Which reminds me that last night, I was talking with an infantry boy—a rifleman in one of the regiments. He had just come back from a hospital in Normandy, having been wounded a month ago from shrapnel from an 88 that was mounted on a tank. He had been hit in the back by a slug as large as three fingers. I was asking him how his life over here had differed from desert maneuvers [in the western U.S.]. He said, "We don't have to walk over here; we only wait. Over there, we hiked 20 miles a day with a full pack. Here, the longest hike was 14 miles with only a light combat pack." But the worst thing about it here is you can't relax; you can't lie down and feel you'll have a couple of hours of undisturbed sleep.

This particular guy had been wounded once before—not seriously in the thigh. This was the second time, and this time more seriously. He was near a road junction when a tank opened fire on him. The fragment threw him across the road and up against a wall. He felt a burning across his back but was afraid to look—afraid his whole back had been shot away. Nobody knew he was hurt, so he tried crawling along a ditch. He crawled about 20 yards when his legs became paralyzed. He fainted and woke up on a stretcher. The hospital was good: sheets, pillows, warm, and good food. But the doctors were rough. The boy in the bed next to him had the muscle in his left arm shot away. His arm—the flesh on the inside of it—was dead from the elbow to the wrist. A doctor pressed a lighted cigarette against it, and it burned, leaving a large blister.

The boy with the back injury was let out after a month, and here he is back again, convalescing ... until he can go back a third time. The amazing thing is he's cheerful, and his only worry [is] that he hasn't heard from his wife since she received the second telegram. The first—for a slight injury—had read your husband has been seriously injured. He was wondering what the second could have said in view of the real seriousness of his last injury....

My love to all, and all my love always to you, Bob

2 March 1945, Germany

My dearest darling,

We are having winter weather again after a month of comparative spring-like weather in February. But tonight, it is clear, and the stars are out bright and clear. I miss you.

Today, I visited a small hamlet that is completely cut off from the rest of the world. I walked down a long winding road, crossed a beautiful little river, followed it around a bend, and there, lo and behold, was a peaceful and very normal-looking pastoral village. In the middle of it and about 60 feet above it on a small hill was the most storybook-like castle I have seen yet. It had the towers of a castle you see in Sir Walter Scott's novels. It is, I was to learn, about 800 years old, and its owner, the count, a young man of 33, was living in it still. He is single and with him was a refugee from another castle in another part of Germany. Also, there was a judge from one of the German lower courts, also taking refuge from the havoc of the war.

The count owns three estates, one other in Germany. The third he was forced to relinquish title to recently. With him still is his old forester, who was 80 years old today and with whom I also talked. His father, grandfather, etc., had all been the game warden and forester for the count's ancestors back to 1500. Around the castle is a woods in which they still hunt wild boar, so they say. I talked with the old forester in his house, which is down in the village. He still wears his forester uniform and looks very much like Robin Hood would have at age 80. He has snow-white hair and a long, flowing beard. In his living room are all kinds of trophies of the hunt—deer heads, boars' horns, hunting knives, and shotguns.

Afterwards, I went up to the castle and saw the count and his two refugee friends. Recently, a great part of the castle was destroyed by fire, only the chapel and long dining room remaining. I saw pictures of the other rooms, and they were everything that Hollywood would have them [be]. [CIC Special Agent] Klimek was with me, and we talked to them about two hours.... They believe, among other things, the following: that the First World War was not entirely Germany's fault; that the Versailles Treaty was a direct cause of this war, mainly the severe reparations; that the resulting economic conditions made possible Hitler for the people wanted bread and work more than anything else; that Hitler gave them, whereas the Weimar Republic didn't ... that 1939 was the turning point in National Socialism and that after that, it slowly but increasingly lost favor ... that the atrocities in France, Poland, etc., had been kept from the German people;

that the German people didn't have the truth; that Bolshevism is the greatest menace in the world today ... that a partition of Germany will provoke a 3rd World War if Russia and the U.S. don't fight each other before ... that every nation has its sadistic cliques; that all Germany—most Germans—wants its original boundaries and colonies; that Roosevelt is an energetic man and Stalin a cut-throat....

It is interesting to get at first hand the opinions of the landed aristocrats. I have also talked to many ... who are very strong Catholics.... They don't seem to understand the complicated Nazi organization any more than our farmers understand the New Deal alphabet agencies. They expect from the Americans fair treatment and order. They are very much against Hitler. One woman, for example, refused the Nazi Iron Cross, which her son had won as he was killed in action.

I have great respect for the Germans I have met so far despite the red on the ledger. They are intelligent, industrious, and straightforward in this region.

All my love always,

Bob

★ ★ ★

7 March 1945

Germany

My dearest darling,

I am still living ... in the town surrounded by rolling hills. I have seen a good deal of the people by now, and I find they differ, but not greatly from the ... people in France and again in Luxembourg.... They work hard from morning to night and are not happy, it seems, especially now when they are saddled with the results of Hitler's folly. They want work as a means of escape from the nightmares they have endured and will endure....

I am impressed, too, with the fact that the people in this area, at least, should not be accused of unclean hands and stigmatized with another war guilt clause. [They] think first of bread, work, family and religion, and after that of the Fatherland…. The simple fact is that the people live in fear once they stray from a course of keeping their nose to the stone. So long as they don't question people and policies but do their work, they have nothing to fear. But the result is no revolution.

The other day, I had the occasion to talk again to the count, his friend—another landed gentleman—who looks more like what a count should than the count: a judge, a businessman, and a notary in the count's castle. There were present also two women who come apparently from well-to-do families but who kept, as a matter of custom, pretty much in the background.

Most of them have lost everything, and I think they are sincere when they blame Hitler for it and not the armies of the Allies…. Helpless resistance is bringing needless destruction, and they, and I think most Germans, see it that way.

The approach to the castle reminds me very much of the road into our cabin [on Lake Namekagon, northwestern Wisconsin], and it makes me homesick every time I travel it. There are the same kinds of trees, the same kind of road, and the same steep hill to climb. But instead of a lake on three sides, there is a beautiful river.

The weather has been rainy ever since the 1st of March, and the ground is a bay of mud again.

I was reading some letters in a Treasury of Great Letters, edited by Lincoln Schuster [co-founder of the publishing company Simon and Schuster]. I never realized how much a part of Napoleon's life women played, or how Babelian Ben Franklin could be, or how terribly young John Keats was—26—when he died…. [132]

Goodnight, my love. Kiss D. for me, and give my love to Mom and Pops.

All my love always,

Bob

11 March 1945

My dearest darling,

The news is good, but they can still prolong it [war] here longer than I would like. My guess is about the end of June, and on that, I have bet about 500 francs. From what Hitler and Goebbels said today on the anniversary of the Heldentag [Heroes' Day], one would gather that they are going to fight for every house in Germany, but at the rate they have been cut up and pocketed in the last month, it seems like so much bravado. The people are sick of it and blame Hitler for unnecessarily prolonging the war....

I have read that the State & War Departments and Foreign Economic Administration have agreed on a force of 500,000 for occupation, which could be made up of 18-year-olds, volunteers, and the regular army. But even that wouldn't affect us [CIC] because of the nature of our work. Still, I can't see how they can hold us more than six months....

To root out the Nazi Party from the German life requires more than merely apprehending Nazis, but even that is a tremendously important job. Creating an attitude of mind in the German people—and we have closer contact than anybody over here—is even more important, though few recognize it as a job. Too many of the persons working at this have no heart for it.... Trying to get a person like this to phrase questions so as to secure confessions or admissions is like squeezing blood from bricks. The best linguist-interpreter is a native-born German who has an axe to grind but not so much arrogance that he refuses to follow any line of questioning but his own.

First things are, sometimes in any work, not put first.... You'd be surprised to see how much a part fear plays in this thing. If it isn't an empty fear of civilians and a conjuring up of what they might be or might do, it is a fear of the person above you and what he might think.

The [CIC] work is interesting ... the rank in CIC inconsequential: Never have we had an opportunity to do so much constructive (in the case of the attitude) and destructive (in the sense of the [Nazi] Party) good in so short a period of time. If only the personnel were impressed with this fact and kept their minds on the ball and not on when they were going home ... they could achieve results they never again would have the opportunity of accomplishing....

Last night, I had a dream about Daidie. She was playing baseball and hit a home run. But the best part about it was how real she seemed—as if I had actually seen her....

My love to Mom, Pop, and D.

All my love always,

Bob

12 March 1945

My dearest darling,

I had a letter post-marked March 1st from you today and a V-mail dated Feb 18th. So you can see the comparative speeds.

We have moved around a lot, and by the time you get this, you will probably know where I am now from the newspapers. The papers seem to do a good job of keeping you informed on the whereabouts of the division, and usually, you know where I have been—the towns, I mean.

Last night, we stayed in a priest's house in a small town of about 200 people. The priest is about 40, a very careful but pleasant sort of person. In his house, too, were his sister, who was also his home-keeper, and a little boy about 10, an orphan the priest had adopted. The boy is a model of politeness ... and was so excited at having us there. He is a very intelligent little boy and showed great interest in our stories. He brought us hot water and wood. Later, when I was sitting by the stove in the kitchen, he came in and started to read his book. Three of his pet chickens flew up to the windowsill and rapped on the window. He brought them in one at a time and gave them some grain so I could see how well he had them trained....

The priest had a radio, and we listened to the news and heard [a summary of] Hitler's and Goebbels's speeches about fighting for every house but at the same time expecting an honorable defeat. It didn't make much sense. Nor does it to the people. The Germans are really suffering now, and though their real reactions aren't apparent because they are so frightened, they will learn a lesson they didn't learn in the last war, when German soil wasn't invaded and German homes and cities destroyed. The destruction is hard to believe even when you see it.

Tonight we are in a farmhouse—vacated by civilians on the outskirts of a town of about 800 persons. The debris we cleaned out of one room—and it's not bad at all as there is a stove and plenty of wood....

We have the soup you sent—the Lipton's—every night before we go to bed. It's wonderful stuff—if you boil it about 10 minutes....

My love to Mom, Pop, and D.

All my love to you,

Bob

P.S. On our farm here, we have a congregation of all the chickens from miles around. There are a few bags of grain they have found, so they come here to lay their eggs. But it's too good to last. The saddest-looking things are the cows, calves, sheep, and pigs.

14 March 1945

My dearest darling,

We had a beautiful summer day today, the best of the year so far. It was actually hot, and the air smelled like the sea, like it did around La Jolla [California]. We are in a valley surrounded by hills with steep sides, and on these hills are acres of grape vines. It's unique the way [farmers] prevent soil erosion. They plaster the soil with slabs of slate, which holds the soil from being washed away but which allows water to filter through.

The buds on the trees are beginning to come out, the grass is getting green, and plants have started to grow. Even the birds have arrived—the warm-weather birds. Somehow, you forget about such things until a day like this hits you, and then you have thoughts from abroad. I can see why "Oh, to be in England now that April's there" was written.

Life continues pretty much the same.... In your last letter, you suggested I make a few requests. Here they are: a few washcloths, that German grammar [book], a German history, a Russian history, and tea.

The news reports say that the Russians have taken Kuestrin and the bay of Danzig [Gdańsk Bay, Poland]. We are closing in [on] the Rhine on this front, and the bridgehead of Remagen was a surprise to everybody....

All my love to you. Kiss D. for me. My love to Mom and Pop.

Bob

23 March 1945

My dearest darling,

I haven't had a chance to get a real letter off to you for quite a while. We have moved fast and furiously in an operation that you no doubt have read all about by now. It is a replica of the Falaise Gap [Western Allies encircled German forces in Normandy, France] debacle that happened way back in August, and until now, there has been nothing to equal it.

The weather here has been unbelievably good, and in fact, the apple blossoms are in bloom. It is very much spring, but I understand that April brings a reversal, and we may have snow again. The scenery is beautiful, but it is difficult to appreciate it now. Today, I had to visit a person who lives in a cottage on top of one of the large, pine-covered hills that are everywhere here. The view was indescribably beautiful.

I wish I could tell you now about some of the experiences we are having because I know I shall forget most of them. Some of the sights and people are hard to imagine.... The reactions of the GIs to the Germans and to the towns laid open to them are too terrible in some cases to describe.

The results of six years of war and of the pasting from the air, the number of lives lost, property wrecked, the fanaticism of some of the Germans in their love for Hitler, the effects of a six-year news blackout and rigid censorship on the thinking of most Germans, the feeling of animosity toward Hitler on the part of most people for unnecessarily prolonging the war, the programs of instruction in the schools under National Socialism, the part played by Protestant churches and Catholic churches in the resistance, the strength of the National Socialist tie, the Germans' views on the peoples of other countries, the great fear of Bolshevism, the blaming of all the sins of the world on England, the fear in which the people perpetually live now, accentuated by the air raids—all of these and many more topics I can't even begin to tell you about in a letter.

The package with the books on Germany came today, and I can hardly wait to read them. It probably seems strange to you that they should be of interest, but anything that sheds more light on the Germans is interesting. The ones you sent hit the nail on the head.... Thank you very much. I shall write Daidie and Mom, too, when I get a chance. My love to them all.

All my love always,

Bob

26 March 1945

My dearest darling,

The box with the lobster and candy and nuts arrived. The lobster was particularly wonderful, and you were sweet to send it. Your letters come regularly and wonderful they are. I can't tell you how happy it makes me to hear from you—and so often.

It's always a big event in my life to have a bath, and I had one today. You can't imagine how clean I feel. I also had my laundry done ... and they did a wonderful job.

You know as well or better than I the progress of the war. What holds it up is the fanaticism of the Nazi core. They are all perfectly willing to fight to the end and destroy Germany with themselves. It seems strange to talk with people who love Adolf Hitler instead of hating him and who, from their point of view, has done a lot of good. It always surprises me to hear someone say they believe in Hitler and National Socialism and think that Germany will still win the war. Most people, however, are not so hypnotized and are now turning against him, saying he has betrayed them. You can't imagine how vast the destruction is until you have talked with them and seen the wrecked cities.

A thing that amazes me, coming from the U.S., is how little inclined the people are to talk politics and how when you ask them their opinion, they always reply, "We were taught that ..." etc. If you ask them how the war started and why they think Hitler did this or that, they always reply that that is too big a question for such unimportant people as they....

Most [Germans] are hard-working people who don't consider politics any of their business, who were taught to love the Führer, and who are only interested in work and their family. The other day, we were in a city half-ruined by bombs. We entered a place [where] they kept party records, found the door locked, so [we] busted it down. Half an hour later, a carpenter appeared from nowhere and had the door fixed in no time. I have never seen such thoroughness and such industry. They have a passion for work.

The enslaved labor is breaking loose now and produces quite a problem—looting everywhere—to say nothing of our own GIs....

My love to Mom, Pop, and D. All my love always to you,

Bob

30 March 1945

My dearest darling,

I have been a little remiss about writing due to the speed of our movement. It all seems a little miraculous to us that we can go for miles and miles into the heart of Germany without encountering any opposition anywhere....

The Germans have lived well off of the rest of Europe and, until recently, in these parts, have not been hard hit at all. There are hundreds of towns we pass by now untouched by plane or artillery—the people never even seeing an American soldier. The foreigners here are raising hell, looting the Germans blind, and wandering all over the landscape. One of the strange sights we see these days—German soldiers marching past us on the roads, no guard on them, with their hands over their heads.

The German civilians we live with and see constantly ... are exceptionally polite and well disciplined.... They are automatons. It matters not who they are working for—just so they are working in their customary groove. They follow our orders as meekly as the Nazis.... On the other hand, there are fanatics around with whom Hitler is a religion and who are suicide cases and consequently dangerous. But it is surprising to be treated so well by the German people. It seems as if they were actually happy and relieved to see us. A few have remarked that they are glad it is the Americans and not the Russians. The fear of the [possible Russian] airplane is amazing to witness. And that is another reason they are glad to see us.

My love to Mom, Pop, and D. All my love always,

Bob

★ ★ ★

8 April 1945

My dearest darling,

For a change, we are having a quiet day. At present, we are probably closer to the Russians than anybody. But still, from the standpoint of apparent activity, we might be far removed from the actual battle scene. Only occasionally can we hear around us machine guns or see the planes diving.

It is Sunday and our first real taste of spring. The violets and daffodils grow in profusion in this fair-sized German town. (You would be surprised to know where we are if, at this moment, you could know where we are.) The German people are dressed in their Sunday clothes and are wandering around watching the GIs fixing tires, washing clothes, etc. They are definitely relieved to have us here in many ways. Although, no one of them can be happy that Germany has lost the war.

We have been with a family—an elderly man and his wife. She has a son on the Russian front and a son-in-law in the Wehrmacht hospital. Nobody has ever treated us with more kindness and hospitality. She is about 55, very plump, and full of kindness for everyone. It is no false front—she is a genuinely good person, and there are many like her here. She pats us affectionately as if we were her sons. She warmed enough water for all of us to take baths and hauled it upstairs to the bathtub. She even dipped into [their] treasured stock of water-softener salts and gave us what she had left of them. The husband opened up his best bottle of wine—the one he had been saving for V-day. He put on his best pair of Oxford striped pants—a little the worse for lack of pressing—and his stiff, starched collar.

She was so worried that we might not like her cooking or might think her modest home too simple for our tastes. She couldn't do enough for us. But it made her happy to have young people around the house again that she could take care of; there was no feeling of animosity at all. That is one of the strange things about war. Both sides recognize the impersonal nature of it, and there is, in most people, little of personal feeling. Yesterday, it was the same story with a woman who had lost two sons in the war and a third [who] was a prisoner in America. But one can never mention the children without receiving a flood of tears....

All my love to you always,

Bob

22 April 1945

My dearest darling,

It's a cold spring day, but the leaves are out, and the grass is green again. We are set up in a pension [guest house or boarding house] in a large German city [Nuremberg] in Bavaria. As in most other larger cities, the damage from bombing has been terrific—literally wiped out except for scattered groups of houses around the fringes.

In this particular house, there happens to be three German women and a Russian man staying on as paying boarders. But they have been [pressed] into service and are now washing the dishes and housekeeping, much to their dislike. One of the women has a fiancé in a prisoner camp in Africa; the other two have lost their husbands on the East Front. They are all from Berlin but have been ausgebombt [bombed out], as they say it. As with others, there is no real hatred of the Allies—save possibly the Russians (whom all Germans make no bones about their fear of)—and they are very much like anybody else. Not that they, especially, shouldn't be, but the notion is supported by the propaganda fact, and the result is people expect the Germans to be a different breed of species altogether. These women have enough perspective and sense of humor to realize that Joe Goebbels has been feeding fiction mixed with fact, that the Americans aren't the lusting and barbarous Semites they are pictured to be (tho sometimes I wonder myself if they are not), [and] that there is something more to life than working, eating, and bearing children for the Fatherland. They wear American-styled clothes, and ... I was surprised to find in this pension (and that's what it's called—complete with an unfilled outdoor swimming pool) a collection of American jazz records—*June in January, Music Goes 'Round and 'Round, Red Sails in the Sunset*, and a collection, also, of English books—one of which *Point Counterpoint* by Huxley I started to read.[133]

We, thru the [interpreter] Austrian Jew Roab, talked about politics and the war. The usual upshot is ... Hitler may have misled the people about the world situation, thus giving them hopes they could never attain, but more probably, he was badly advised, so the war guilt is placed on his advisers and on England. The U.S. is always omitted by courtesy, but they probably blame us as much. The bombings of cities indiscriminately is the sorest point as they never learned about Coventry or the haphazard effects of V-1 and 2. [Also:] The U.S. is misled and will someday realize Russia is the real enemy....

It is difficult to assess how much the German mind has been turned by 13 years of Nazism—especially so when there was never a very clear understanding of the German mentality and psychology before 1933. But to me, the German one finds in the mass is very little different than the average American, despite the fact we refer in prose and poetry to ourselves as the Christians and to them as the pagans ... the standards of right and wrong are much the same. As a matter of fact, except for the tough Nazi, I think most Germans may have a higher regard for morality than many Americans.

Most Germans are courteous, careful, conservative, law-abiding people—the discipline is everything it is said to be. No one is genuinely more shocked and more ashamed than the average German when he learns of the SS atrocities in the prison camps. Back at Ohrdruf [concentration camp] ... the mayor of Ohrdruf and the whole population were marched thru the camp—a place they had before never been allowed to set eyes on—so they could see and hear about the murder of 250 [Jewish] prisoners by the SS the day before we arrived. The result was that the mayor committed suicide—his disillusionment was so great. The same is true in many other cases.... All this supports making a division between the mass of Germans who are good and the corrupt minority who led them astray. Making such a division is usually ridiculed, especially after the effects of the last war, for in a way, it absolves the German people from responsibility in this thing. The fact is theirs is not the great responsibility, for they never saw or could see to what ends they were being manipulated....

The blame lies on the leaders; the great mass of people are suffering now and will continue to suffer for a long time for their part as tools in a game that was too big for them to grasp the meaning of. And such would be the case if the shoe were on the other foot, for people, by and large, are essentially the same everywhere, I believe. There are people over here who believe all Germans are criminals and should be treated that way. Only the most ignorant believe that.... I don't believe that turning the other cheek is a good policy, but it seems to me that vengeful action now produces in the future in Germany an equal and opposite reaction as surely as it does in the realm of Newtonian physics.

My love to all. Kiss D. for me. All my love, always.

Bob

26 April 1945

My dearest darling,

You always seem to be wondering if we are staying with the 80th [Division]. We are.

We are in a city [Nuremberg] now that is a mass of ruins. Near the center of the city is the old city, and below the old city, extending for miles in every direction, are medieval labyrinths mixed with modern dwellings. It extends down at least five levels below ground and is stocked with everything imaginable.

Tonight we went down—another guy and myself. There is still a lot of sniping at night, and we could hear shots ringing out on all sides. Most, I think, must have been G[ermans] firing at their own shadows.

Some people think that quite a few Nazis still are hanging out down below with enough stuff to cause some trouble.

The ruins were eerie in a bright moonlight.

We went into the cells they kept the Russians and Poles in—like the dungeon [from Lord Byron's poem, "The Prisoner of Chillon"] the prisoner of Chillon was kept in.[134]

We are in a part of Germany where there is really nobody who isn't pro-Nazi—who doesn't have a great love and admiration for Hitler, even in defeat. The other day, I came across a person who was the first person to arrest Hitler back in 1920. He still hates him but hasn't been able to be very effective in his work against him. We have run into other interesting cases in this town—some of the old fighters, early Party members.

Your letters are wonderful.... My love to Mom, Pop, and Daidie.

All my love always,

Bob

7 May 1945*

My dearest darling,

The last place I told you we were at was Limbach near Chemnitz. After that, we retraced our steps to Erfurt and headed south to attack the forces thought to be congregating in the National Redoubt. We went to Coburg—to a place called Schesslitz and then south to Nuremberg. At [Nuremberg], we stayed ... in the only part of the city that seemed to be relatively untouched by bombs. The old part of the city inside the Ring is completely flattened—a mass of rubble. Underneath is a city beneath a city, which was the strong point of resistance up until the day before we entered. Even after that, sniping and fighting went on in the labyrinth of tunnels. I went thru most of them, and they are exactly as you read about them in the *NY* [*New York*] *Times*—modern living apartments, ventilation system, tremendous stores of food, clothing, and records. They are connected by tunnels and are on three levels below the ground.

You can enter the underground city at any number of places. Outside the city—on the outskirts—are the huge headquarters of the SS and the Party Stadium and Congress Meeting Place— famous in newsreels. Nuremberg, as you know, is an ancient stronghold of Nazism, and we expected trouble there from a CIC standpoint.

After [Nuremberg], we went to Regensburg—called Ratisbon in the Browning poem "An Incident in a French Camp." This wasn't badly hit, but we lived in a lousy section on the outskirts. Here, we picked up a couple of police dog puppies eight weeks old— schäeferhunds, they call them here. One "Sherry," a female, is black; the other—mine—"Shep" is a male and lighter in color. The other day, I gave Shep away as we were moving too much to give him a good time. The other [CIC] fellow, Raab, still has Sherry.

Regensburg is on the Danube. The river was very grey where we crossed it, with low-lying banks. But the country is beautiful. We moved south fast, stopping at the Isar River at Griessenbach for a day before crossing this, the swiftest river of all. Then we went SE in a long march to the Inn River to a town called Winhöring. The people here lined the roads waving white flags, clapping, and seem[ed] very happy to have the war over and [having] us, not the Russians, as their hosts. There is an ungodly fear of the Russians....

*In *A Search for Adventure, Part II, The War Years: 1940–1946* [self-published in 1980 by Robert Eliot Matteson], Matteson writes: "On the 1st of May [1945] we moved on to Regensburg and then southeast to Winhöring on the River Inn.... Winhöring was the location of a beautiful 11th-century castle owned by Count Karl Theodor of Toerring-Jettenbach age 45 in 1945.... He admitted that he had been an economic collaborator. He also said he had stored in his castle a large part of Heinrich Hoffmann's collection of Hitler photographs. Hoffmann was Hitler's official photographer. I reported the collection to the Battalion HQ. We picked them up, and the pictures later were used at the Nuremberg trial. The count gave me one book of Hoffmann's pictures [that] Hoffmann had given him. At the trial, Hoffmann himself later gave me more pictures....*

"On May 2nd, we moved into Braunau, Hitler's birthplace, just across the Inn River in Austria. By coincidence, it was here that I first heard that Hitler, Goebbels, and Eva Braun had committed suicide in the Führer's bunker in Berlin on April 30th....

"Then, at 2:41 a.m., May 7th, General Alfred Jodl signed, on behalf of the German government, the surrender document [that] indicated all hostilities would cease at midnight May 8th. General Eisenhower, in the early hours of May 7th, communicated this to General Bradley, and he, in turn, to General Patton with the order that 'We are to hold in place everywhere up and down the line. There is no sense in taking any more casualties now.' But for us in the CIC, the war was not yet over.

"On the same day that General Jodl was signing the surrender document, May 7th, I received the first solid indication the Allies had on where SS General Ernst Kaltenbrunner was. Kaltenbrunner, we knew as the head of the Reich Main Security Office, which contained the dreaded Gestapo, Kripo, and Intelligence Services of the Nazi Reich. We were to learn later that he was in charge of the Alpine Fortress, or National Redoubt, where the fanatic Nazis were said to be congregating to make their last Götterdämmerung-type stand. So, as the European war formally ended, the chase into the National Redoubt after one of the most-wanted of the Nazi war criminals began."

18 May 1945

My dearest darling,

It happened that we hit a hot spot and have been busier than ever before. I wish I could describe everything that has happened in the past week or 10 days. The last time I wrote, we had just crossed into Austria, and that was over a week ago. For the past nine days ... [CIC agents] Bruskin, Motel, and I have been operating in a small mountain village on a beautiful lake in the Austrian Alps. The scenery is indescribable. We have rooms in one of the hotels complete with table and chairs—and my window—a huge thing, looks out over the lake—much like Lake Louise in the Rockies ... but there I had you, and here I have not you.

We eat in the dining room like civilized persons and have our office a block down the little street. It's a tiny village but fraught with problems of the kind we are interested in—for here, the National Redoubt is no myth. I have never known intrigue and silk-like skullduggery until I came here. These Austrians carry a smile on their face and a dagger in their walking stick. And when you mix that with a good group of Nazis, who are fighting each other, plus several families with famous antecedents, plus a colony of Viennese screen, stage, radio, and music stars, plus a collection I can say no more about, you get the beginning of what should be the background for one of the Grand Hotel plays. One night, I refuse an invitation to have dinner with the prince, the next with the countess so and so, and end up by agreeing to spend a couple of here, there, and everywhere—all the time picking up tips on who is what and where.

I came up here to operate with a task force in cleaning out SS troops and ran into a hotbed of our work. The other day, I had the opportunity to go out with a patrol and some Austrians I got together. We started at 12 midnight to climb a snow-capped mountain, and we were still climbing when the sky became light at 4:30, reaching our destination at 6 a.m. It was wonderful exercise, and god, what beautiful country. Especially as the sun rose in the morning and made possible a view in all directions. We went up past the timberline, way up into the snow that at the pass was 30 feet deep.

We have run into all kinds of cases up here. Which reminds me, if you happen to see anything in the paper about a Nazi named Kaltenbrunner in the papers between May 14th and May 21st, please let me know what....

Over here—especially in Austria—there is an unholy fear of Russia [amid] civilians. Everybody predicts a war with Russia, and of course, Austria and Germany are doing their best to bring it about—to bring [the] U.S. into it.

You ask what the future holds. We have heard nothing at all. There was an order May 10th divorcing theoretically all but 5 CIC men from the Division, but with the provision, the Division could keep them as long as they need them. Nobody knows, and I'm so far from the CP [Command Post] that I get no news at all. Some say the 3rd Army (without all of its units) is the Occupation Army. Some say the 15th [Army] is. But a decision should be forthcoming soon, as the war with Japan must be won first. Some say military government will be here 2 years—others say 6 months. CIC—no one knows.

Please send some canned fruit.

My love to Mom, Pop, and kiss D. for me. How is [the dog] Plato?

All my love always,

Bob

23 May 1945

My dearest darling,

Your birthday, and I'm thinking of you every minute—of days that are longer now that the war is over. How I wish I could be with you and D. to celebrate, but I am sure that no matter what happens, I shall be with you on the next one....

I am in the same spot I was in 2 weeks ago and have been here continuously except for excursions over the territory. I am responsible for a couple of trips into the mountains. If only you were here, life could be so wonderful, and you would love it in more ways than anyone I know. I am staying in a beautiful hotel that faces close to the mountains. I have a little veranda—portico off the room from which I'm now writing—and the view defies description. In the distance—not too distant—are snow-capped peaks, and right here below me is a mountain lake beside which rise the rocky cliffs of the mountains. The water is like Lake George—very clear and cold.

We have been very busy, but about this time at night, we have a chance to relax, and God, how I wish you were here to talk to. Austria is a dreamland of beautiful scenery, interesting people (from Vienna, Linz, Graz, Berlin), and terrific intrigue and drama. Life couldn't be more interesting, but it lacks you and Daidie.

We have here a film colony that is trying to ingratiate itself with the Americans—happier than you can imagine that the Russians aren't here. That is a story in itself. Celie Koch and Kurt Von Klipstein, Peter Kreuder, Franz Lehar are all here and many more that are always handing us hot tips and asking us over for a drink after dinner. Also, a prince who was married to Mabel Cochrane of NY—and divorced—and innumerable countesses, etc., one of whom is the mistress of Dr. Ernst Kaltenbrunner—a man whom I shall tell you about at a later date.

Some of the people we have picked up here had connections with our State Department in a movement [that] is [a] story by itself. Another guy we ran across you have heard on the radio from Germany. There are people from the Balkans and Baltic countries that held prominent positions and others in industry from Vienna. More I can't say.

Your wonderful packages arrived today with all the books I want to read. Thanks for the interesting selection.

There is so much I want to tell you, but I can't. It looks now like I shall be here for a while—two or so months anyway. More I don't know. Anything can happen.

All my love,

Bob

25 May 1945

My adorable darling,

American knowledge of German Intelligence [Services] is small, mainly because it (GIS) was so well guarded. Even among staff personnel over here—except for CIC and OSS—it is small. So let me do a little tooting.

German Intelligence Services is the vast intelligence network [that] the Nazi Party built up out of what existed before and what they created after 1933. All intelligence centers in the

Reichssicherheitshauptamt (RSHA), which controls all political intelligence at home and abroad, and since June '44, all military intelligence. It is divided into eight offices or subdivisions called Amts. Amts I and II aren't important—Personnel and Finances. Amt III is the central headquarters of the super secret SD or security service of the SS and the center of all internal political security in the hub of the RSHA. It, in effect, controls Amt IV (Gestapo) and Amt V (Kriminal Police or Kripo)—for which ... it also enlists the services of Amt VI—espionage abroad, [and] the Military Amt (no number), which was the Military Intelligence, and Amt VII (or Ideological Research), which consists of only 14 men (one of which I arrested two weeks ago). This last Amt VII had the job of shaping the German "World Outlook."

In the home of the man I arrested, I found part of the secret library of the RSHA. The books dealt with theosophy, mysticism, freemasonry, religion, astrology [and] gives an idea of their trend with thought. The head of this entire RSHA is the chief for the Reich of the SIPO and SD—general of the SS and Obergruppenführer, Dr. Ernst Kaltenbrunner—little known to people over there or over here. Better known were the Gestapo ... the gas chambers and concentration camps, which he controlled.

Tomorrow, I shall immediately tell you how I captured him—Kaltenbrunner. It makes a good story, but the censorship of the press forbids names, and the limited knowledge of German Intelligence and personalities in it hinders a realization of his importance. Only Himmler was a worse Nazi, and he committed suicide.

Forgive me, but I had to tell somebody what it is all about.

All my love,

Bob

26 May 1945

My dearest darling,

I am—and have been for the past 16 days—in Alt Aussee, Austria—on the map S.E. of Salzburg, near Bad Ischl, and four kms. from Bad Aussee. It is a village of 4,000 persons, filled with the most fascinating problems from our point of view I have yet encountered.

There is a film and music colony from Vienna, a few countesses, including the mistress of Kaltenbrunner, plus a nest of SD men, German foreign agents, Nazi puppet governments, and local townspeople that form a nest of intrigue and excitement I haven't come across before. I am here in charge of CIC in this town and a territory extending many miles south and east.

I came in with the task force that took the town the day before the war ended and have been here ever since. It is the hottest spot in Austria, and the number of correspondents, OSS, and brass indicate it. The town is on the side of the Austrian Alps—a rich man's mountain resort for Linz, Vienna, and Graz—and holds within it a class of people and art treasures you would never believe. One night, we are invited to Peter Kreuder's, the Cole Porter of Austria; the next night to Cecile Koch, the Greta Garbo of Germany; the next night to Prince Hohenlohe's; and the next to Kaltenbrunner's mistress. These Austrians are clever, charming, and deceitful. Intrigue is rife. Bad Aussee—only four kms. away—is also full of CIC problems.

Today in your letter, you mentioned reading about a special agent of 80th CIC capturing a Nazi fiend in the mountains with the aid of Free Austrian troops. That was me, but censorship on the press prevented them from telling who it was—an old CIC policy. We get no publicity, no rank, no nothing—but we lead a wonderful life doing exciting things ... posing now as a captain, then as colonel, and getting away with as much or more than if we were all generals.

Ten days ago, I received a tip from a forester that Dr. Ernst Kaltenbrunner, his adjutant, and two SS men were on top of the Totes Gebirge—a range of the Austrian Alps—in a cabin. I asked a friend in the Free Austria Movement for a guide to lead me on the six-hour trip into the mountains to the hut. Because the head of our task force thought there would be SS troops in the area, he gave me a squad of soldiers. I, with four Austrian mountain climbers and the squad of GIs, started at midnight for this hut, hoping to get across the snow in the night while it was still hard, while the SS were still in bed, and while we could approach the cabin under cover of darkness, as it was way above the timberline in the deep snow barrens. I went dressed as an Austrian in lederhosen, green jacket, and an Alpine [walking] stick, and no weapon.

The idea was for me to approach the cabin as a passerby and find out what was there. Then call for the troops if necessary. The prize was Kaltenbrunner—from a CIC standpoint, the biggest catch in Germany. He is not well known to the public. In 1943, he succeeded Heydrich (The Hangman) as chief of the Gestapo, Criminal Police, and SD for all Germany. The SD is the intelligence agency for all German intelligence, including all military intelligence, and under it operates agents (such as those caught in the U.S. coming ashore from submarines) all over the world. Kaltenbrunner was the head of all of this—under him also operated Skorzeny—the liberator of Mussolini and the head of the famed Brandenburg Division, which operated behind our lines and made several attempts on Eisenhower's life.

Kaltenbrunner, his assistant Scheidler, and two SS men were supposed to be hiding out in the cabin. We started at 12:00 [midnight] and after a long hard climb—over snow 30 feet deep at the pass—reached a position 250 yards from the hut at 6:00. I went up on the porch and knocked on the door, not knowing what to expect.

I aroused one person, at first thinking the cabin was deserted because it was all locked up and there were no fresh footprints on the snow. The person opened the shutter and asked me what I wanted. I said Mrs. Scheidler and Kaltenbrunner sent me to ask S. and K. to come down peaceably before the Russians (of whom they all have an ungodly fear) come. The person, an SS man, went over [and] picked up a pistol, put it in his pocket, and told me he didn't know K. or S. and that nobody had been there at the cabin. Seeing my four Austrian guides approaching, he shut the shutter. I motioned the Infantry to come up around the house and got off the porch as I thought they would start shooting. (K., awhile before, had shot the head of the police in Linz, and I knew he was capable of doing anything. He was also a general in the SS.)

Ten minutes later, the SS man opened the door. I reappeared on the porch. He saw the Infantry coming up and went in and bolted the door. I yelled out an ultimatum, and the GIs started knocking the door down. Then they came out. We found cartons of tax-free American cigarettes, French bon-bons, machine pistols, rifles, pistols, burp guns, etc. inside and identification cards of K. and S. None admitted being K. or S., and K., I found out later, after three hours, posed as a doctor under a false name; the other, S, also went under an assumed name.

We marched them down the mountain, and as we entered the village, Frau Scheidler rushed up and threw her arms around her husband, immediately identifying him. Prince Hohenlohe identified K. also ... I [had] found a picture of K. and his family (four days before I had arrested his wife, which is another story) and so knew that she in the picture was Mrs. K. and that he must be Mr. K. He admitted it to me, as did S. Needless to say the 80th, the XX Corps, the Third Army were all excited about it, and several correspondents appeared to write the story you read.

That night, Mrs. Scheidler and the mistress of K. invited me for dinner. I went, not knowing whether I would be poisoned or questioned. It was the latter. They are only about 28 years old. The mistress—the Countess von Westarp—the blonde, had had eight weeks ago twins by K. Mrs. S is six months along with hers, having divorced another—a man I arrested today, a prominent Vienna surgeon, on incompatibility grounds.

28 May 1945

My adorable lover,

What ecstasy to be able to write what I feel like writing and know that someone I know, besides you, is not reading every line. Our letters have been used as a way to test morale, attitude, etc., as a check on what we are doing.

I love you, my darling, with all my soul, and if I don't repeat it more often now, it is for fear it will become tiresome to you, and if I did not before, it was because [commanding officer] McMillen was devouring every line of it.

Today, Sunday, has been a beautiful, sunny day. The mountain air is cool, and all the meadow and mountain flowers are in full bloom. Being Sunday, all the village people were in full regalia—the men in their little Alpine hats with a proud feather sticking up behind. The feather or brush is only worn for dress. The lederhose, dark green stockings up to their knees, polished dark brown oxfords, green jackets, white shirts, and dark green neckties. The women wear dirndls, and how I love to see them. I think they are the prettiest dress there is, each with bright colored skirts, white puffs at the shoulder, shirt sleeves, and bright colored bodice....

The nice thing about CIC is the lack of the army [protocols] ... we live where we like, with whom we like, and do what we like. The work is interesting—the best job in the service as we deal with only the most interesting civilians—the Nazi agents, politicos, big business, SD, Gestapo, and anybody else we want to. For the officers and GIs, non-fraternization is the rule. For us, it is our business to fraternize. I could not, if I wanted to, think of a better excuse for talking with people here in Europe, seeing their problems, and finding out what they are like, than being in CIC and doing what I am doing. The penalties are two: We continue to work as if the war were still on and get no rest or furlough; we have ranks lower than anybody else in the army by comparison with the type of work we are responsible for. But rank only stands in the way occasionally. We work very closely with Military Government naturally, and they have the rank on us.

I am the head of a CIC detachment for a regiment and have the rank of Tech[nical] Sgt. The head of the Mil Gov't detachment for the same regiment is a major, although the caliber of our work is the same. Consequently, the Mil. Gov't officer tries, because of his superior rank, to keep us under his thumb, although we are not an agency of Military Gov't and have our own channel of command.

McMillen is only a captain, and he is the head of a Division CIC. The head of Mil Gov't of Division is a Lt. Col. Twice I have refused to obey orders of the Mil. Gov't major of our regiment because I am not responsible to him, and twice I have come within an ace of being court-martialed. I told him to, if he wanted to, the last time, but he was afraid of the repercussions. That sort of thing only happens occasionally. Otherwise, I live and act like a 5-star general.

I never told you that in January, I was offered a battlefield commission, passed an examining board of officers, but was prevented from receiving it when ETO CIC ordered all commissions in CIC stopped for some unknown reason....

I love you and miss you. It hurts to know we are missing so much together. You would love it here in the Alps. It is the most perfect country in the world.

My love to Mom, Pop, and kiss D. for me, and [the dog] Plato, too.

All of my love, my dearest,

Bob

31 May 1945

My dearest darling,

It pains me to realize in your letters that you haven't received a letter from me in days. For a while, I was unable to write as we were busy every night. But now I have things under control in my territory, and the Free Austrian Movement is doing a tremendous job in assisting us in this area. I have an area that is about 50 kms. long in Austria and am still headquartered in my favorite little town of Alt Aussee, on the side of the Austrian Alps.

Never in my life have I met so many interesting personalities whom we have to interview as part of our job. I have been here now three weeks today, and we are well known as the American Gestapo in the entire area. We have our own Viennese Symphony Orchestra of 50 men that plays for us at night, our own radio station that broadcasts our policies and announcements. We are given the privileges and consideration of generals. As you know, we wear no stripes on our sleeves and only U.S. on our collars so that no one knows whether we are a colonel or what. It helps us to do our job and have privileges we otherwise would never have. CIC is by far the most interesting job in the army, including Military Gov't, which is quite dull....

Intrigue is still rife, and CIC is at the center of it all. Everybody from the general on down tries to assist our work, always messing things up so that it is really no assistance at all.

You asked about the details of [CIC colleague Alfred Etcheverry] Etch's death. I wrote Marion [Etch's wife], I think, everything that happened. One thing I didn't tell her [however] was that it was the wheel of fortune that put Etch in the spot and not me that day. Every day, Klimek and I had visited this little town of Goesdorf [in Luxembourg]—high above the river. I would always check the situation in one place, Klimek in another. The day Etch got it, McMillen asked me to interview some boys who were interested in getting into CIC work. So Etch went instead, and as he was talking to a civilian in the courtyard in front of a barn, a mortar shell lit right beside him. A fellow who saw it said Etch's helmet flew 25 feet into the air and lit on the barn roof. He was hit in the back of the head, blowing his head to pieces, [and] in the arm and leg. The civilian also was killed instantly.

Etch was a fine person—one I liked as well as any I've met. And though we had been together only 2 or 3 weeks, it was a great personal loss....

It rains like hell here every 4th day, lasting 24–36 hours. But when it is nice, it is beautiful. The other night, when the moon was coming up over the mountain, I went rowing with our IPW boy—interrogator of prisoners of war—over the mountain lake. It was too beautiful to put into words, and God, how I wished you could be there....

Last night, our little orchestra played [Edvard] Grieg's "Peer Gynt," songs from Mozart, a Haydn march, and selections from Beethoven. "Peer Gynt," especially, was beautiful. The audience was small, but you felt they were there because they loved it, not because it was the thing to do or the place to be. The same with the orchestra. People here know and love music, like few I've met before.

All my love always, my lover,

Bob

3 June 1945, Austria

My dearest adorable lover,

Still you have received no letter from me, and it hurts me as much as it does you.... Now it is possible to write more often as things have calmed down considerably, tho we are still in our little paradise in Alt Aussee, with intrigue rife. Everyone is a countess or princess or baron, and there are so many cliques vying for influence with the Americans, especially the much-feared American Gestapo—CIC. They all bite each other, pass clandestine notes to us, and all in all, I feel quite dizzy.

But God, what scenery. Today, for the 1st time in months, I closed the office—Sunday—for half a day, and we went to ... the mountainside and soaked up sun. It was wonderful, and it made me so homesick for you and for Daidie. There is a little lake near here we can go swimming in, that is warm enough now. The lake we are on, tho small, is too deep and consequently very cold—fed straight from the surrounding snow-topped mountains. These alms are beautiful, grassy meadows full of the most gorgeously brilliant mountain flowers of all varieties.

I heard today that I am to stay with a CIC detachment in Europe for a while. Captain McMillen is the head of it—Axtell, Vance, Klimek, and several others you don't know so well—including some who have just joined us from the States.... In a couple of weeks, we expect to leave the [80th] Division, which will be sad in many ways.

Please give my love to Mom and Pop. Kiss little D. for me, and Plato [the dog].

I love you forever,

All my love,

Bob

5 June 1945

My dearest lover,

Today, in a simple ceremony, they—the colonel—gave me the Silver Star. Besides the G-2 staff and CIC, there was the G-3 staff, including good old Colonel Kerr, who now is with G-3 instead of G-2, and who was really genuinely happy and excited to see me get it.

The audience lined the walls of the room. I stood in front while the G-2 read the general order, which I am enclosing. He then pinned the thing on, shook hands with me, I saluted, and it was over. It was the only one given to a person in Division Headquarters, including the Headquarters staff and attached Intelligence teams during the war, so they were unusually nice in extending congratulations.

When it was all over, Colonel Fleisher—my old G-2 boss—came out to tell me I really deserved it and a few other nice things.... The star is in a nice case. It is a large gold star with a tiny silver star at the center suspended from a ribbon, which is blue, white, red, white, blue. On the back is inscribed "For Gallantry in Action." With it comes a ribbon to be worn and a little metal ribbon to be worn on civilian clothes in the lapel....

I love you always. My love to Mom and Pop, and kiss D. for me.

All my love forever,

Bob

[The 8 June 1945 letter—continuation of letters from Bob to Jane—below is from a typewritten excerpt of the original letter, so we present it here as typed.]

8 June 1945

In one of the towns in my territory is Franz Lehár [1870–1948, Austro-Hungarian composer of operettas, best known for The Merry Widow]. Today, noticing an article in Stars and Stripes about him, I decided to stop in and see him to give him the article. So, with an interpreter, I went into this quaint old house along the Traun Streams that flows out of the Alps into the Enns River and thence the Danube. The house is on Franz Lehár Quai. Very graciously, the old man met me (he is 75) and talked with light in his eye about the US, "the land of smiles"; his operetta was to be produced by Schubert Inc. in NY, but they wanted to change it, so he refused, and consequently they never produced it. To change it from the original would have destroyed it.

I was fascinated by the numerous Chinese tapestries and cabinets he had. His wife was there, too, an old Viennese actress—Jewish—who ... was very nice. He brought out a bottle of brandy, and we talked for an hour. [He said] only Frederica was banned by the Nazis. Merry Widow was Hitler's favorite, but when it was produced in Berlin, it was so over-staged that it collapsed from sheer weight.

Mrs. Lehár ... has a Jewish brother in NY ... whom she hasn't heard from in five years. So I agreed to take a letter from her, give it to a friend who lives near him in NYC whose wife would deliver it. As we left, I gave him [Lehár] my name and address, and he gave me a picture of himself with my name, his, a salutation, and a bar of music from the Merry Widow. I shall try and bring it home in one piece. He has a beautiful home in Vienna—250 years old—but he left it two years ago because he hated the Nazis and their rule. He still doesn't know what happened to it.

Today, I hit with my fist my third Nazi. He is a friend of Hitler's, marched into Austria with him, was a partner to the murder of Dollfuss, was manager of a Nazi bank to organize Jewish property, was a Standartenführer in the NSKK [National Socialist Motor Corps], and a member of the Party since 1932. He claimed he hadn't been a Nazi and couldn't understand why we had arrested him. (He is the clever, diabolical type.) So I stood up and let go with a right that caught him flush on the mouth. Three teeth fell out on the floor, and blood was over everything. I hit him once more, and he collapsed. His last remark was "Ist das Amerika?"

Everybody thinks America is soft and plays us for a big, generous, soft-hearted sucker. So I'm starting a one-man campaign to correct it. As a result, I and my team are the best-hated people in this part of Austria. I have arrested heads of national banks, heads of puppet state govts, cabinet ministers, many Gestapo and Intelligence men, Foreign Office people, Nazi Party officials, and members of the SS. Methinks that our life in America will be haunted by people trying to get even, whose one purpose is find that son of a bitch who imprisoned them—not the least of whom is Kaltenbrunner.

[The 10 June 1945 letter below is from a typewritten excerpt of the original letter, so we present it here as typed.]

10 June 1945

I am leaving this little paradise of ours, Alt Aussee, the 12th of June for a new area of Germany near Munich. Today, I have been here a month, and so much has happened that it has been the most interesting experience I have had yet in CIC.

I arrested the chief of construction of V-2 and had an interesting talk with him. Then today it was an Argentine with German citizenship—prominent as the head, former, of all German pharmaceutical industries, including IG Farben [prominent Reich industry that was the "fourth largest corporation in the world and the largest in Europe" at the start of World War II].[135] He held many interesting jobs and is the kind of international high finance bastard on which Nazism rests and by whom wars are created. He owns controlling stock in more companies in more countries than you can count.

12 June 1945

My dearest darling,

Enclosed is a second picture Franz Lehár gave me yesterday after I stopped in to pick up a letter his wife wanted sent to her brother, Hans Parker, in NYC. He is too good to be living in this world. He loves people and, though 75 years old, becomes more rested and relaxed the more he talks. He poured a drink of some Czech stuff that was as powerful as the French Eau de vie de Poire [pear brandy].

As he said, he loves Americans because they are so frank and friendly. He said he can tell Americans anywhere as they breathe freedom. Again, he described how awful it was with the Nazis. You had to whisper when you talked; you could never be sure (his wife is Jewish) that the Nazis weren't coming to arrest you or expel you. He asked if I wouldn't write him around whenever I heard one of his operettas wherever I was, to send him a program. Wasn't that cute? The large picture with a bar from Merry Widow I'll bring with me.

Yesterday, when we left our little Alt Aussee, the mistress of Kaltenbrunner Gisela von Westarp came over to me and, with tears in her eyes, handed me a 150-year-old scarf for you from Alt Aussee, with special thanks for not killing her man, but bringing him back alive.

Peter Kreuder, the Cole Porter of Austria, brought [a] ... picture, and with tears in his eyes, said good-bye. And the Bürgermeister of Bad and Alt Aussee—the wonderful Georg Schumacher (alias Albrecht Gaiswinkler), who was parachuted into the area before the Americans came to organize resistance—gave me a silver, hand-carved cigarette case from the people of Alt Aussee inscribed with "To the liberator of the people of Bad Aussee," signed A. Gaiswinkler, Bürgermeister. Also, he gave me a hand-made pair of leather boots and half-shoes and a phenomenal small camera 1" by 3", used by the Gestapo to take pictures thru key-holes [and in] more subtle ways. It cost something like $300.

You can imagine my sadness at leaving what had become my little home in Europe. Everyone was so nice and so sad to see us go.

I love Austria with all my heart. They are a wonderful people in a wonderful land.

But this is meant for you on our 5th anniversary. May it be the last we are not together again. I shall be thinking of you on that day.

All my love,

Bob

[The 15 June 1945 letter below is from a typewritten excerpt of the original letter, so we present it as typed.]

15 June 1945

Growing up every wall are huge banks of red roses. Red poppies are in the fields around and all sorts of wildflowers. I have never known more picturesque people than the Austrians in summer. They all wear bright colored dresses or socks or ties—hats, shawls.... Everyone is sunburned a deep dark reddish brown from the hot sun and mountain air.

Norman Baillie-Stewart, who started the Lord Haw-Haw programs, was another one that I arrested. I got him by chance in Alt Aussee.

He came into the office one day as interpreter for a Dutchman. I knew enough German to know he was mistranslating. So I nabbed him. He gave me his story after some parrying. He is a blue-blood. He went to Sandhurst, Royal College of Dartmouth, served a period in India as member of the Coldstream Guards. Was disgusted with England. Volunteered in '20s for German Secret Service, given a mission in England. Discovered by English censors. Imprisoned for five years in Tower of London. Influence of his mother got him out. More embittered than ever, went to Vienna. Followed by both Eng. Secret Service and Gestapo, as no one knew what side he was on. Went into business with two Jews to avoid suspicion. Criticized Germany's Eng. propaganda so was invited to improve it. Went to Berlin as advisor to Goebbels. Started Lord Haw-Haw program and edited ... paper put out by Nazis. Got into fight with someone in propaganda office so switched to German Foreign Office. He was a nice-looking, young (34) English aristocrat who was against everything and everybody.

Nobody he lived with knew the real story, but he proudly told me about it, and I listened with such sympathy that he told me enough to hang him.

★ ★ ★

[The 22 July 1945 letter below is from a typewritten excerpt of the original letter, so we present it here as typed.]

22 July 1945 [Fussen]

Hannah—a half-Jewish girl who works for us as a stenographer and secretary. Because she is half-Jewish, she has not been allowed to get married, to dance, to hold a good job, to do anything with the freedom that normal German girls were permitted. She is 25. Her mother (who is all Jewish), her father, and her only sister live in Frankfurt. She is very independent and so left her family about a year and a half ago to come to Fussen to make her own living. She speaks perfect English, is a 1st rate stenographer, and runs the routine side of the office.

She was 13 when Hitler came to power and attended the usual public schools in Frankfurt. She was taught National Socialism like everyone else and, like all children, believed in most of the principles. This despite the fact that her father and mother were violently opposed. She excuses her belief by saying that the ideals of the program were beautiful as presented to the children. But as the years passed and she came out of the world of books into a world of action, the ideals dissolved and were replaced by actualities.

Her mother, in 1938, was sent to a concentration camp. She and her sister were not allowed to be in the company of German Aryan boys. And [there's] a continuation of the same things you have heard so often that so many in the same position suffered. During those years, she travelled to Sweden and to London with her father, who had an export textile business. In Sweden, she learned and felt the difference in atmosphere between the two countries.

She was in love with a German boy whom she saw on the sly. He was killed at Stalingrad. In 1944, March 22, Frankfurt was hit by a 2,000-plane raid that destroyed 80% of the city. All of the houses around hers were completely destroyed. Her house was hit by three incendiaries that they put out. But a huge bomb landed 100 yards from the house, and that concussion caved in the walls and blew all the windows and doors in. Her father's factory was destroyed completely. But her father rejoiced every time there was a raid, and the more Germany was destroyed, the better he liked it. Hannah felt differently. She hated the raids and will never be able to excuse the mass saturation bombings that bombed military and civilian targets alike. Being unusually sensitive, she could stand the raids no longer. So in April '44, she came to Fussen.... In a way, she is a minor edition of Virginia Woolf.

[The 5 August 1945 and 20 September 1945 letters below are from typewritten excerpts of the original letter, so we present them here as typed.]

5 August 1945

It doesn't add to the atmosphere to be living in a conquered country. The people don't have much to eat—very little to buy. Most of them are from bombed-out cities and have lost everything. Sons, husbands, brothers are still missing—they don't know whether they are dead or alive. There are no communications, little travel, and most people do not live where their family home was.

Everyone looks to the winter with great dread, for it is cold near the mountains. Fuel is scarce and food very scarce. Most of the people are nice and accept it far more stoically than the Americans would.

The fear of Russia continues to be great. Communists appear strong in every German locality, but they are not more than a strong vocal minority.

Interrogation reports from higher headquarters on K. and Höttl and Waneck (all arrested at Alt Aussee) have reached us finally. They are extremely interesting. The inside picture of the RSHA—of Himmler and Hitler—and the great suspicion and jealousy of all big shots for their subordinates and among themselves, and the fights going on inside is even more a fact than I had imagined. Kaltenbrunner was ranked with Hitler, Himmler, and Bormann as the four greatest war criminals and most powerful men in Germany, not excepting Göring and Goebbels. Göring's role especially waned the last few years as Bormann's, K's, and Himmler's roles increased....

Thursday, 20 September 1945

My dearest,

Thank you for the cable I received on my birthday and also for the books that arrived shortly afterwards....

We moved to Garmisch [Partenkirchen] last week and, as I think I have told you, are living in a wonderful small hotel in Hemmersbach right under the Zugspitze [highest mountain in Germany]. The office is in the center of Garmisch. The Division area for which I am responsible from a CIC standpoint has been enlarged considerably and involves a lot of traveling. But life is very simple now that I am my own boss and only have to coordinate. As a result, I have set up a good working schedule, with Saturdays and Sundays off....

Last weekend, [CIC's] Motell and I motored down to Alt Aussee. We started at 6 p.m. Friday night and arrived there at 11 p.m., going through Salzburg, St. Wolfgang, Ischl. We stayed at our old place, Eibl Hotel.... The next day, we were invited [by] Gisela and Iris for a trout dinner (Remember them? K.'s mistress and wife of SS Obergruppenführer Wolf, and the wife of Scheidler—K.'s adjutant). They are very interesting to talk to. Iris just had her baby. Gisela's twins are very healthy and mature looking at six months.... Gisela asked if we would take her back to Hindelang (near Fussen), where her mother and child by Wolf are living. We started at 4 a.m. to get back here by 9 a.m. The car broke down coming over the Pötschen Pass, and we had to stay at St. Wolfgang for 12 hours until it was fixed. It was a beautiful fall day, with blue sky and the leaves turning red and gold. As we came through Salzburg, about 10 p.m., Gisela burst into a flood of tears. Salzburg was her place of rendezvous with K. when he was in Graz and she in Hindelang. It was the first time she had been there since the end of the war. She told us more about K. and herself. The amazing thing about her appearance now is how fat she has become in three months. She knows he will be hung and so doesn't give a damn about anything except her babies....

Give Mom and Pop my love and kiss D. for me. I wish I had more time to describe a few of the funny situations we are always running into around here.

All of my love always,

Bob

25 October 1945

My dearest darling,

We never get any mail these days since our change of address, but I hope it comes thru soon.... I am trying to get into the War Crimes Trial at [Nuremberg] starting the 20th of November, and everyone thinks the chances are good. There will be over 200 correspondents, and from the size of the room, I don't see how they will get anyone else in.

On Saturday morning, Roach, an Austrian civilian who lives in Wien [the German word for Vienna], Gisela von Westarp, and I are going to Alt Aussee. You will no doubt be horrified at my taking Gisela back from Hindelang to Alt Aussee, but there is good reason—purely to get her to talk. No one has gotten much information from the group that lived in the Führerhauptquartier. Kaltenbrunner has refused to talk, as has Gisela. But on the trip five weeks ago from Alt Aussee, she started to break down. Now that she knows K.'s fate is determined, she should not be as afraid of saying things she might have thought might be used against him. In fact, she should figure that her talking might help in some way. At least that is the line I shall play....

Military government [MG] like CIC has had a spotty record over here. But MG, of the two, is the worse.... The case was this: A certain Dr. Lieffers was employed by MG as a civilian adviser and investigator, [but] CIC informed MG that Lieffers was a member of the SA (Stormtroopers) since 1933, NSDAP [National Socialist Democratic A Party] member since 1938, [and] an employee of the Reich Forschungsamt [Research Office of the Reich Air

Ministry] since 1938. The latter agency was the intelligence agency of Göring [that] he had built up for his own personal information, not trusting the information given him by the regular intelligence agencies. Lieffers held a position that was high enough to make him an automatic arrest by our arrest categories. MG had been informed of this but refused even to dismiss him. So the CIC agent said he was going to arrest him on security grounds. They asked to know why. They put in a protest to their higher headquarters in Augsburg. That is where I came into the picture. I have seldom had as much fun in my life in damning a person ... as I did the MG person, captain, and two Lts. [lieutenants].

The upshot was we arrested the guy immediately and embarrassed them by threatening publicity on their policy. They insisted on giving protection to a Nazi who had been in an intelligence agency and who had access to everything they were doing. In most of those cases, when you get to the bottom of it, you find that some officer is receiving favors of one sort or another. Cases like that happen every day, but we (i.e., the operating teams) have enough to do in investigating the security threats and Nazis without investigating our own military [government] personnel....

It is easy to become disgusted and disillusioned with our occupation policy or lack of it and the execution of it, and it is another thing to do something about it. There is nothing to be lost in these last weeks over here by blasting some of the rampant corruption and lack of efficiency.

Today, our eight-week-old puppy arrived fresh from its mother and brothers and sisters. It is a police dog, or schäeferhund as they call them, and looks like a ball of grey cotton. We call him "Hercules," which was the code name for the 80th Division. Naturally, he is homesick today, but he gets so much attention from all of the civilian employees that he should very soon be spoiled beyond repair.

The deer season is on, and Marty—the right-hand man—has shot three already. Tomorrow, we shall have venison, and my mouth is already watering.

Rumors persist that Stalin is dead. Incidents continue in which Russians shoot Americans or vice versa along the border zone. It is not so much the program but the ruthless, aggressive, and unfriendly manner [in which] the Russians execute it that is the root of the anti-Russian feeling here.

Please give my love to Mom and Pop. Kiss D. for me.

All of my love forever, Bob

29 October 1945

My dearest darling,

Still no mail, but I know it is not your fault. Our change of address has screwed everything up....

Over the weekend, I finally completed a mission that began last May—getting enough information from Gisela re K. so that there would be nothing lost by arresting her. Besides, now her twins are big enough to live alone and like it. When we brought her back to Hindelang from Alt Aussee so that she could see her family and other child (by Wolf), we made a half-promise that we would be going again to Aussee. So after 6 weeks back, we went again. This time, Roach, who was in Aussee with me in May, came along and also Erwin Rodin, who lives in Wien [Vienna], and who has been working for us in CIC since V-E Day.... Iris with her offspring was still there in Aussee. Iris is actually going crazy. She talks about suicide, and she looks like she means it.... After the life of glamour she once led, it is hard for her to take.

I left a memo with the CIC there giving the facts on Gisela so they can make out an arrest report. She is a security threat in as much she is intelligent, has the contacts, and still retains her Nazi sympathies. Friday night, I drove down to Hindelang, which is within my sub-region, and picked her up. Her mother, Gräfin von Westarp, and her sister were there. They have been forced out of their large house and live with three children in one room with three beds. There is no heat and little food. I didn't feel sorry for them either.

Gisela was a secretary for Himmler for a while. She is a great friend of Dr. Brandt, Hitler's personal physician. She knows Eva Braun and Fegelein's wife. So she is a good sounding board for Nazi personalities. To her, Ley was crazy, as was Streicher. Goebbels and Hitler were okay, of course. Ribbentrop was stupid, Himmler sadistic. Bormann was the devil incarnate. So what she says jibes with one-word characterizations that most give. I showed her the articles you sent me written by Bernadotte, and she was visibly affected by the bad things they had to say about K.

I asked her why most Nazis took a mistress. She said it was not just the Nazis but customary with the Germans. Also, she said it was the rule, especially in the SS. Usually when a young SS man married, he married a young gal in the BDM [Bund Deutscher Mädel – Band of German Maidens] of the same rank. Usually, the man outgrew the gal, and as he rose to the higher ranks, he grew tired of a wife whose horizon was limited, so he took on something more interesting and younger. I asked her about her and K. She said that Mrs. K. was serious and coldly intelligent—that K. had a lot of feeling and warmth. He needed somebody else. So-o-o having had only three children in 12 years, he took on G.

Wannsee—the RSHA guest house—was a beautiful spot with a lake and trees, and in one year, G had produced twins. K. was very proud of her, she said, and she herself thought she should get the Mother's Cross [Cross of Honour of the German Mother].

All the wives of the people we arrested descended on us when they heard we were there and begged for word of their men. They brought letters, which they hoped we would deliver. Most of them had just had babies, and I was wondering if it was the right thing to say to husbands they hadn't seen for such a long time. Iris was more interested in seeing her divorced husband, Dr. Praxmarer—the Viennese physician who I arrested 16 May as a collaborator of K's. He had given him weapons and fixed up K.'s disguise as a doctor. She had found out he was in a camp near Salzburg, which was on the way back, so, wanting to see the inside of one of our concentration camps, which the Nazis claim were worse than theirs, I consented to take her along.

The camp, Marcus W. Orr, is an old German military camp. It houses 8,000 PWs. I found Dr. Prax in Compound II. He was the head of the PW hospital. Iris had read us a menu that had been smuggled out, and she was sure Dr. Prax was starving. But Dr. Prax never looked better in his life, and he didn't seem too unhappy. But I was amazed at the little food they get. Most have lost quite a bit of weight. I inspected the entire camp to be able to compare it to what I had seen at Dachau and Ebensee. The men sleep on the floor on boards. They have six spigots of water for 150 men for washing and their laundry. They get little soap. Their menu—one cup of ersatz coffee without sugar or milk for breakfast, and that is all. One bowl of soup made of cabbage leaves and meat for lunch. I sampled it, and it tasted good, but it only made you want more. A hunk of bread and a piece of cheese for supper. Men who worked had a couple of squares of chocolate added. In addition, they are allowed packages from home—if any ever arrive. But the camp was clean, especially the kitchen and washrooms. The number of sick isn't high. They only have the clothes on their backs. No political education is given, although they are all political PWs. They have language classes taught by their own men. I asked my interpreter why he was in. Only a Party member. I said it was impossible. Seeing I wasn't convinced, he said he did join the Allgemeine SS [major branch of the SS paramilitary forces] and was an Unterfturmführer (SS paramilitary rank). I didn't have to ask him anymore....

I have had no more news about redeployment, but I still guess it should start for me the end of November. I hope so.

We have a cute puppy police dog who is very intelligent. He is getting strong and has lost his fear and homesickness. He loves it and everyone loves him. Already he is house-broken....

Please send me the accounts of the trials, as we never see anything written anymore—not even the Stars and Stripes.

My love to Mom and Pop. And tell D. I am expecting to see her soon and be able to really kiss her.

All my love forever,

Bob

[The 3 November 1945 letter below is from a typewritten excerpt of the original letter, so we present it here as typed.]

3 November 1945

Yesterday, I received word simultaneously of two things [that] counteract each other. I received orders that I was to leave for home from USFET CIC Hq on the 8 Nov, meaning I would be home in the US probably by the 15 December. But at the same time, I was "requested" by the CO of CIC (which means ordered) to remain in Europe until the completion of a special mission. The mission I find today is to take charge of security for all distinguished personnel at the Nuremberg War Crime Trials. The job starts today so I am moving to Nuremberg immediately. It should be interesting, however, as I shall have contact with everybody of interest at the trials, including all of the judges, generals, ambassadors, and what have you. The best part will be constant access to the courtroom and the trial itself.

I have never done a job like this before, and tho I wouldn't relish it as a life profession, it will be interesting this time because of the occasion. There is a Colonel Sutherland who will be responsible for the general security—the placing of the guards, etc., but we have all counter-intelligence functions, including supervising the daily schedules of the big shots. I am taking Roach and Marks with me and will have the CIC in Nuremberg, also. There is fear that the Nazis will pull something at the trials, and the repercussions would be bad inasmuch as they are held in American territory. There will probably be hundreds of Russian secret servicemen around, and they no doubt will cause more trouble than the Nazis. The setting up of the security plan should not take more than two weeks, but it is possible I shall be held for the entire trial, which will last about six weeks. After that, there is nothing more to hold me....

Please give my love to Mom and Pop. Kiss D. for me.

All of my love forever, Bob

APPENDIX D
"SECRET" CIC Report, 8 June 1945

HEADQUARTERS 80th INFANTRY DIVISION
80th CIC DETACHMENT
APO #80
U.S. ARMY
SUBJECT: After Action Report

May 1945

TO: Asst. Chief of Staff, G-2 80th Inf. Div.

During the month of May 1945, the 80th CIC Detachment directed most of its attention toward counter-intelligence personalities from the Salzkammergut section of the National Redoubt. The net results of this operation, in terms of arrests, is as follows:

Agents	13
Security Arrests	111
Political Arrests	648
Total:	772

The most notable individual apprehended was SS *Obergruppenführer*, Dr. Kaltenbrunner, chief of all police agencies in the Reich, who was apprehended along with his adjutant, Arthur

Scheidler, and two SS guards. Information was received that the party was hiding with false papers, heavily armed, in a remote cabin near Alt Aussee. Special Agent Robert E. Matteson of the 80th CIC Detachment organized and led a patrol to effect the arrest, climbing over mountainous and glacial terrain for six hours in darkness and personally confronted his suspects alone and unarmed. For this exploit, Agent Matteson was awarded the Silver Star for gallantry in action.

Subsequent investigation also implicated Dr. Rudolf Praxmarer in the hideout plot. This physician, who was director of an SS hospital in Alt Aussee, and was Orts Kommandant of the town, had been secretly active in several Nazi and SS plans and was evacuated as a security threat. Likewise evacuated after subsequent investigation was Kaltenbrunner's wife, Elizabeth.

In the same area as Kaltenbrunner, and operating under his directions, was a group of Sicherheitsdienst officials led by Wilhelm Waneck, chief of Amt VI-E of the SD. Along with him was Werner Göttsch, who was the leader of an SD group whose mission was to draw the United States into war against Russia, and Dr. Wil Höttl, a representative from this group who assertedly had met with members of the U.S. State Department in Switzerland. All were arrested, along with five other SD officials and a radio transmitter, which had been in contact with Washington and other capitals. Simultaneously but by independent investigation, seven more members of the group, including Paul [——], Göttsch's chief of staff, were arrested, operating three more radio sets in another valley some 50 miles away from the original group....

Two investigations of special interest were conducted by this office. The first was concerned with a large counterfeit plant controlled by the Abwehr at Zipf [Redl-Zipf concentration camp, a sub-camp of the Mauthausen concentration camp, operating 1943–1945]. Operated by conscripted Jewish engravers and professional counterfeiters, this unit was equipped to turn out excellent reproduction of British, American, and other currency, as well as false credentials and official stationery. Personnel from the plant was located at various concentration camps in the area, and its products have been recovered from the [Austrian locales:] Enns River, [Lake] Toplitz See [Toplitzsee], and Lake Gmunden [Traunsee]. The investigation has been taken over by higher headquarters.

The second matter of interest was the [Austrian] Chemical and Physical Experimental Laboratory for Rockets (underwater), which was found on Grundlsee [Lake Grundlsee] at Gossl. Under the direction of Dr. Hermann Determann, this unit had moved from Kiel [on the Baltic Sea] and was working, among other things, to perfect a rocket that could be fired from a submerged submarine. Beside Determann and a dozen of his technicians, the Detachment arrested Walter Riedel, who had been chief of the construction section of [the] V-2 experimental plant on the island of Usedom [divided between Germany and Poland] in the [southern] Baltic Sea.

During this period, about half of the Detachment personnel was occupied in screening over 100,000 [prisoners of war] who were being discharged. A large number of arrests are being made at this point, the final results of which are not included in this report.

Thomas R. McMillen

Captain, Infantry

CIC Det.

APPENDIX E

Robert B. Persinger on 6 May 1945 Liberation of Ebensee Concentration Camp[136] – 6 October 2009 Email to Sumner Matteson

Robert Persinger served with General Patton's Third Army Third Cavalry and commandeered the first tank that liberated Ebensee on 6 May 1945. Bob passed away in Rockford, Illinois, at age 95 on 19 November 2018.

> Subject: Ebensee
> Date: 10/6/09 4:52:47 PM
> From: "Robert B Persinger" <bpersinger@juno.com>
> To: smat1@charter.net
>
> Dear Sumner,
>
> Sounds like your father arrived that same day as we did. The weather was beautiful compared to the weather we had in the days before.
>
> As I told you [over the phone], I took my tank and another to the camp. When we were about two hundred yards from the gate, we started to smell that terrible smell of decaying bodies and the terrible filth. When we got to the gate, we just stopped the tanks to look around to see if there was any SS troops or

anything beside the Volkssturm, who were very thankful that we had arrived. The prisoners were standing in filth and mud up to their ankles. Some were half-clothed, others with nothing. There were dead bodies everywhere. They looked like ghosts with the averaged weight of sixty-five to seventy-five pounds. However, they were cheering and celebrating so much to see us.

We entered the camp, and eventually, we dismounted the tanks and were immediately hugged as we walked to the kitchen. They were filthy, also open sores and loaded with lice. We went through a barracks, most of them in their bunks were so ill that they never saw us. They were dying, and the smell made you sick. Then came the crematorium, which was worse, if that was possible. There were stacks of bodies stacked like cord wood four or five bodies high waiting to be burned in the furnaces. We had seen enough and became more sick, and vomiting followed. All of this is glued in my memory, so I will never forget it as long as I live.

The camp was in an area that was wooded; however, there was an area that was open for the roll call each morning. I do not think it was concealed in any way.

You asked for some ex-prisoners' addresses. I will get them together in the next few days and send them to you.

Sincerely,

Bob

APPENDIX F

Compiled Emails from
Samuel Goetz to Sumner Matteson,
29 November 2009 – 29 April 2010,
Regarding Nazi Concentration Camps,
Especially Ebensee in Austria

Sam Goetz survived four concentration camps from age 14 to 16, with the last being Ebensee, a subcamp of Mauthausen. Sam was present when Robert Matteson appeared at Ebensee on the same day (6 May 1945) as Robert Persinger, but Goetz and Matteson did not meet. The first email presented is a composite of three received in response to questions posed by Sumner during 29 November – 4 December 2009.

Sam was an optometrist for 50 years and was the leader in establishing a Holocaust studies chair at UCLA—the first ever in the U.S. at a public university. He passed away on 24 October 2013.

Sam's family—Poland, 1938. **From left:** Sam, age 10; his brother Bernard, age 17; his mother, age 39; and his father, age 39.

Sam at UCLA, upon opening the 1939 Club Chair on Holocaust studies.

Photos from *I Never Saw My Face* (Rutledge Books, 2001) by Samuel Goetz. Sam last saw his parents—both the same age in their early 40s—in Tarnow, Poland, on 15 June 1942, when the SS police took them away.

Dates: 29 November-4 December 2009
From: "SAM GOETZ" <samg28@sbcglobal.net>
To: smat1@charter.net
Subject: Ebensee

Hi Sumner,

I arrived in Ebensee late January 1945, following a death march and a stop at Mauthausen. The death march was from a subcamp of GROSS ROSEN—the concentration camp Falkenberg south of Berlin to Reichenburg. The death march lasted two weeks and got us to a railroad station on a German-Czechoslovakian border (Reichenburg). Three days later, the train arrived in Mauthausen. Those of us alive helped to unload the dead from the train, and we spent a day in Mauthausen, and [then] were shipped to Ebensee via San Valentin.

There on the bridge over the Danube, I witnessed an air raid with dozens of American planes, rather high up in the sky. The SS guards jumped off the train, but we were not the target.

I have no answer to your question, what gave me strength. I did have faith in God, but I was very young and had hardly time to rationalize my faith and my misfortune. You lived for the moment. It was a miracle to be able to survive. The hunger, the cold, the lack of shoes, and constant beating or harassment by the SS guards, and the 12-hour work required a Herculean effort to make it.

I had my moments of desperation in Ebensee; there were times at the very end that I ate charcoal, was getting weak, and doubted that I could survive. Inmates were dropping dead as we were walking to work from the camp to the tunnels, but one was oblivious, since death was all around us. Tunnels were used by the Nazis to protect the weapon system from bombardments. In Ebensee, the tunnels were huge completed, and the Nazis were assembling part of tank engines, as well as possibly some of the rocket parts.

In early April 1945, a group of inmates arrived in Ebensee. They were dressed differently and had full-length hair. After liberation,

I befriended one of the inmates who told me they were making counterfeit money in Sachsenhausen concentration camp and transferred to Ebensee when the Russian armies were moving toward Berlin. There was no counterfeit money-making in Ebensee (to the best of my knowledge). Ebensee was one of the worst of the 5 camps that I went through; there was no peace and quiet. You were surrounded by death.

Food was very scarce, particularly during the last few months of the war. A small portion of bread, black coffee (not real), and a watery soup. People were dying of starvation. The work in the tunnels, particularly in Falkenberg camp, consisted of removing stones, debris following an explosion. In Falkenberg, we began to build tunnels. In Ebensee, tunnels were completed and even trains were able to deliver the weapon systems to be assembled. No sympathy ever from SS guards. Just the opposite: they were human beasts.

When I was liberated, I was 16. What lessons? To beware of dictatorships, to maintain strong democratic values, and to be tolerant of fellow human beings.

Sam

Date: Thu, 4 Mar 2010 21:37:31 -0800 (PST)
From: SAM GOETZ <samg28@sbcglobal.net>
To: smat1@charter.net
Subject: Re: Dad's memoirs

Hello Sumner. The actual capture of Kaltenbrunner, a single-handed act, was a rather heroic one. Your dad was in great danger as he entered the lodge. The back soldiers were some distance away from the mountain lodge. Your dad showed great courage the way he describes the act of identifying the capture of one [of] the most feared human beings in Nazi-occupied Europe. As I mentioned to you in my previous email of Feb 18, your dad's memoirs provide a footnote to the history of a dark age in Europe's XX century, and it is a very valuable document for the historians.

With best regards,

Sam

Date: 4/29/10 7:34:54 AM
From: "SAM GOETZ" <samg28@sbcglobal.net>
To: smat1@charter.net
Subject: I Never Saw My Face

Hi Sumner. We spoke the day I was leaving for Europe. We arrived last night very late from Austria. I read your email late last night, and I reply still on a bad jet lag.

By Saturday I should be able to function well. Let me know if you can call me on Saturday, at what time Calif. Time, and I will stand by. In addition, I have funerals to attend; a close friend of 98 passed away.

The Italian experience was exhausting and exhilarating. The publisher had us speak [on Sam's book *I Never Saw My Face*] in towns and high schools with over 1,000 students in several high schools, etc. Lots of media of Salento region, Bari, Lecce, etc. We were exhausted, not getting to sleep till late after 12. They were very kind, and we have no idea how many books we signed; we were too tired to care.

With best regards,

Sam

APPENDIX G

Email from Phyllis Bausher, Daughter of Sydney Bruskin—Robert Matteson's Interpreter and Traveling Companion in the Final Days of the War

From: Phyllis Bausher
Date: Wed, May 19, 2010 at 7:35 PM
Subject: Re: Materials
To: <smat1@charter.net>

Hi Sumner,

I will try to give you more information about my father. A big part of his (and my mother's) lives was his bicycle business—Bruskin's Bicycle Center. It was in downtown New Haven and catered to Yale students as well as "townies." It seems like everyone in our area bought at least one bike from my father. Whenever we would go somewhere with him, someone would always come up to him and say hello and talk about their bike. My father also officiated at college bicycle races in the area. When the Special Olympics were in New Haven about 15 years ago, he also volunteered in bicycle events, too.

His store was on the main drag in New Haven. In addition to bicycle aficionados who would stop by the store to visit and chat, other local "characters" stopped by also. Another notable aspect of the bike store was the fact that over the years, starting during the war, various relatives worked there.

My mother, Shirley, developed health problems in 1974. It was a degenerative muscle disease called polymyositis. She passed away in 1990. During those years, my father devoted an increasing amount of time to her care. They also had many home health aides during the last few years. My father sold the bike business in 1984.

Once he retired, he volunteered at the Jewish Home for the Aged and joined a conversational Yiddish group. He did some traveling. After my mother's death, he spent part of the winter in Florida for about 10 years. Before my mother's illness, my parents took wonderful vacations and traveled to South America, Australia and New Zealand, Africa, Israel, Mexico, and the Caribbean.

As a pastime, my father loved to play cards. For many years, he played poker—he even was part of a poker group when he was in assisted living. He also played a lot of Scrabble. He was a very good player. Later in life he learned to play bridge. My mother had always been an avid bridge player. I play a lot and met my husband at a bridge tournament. So I guess that card playing runs in our family.

Family was always very important to my father. He tried to stay in touch with extended family members in various parts of the USA. He was very close to our son and enjoyed sharing stories of his early life and of the war. He faithfully attended all of our son's piano recitals, school concerts, plays, etc.

Syd would have loved being a great-grandfather. Our granddaughter was born 10 months ago and aptly named Lilah Sydney Bausher. [Lilah, age 14 in 2023 and a freshman in high school, has a younger sister, Hallie, age 11, and in sixth grade in 2023.]

My father was also very close with his nephew, Sam Bruskin, whose father was my father's brother. In 2004, Sam, living in New

Orleans at the time, came to Connecticut for our son's wedding. While Sam was here he spent a lot of time with my father and brought along his camcorder. When I recently emailed Sam (now in LA) and told him about your project, he became very interested. He has the videotape of my father (probably somewhat similar to the tape I sent you) and other recollections about my father that he would like to share.

I hope this helps. If I think of more things, I will certainly send them along to you.

Phyllis

Sydney Bruskin, May 1945, posting civilian guards at an Alt Aussee building to guard "arrested Nazi Party functionaries." Photo a gift of Bruskin's daughter, Phyllis Bausher.

APPENDIX H

Lloyd Roach Letter to Jane Matteson, 15 January 2000

Lloyd M. Roach

Tyler, Texas

1/15/2000

Dear friend Jane,

I was glad to get your Christmas card with your family portrait. This letter is your word from me that I cherish[ed] having Bob as my partner, and he was kind enough to let me share part of the way his "adventure," as he so aptly dubbed it.

It is easy to drop a friend out of a modern-day busy life. The wonder is that we allow it to happen—then regret. I believe it to be a fact that Bob and I met as total strangers—nothing in common—and served together as friends at the historical trial of Kaltenbrunner and the others. Of course, we parted at the water's edge, but the memories for me are eternal....

Sincerely,

Lloyd

APPENDIX I

Letter from George Griebenow to Robert E. Matteson, 7 November 1978

Mr. Griebenow—on his birthday—was one of the GIs who accompanied Matteson up to Wildensee Hütte to capture Kaltenbrunner.

Dear Bob:

I thoroughly enjoyed the phone call.... As you told me, we left the village for Kaltenbrunner's ski cabin at midnight May 12th, 1945, arriving on site soon after dawn. We were 18 in number, all volunteers, but by the time we got to the cabin 4 to 6 people had dropped out because of fatigue or break throughs in the snow and ice crust.

1) We carried conventional infantry squad weapons—I had a BAR [Browning Automatic Rifle] picked up at Bastogne. Others had M-1s [M1 Garland] and carbines [short-barreled rifles].

2) After getting to the cabin, we stood in a semi-circle pending your approach to the cabin, then "rushed" the cabin and Nesselrodt, and banged in the door with rifle butts.

3) The occupants were in various stages of undress, having recently risen from bed. You were most deliberate on

identification, papers, rapid interrogation, and poison detection. Fearful of SS troops possibly being nearby, we gathered evidence, including US twenty-dollar gold pieces, tax-free cigarettes, chocolate bars—packed up and left. Kaltenbrunner, with a heart condition, set his own pace, but soon was "skiing" on his own shoes and being passed from one soldier to the next.

4) The descent was rapid. We picked up the stragglers and arrived amidst some civilian excitement at Alt Aussee. We soon went for food and rest. At age 19 we were not too concerned with protocol, interrogation, etc. Others seemed to have things well in hand.

5) There were several bags of $20 gold pieces. Some were kept for souvenirs, but the bulk was tagged for regimental HQ.

6) There were some small arms in the cabin.

7) Kaltenbrunner, once firmly treated, was placid and cooperative. His staff stayed somewhat agitated.

Best regards. I note we have a most valuable mutual friend in Sigurd Olson. I have talked to Jim Klobuchar [Senator Amy Klobuchar's father] about the Kaltenbrunner adventure.

George Griebenow

APPENDIX J

1945 Letters to Marion Etcheverry from Thomas McMillen and Robert Matteson

Somewhere in Luxembourg

13 January 1945

Mrs. Alfred Etcheverry
301 East 21st Street
New York, N.Y.

My dear Mrs. Etcheverry,

As you have been informed, your husband Pvt. Alfred S. Etcheverry, 421301151, was killed today. He was on a mission in our forward areas when caught in artillery fire. He was killed instantly, along with a local civilian with whom he was talking.

To me it is significant that your husband died side by side with a peace-loving farmer who, like himself, was being swept along by the storm of war. He possessed a deep feeling for human relations and was doing what he seemed to enjoy most, where he was of most value—working with people.

During the comparatively short period that Pvt. Etcheverry served with my organization, I had acquired a growing admiration for his character and his ability. Although he was doing what I believe to be one of the most exacting jobs in the army and among the finest group of men in the works, he had already distinguished himself as one of outstanding promise. I say these things with all sincerity. Your pride, as your loss, should be the greater.

With deepest sympathy,

Thomas R. McMillen
Captain, Infantry
C.O. 80th CIC Det.

From:

Lt. Robert E. Matteson 02026331
C.O. 80th CIC Detachment
G-2, 80th Inf Div HQ
APO 80, c/o PM, NY, NY.

25 September 1945

Dear Marion,

Excuse the typewriter, but I think you would prefer it to my handwriting which even Jane can't read. The pictures of Etch arrived yesterday along with your good letter. I am extremely happy to have one, and I know John Klimek will be too. I agree that it looks very much like him. He made such a definite and strong impression that the chapter in our lives which we shared would not be complete without the picture. Thank you for the trouble you went to.

Tell Nick that I should be extremely happy if he would marry D and that the Fourth of July would probably be the most appropriate day. From what Jane writes, Nick is a tough guy with a soul and Michele a charming angel. I love them already. And from what I can gather, you are a phenomenon that occurs only one in a thousand years. The three of you and Pinnacle Valley have given J and D the most enjoyable summer they could have possibly spent.

We have just heard that the 80th is to be a closing out force, which will not leave until the late spring. But the army has no embarrassment about changing its mind every other day so not much heart is lost by its periodic, president-like proclamations. Furthermore, I have 75 points which according to the present critical entitles me to discharge as soon as my ticket comes up to ship. I hope, therefore, to have the chance to talk to you in the not-too-distant future.

At present, the 80th is half in Czechoslovakia, half in Bavaria with a gap of 300 miles betwixt. It complicated CIC work as there is no communication system. I have elected to stay here in Garmisch, probably for no other reason than that it is Garmisch.

Please give my best to Nick and Michele. Hope to see you all soon.

Affectionately,

Bob

465 West Macon Street
Decatur 4, Illinois

26 December 1945

My dear Mrs. Etcheverry,

You may feel that I have forgotten you and your husband, but quite the contrary is true. The events of a year ago seem unusually clear at this time, and I have thought of you often.

The material on Luxembourg is not quite what I wanted, but it is apparently hard to come by. This I obtained at the Luxembourg Legation when I was in Washington recently.

You will observe that I have underlined three towns on the map in the January 1945 issues of the Luxembourg Bulletin. Heiderscheidergrund is where Matteson, Klimek, and your husband were living. Goesdorf is where your husband was killed, the Germans being generally east and northeast; as a matter of fact, we had not taken the ground to the north or the west at the time, so that they were on a salient, which protected our crossing of the Sure River. Etch is buried at Hamm, the third town marked, accounting to Ken Clark's information. You will remember that General Patton chose to be interred there with his men.

I hope this letter finds you and your children in good health. May the new year bring you increasing happiness and contentment.

Very sincerely yours,

Thomas R. McMillen

APPENDIX K

Kaltenbrunner Recollections, September 19, 1978

by Sergeant Sydney Bruskin, 80th Infantry Division, 318th Regiment, WW II

(Many thanks to Mr. Bruskin's daughter,
Phyllis Bausher, for sending this to S. Matteson.)

Even though it is 33 years ago that I spent several memorable months with the CIC in Alt Aussee, Austria, I recall clearly events [that] occurred there. I remember interrogating and writing arrest reports on several prominent Nazis, such as the German ambassador to Latvia; Lord Baillie-Stewart; and Frau Eigruber, the wife of the Gauleiter of Austria. With some research through some memorabilia [that] I have kept since World War II, I hope to some day find copies of same arrest reports. However, the most important event was the capture, and preceding events to same, of Ernst Kaltenbrunner, the man who succeeded Reinhard Heydrich as head of the Gestapo. This is what I shall deal with here.

Driving to Alt Aussee just after VE-Day, Bob Matteson and I stopped to visit Kaltenbrunner's wife, who was at odds with her husband since he had been living with his mistress [Gisela von Westarp]. She gave information as to his possible hideout. Further on toward Alt Aussee, I remember the eerie feeling of just Bob and myself driving past thousands of SS troops who had just laid down their arms.

Once in Alt Aussee, we set up headquarters in the house [that] previously had been the headquarters of the local NASDP [National Socialist German Workers' Party or Nazi Party]. After a number of arrests, we settled down to the matter of Kaltenbrunner. The home of Kaltenbrunner's mistress, her newborn twins by him, and Frau Scheidler, the wife of Kaltenbrunner's adjutant, was just across the road from the hotel where we were billeted. We became quite friendly with the two women, having an ulterior motive in seeking information as to where Kaltenbrunner and Scheidler might be hiding. As subtle as we were, they were just as curious as to what we were up to.

One day, I inveigled the two to invite us to a Wienerschnitzel dinner, which was quite delicious and replete with fine wine and all the fixings. Half-way through dinner we heard rustling outside, which we decided was that of persons spying on us.

Other informants furnished data on the possible whereabouts of the two men we were seeking. Finally, the moment of the possible capture arrived. Bob was to go to the top of a mountain, accompanied by a platoon of infantry from the 80th Division. He was dressed in lederhosen, etc., to make him appear as a native hunter. My task was to hold everybody in the Scheidler household under arrest and to keep all there from leaving the house all night until permitted.

I entered there just after dark, took out my 45-revolver, and ordered everybody not to leave. Much emotion was displayed, particularly by Frau Scheidler, and many questions were excitedly asked. I refused to answer any queries and told them that I would shoot any person leaving. I had no sleep the whole night, sitting at a table (I believe in the kitchen) with gun in hand.

The following morning, about 9 a.m. I believe, we heard a slight commotion outside. Looking through the window, we saw a group of sleepy GI's; Bob Matteson in traditional Austrian garb and two grim-looking men—also in lederhosen, etc. At this point, I learned later, it was still uncertain that the two men being closely guarded by soldiers with pointed rifles were the men being sought. Just before this contingent passed the house I permitted everybody to go out on the porch. As the walking group passed us by, Frau Scheidler rushed out and embraced her husband.

At least we knew that we had Scheidler. Apparently not wishing to disclose his identity, K's mistress showed no emotion as did her friend [Kaltenbrunner]. So, we still did not know if we had our star person. However, soon thereafter, it was established that the other man was Ernst Kaltenbrunner. He was marched over to our CIC office. Bob went into one room where he telephoned to make arrangements for high-security transportation of K to a prison. While Bob was doing this, K and his mistress requested a few moments together, in private. Privacy was denied, but I remained with drawn revolver a few feet from the two in the same small room while they conversed. Actually, they both said very little to each other. Kalenbrunner appeared very dejected and resigned, apparently sensing his future.

ACKNOWLEDGMENTS

Compiled by Sumner and Fredric Matteson based on conversations with, and writings by, Robert E. Matteson.

A special thanks to the heroic men and women of the U.S. Armed Forces, to our European Allies, who helped bring the war to a close, and to the brave French and German civilians who sheltered and fed our CIC operatives in the European Theater during the war's final months.

There is no way to express the great personal sorrow at losing close CIC colleague, Alfred Etcheverry, in January 1945. To his son, Nick Etcheverry, thank you for sharing a copy of your father's last letter, dated 14 December 1944. His sacrifice will never be forgotten. To his daughter, Michelle, thank you for your support and remembrances.

Special thanks to Major Ralph Pearson—the commanding officer of the 80th CIC detachment, and to Captain McMillen, supervising officer, for their support of the plan to capture Kaltenbrunner, and to each of the reluctant GIs who, after the war had ended, served with distinction in assisting Kaltenbrunner's capture high in the Austrian Alps.

Pursuing Nazi officials wanted by CIC during the last days of the war, as well as the journey to capture Kaltenbrunner, would not have been possible without the aid of interpreter Sydney Bruskin, whose skill and dedication to the CIC mission were invaluable. No less important were the bravery and fearlessness of CIC agents Lloyd Roach and David Marks in the war's final days, who carefully and judiciously assisted with testing military security at the Nuremberg trials.

Finally, a hearty and special thank you to the bravery and courage of the four Austrian guides, Karl Moser, Johann Wimmer, Joseph Frosch, and Willie Pucher, who led the way to the Alpine hut where Kaltenbrunner hid on 12 May 1945.

Last and by no means least, words fail to describe the tireless, emotional support of Jane Paetzold Matteson—no better companion in the world—who held down the fort at home with daughter Daidie during 18 months of separation.

The editors are grateful to Adelaide "Daidie" Donnelley for her edits and for endnote materials provided by writer and friend John Michlig. Special thanks to Samuel Goetz, Robert Persinger, George Griebenow, and Lloyd Roach for their vivid remembrances and impressions. Many thanks especially to Peter Black, author of the definitive biography to date—*Ernst Kaltenbrunner, Ideological Soldier of the Third Reich*, for his excellent critique, including corrections and suggestions to improve the manuscript.

We extend a heartfelt thank-you to Phyllis Bausher for graciously sharing remembrances and photos from her father, Sydney Bruskin.

We also wish to thank Shannon Booth for her careful and superb editing of the entire document; and to the incomparable leader of Little Creek Press, Kristin Mitchell, we greatly appreciate your meticulous and creative layout of the book, and thank you for your substantial patience with the brothers Matteson for last-minute additions and edits.

Finally, last but not least, we appreciate the courtesy and generosity of the Wisconsin Veterans Museum and Russell Horton in allowing publication of selected historical photos from the Robert E. Matteson collection.

ABOUT THE AUTHOR

St. Paul, Minnesota, native Robert Eliot Matteson (1914–1994) graduated from St. Paul Academy in 1933. He stayed near home for college and graduated cum laude in 1937 with a BA in history and political science from Carleton College in Northfield, Minnesota. In his college senior year, he was elected student body president, and as football co-captain and quarterback, he led his team to the Midwest Conference championship. In 1940, he received an MA in international relations from Harvard University's Littauer Center of Public Administration.

He returned to Carleton in the fall of 1940 as a political science instructor. He departed in 1943 to become a desk officer in the U.S. State Department's Division of Latin American Republics before enlisting as a private in Patton's Third Army later in 1943. While in the army, he transitioned to serve as agent and special agent in the 80th Infantry Division's Counter Intelligence Corps (CIC). As a CIC agent, he led an army team into the Austrian Alps to capture, on 12 May 1945, SS General Ernst Kaltenbrunnner, chief of Hitler's Gestapo, Criminal Police, and Intelligence Services. For his bravery and leadership, he received the Silver Star Medal.

After the war, from 1946 to 1948, Matteson served as a research assistant to Harold Stassen, candidate for U.S. president during 1948. He then worked as an assistant to the president of the University of Pennsylvania and as assistant professor of Political Science at the same university from 1948 to 1952.

After 1952, Matteson began a long and distinguished federal government career as follows: Assistant Director, Mutual Security Administration (1953); Assistant Director, Foreign Operations Administration (1953-1955); Director of President Eisenhower's White House Disarmament Staff (1955-1958); Assistant to Sherman Adams, Eisenhower's Chief of Staff (1958); Member, CIA's Board of National Intelligence Estimates (1959-1962); Director of Policy Staff, U.S. Disarmament Administration (1961-1962). During this period, he thought of and advocated for a U.S. complete arms control and disarmament policy under President Kennedy in a March 1961 session with Presidential Adviser John J. McCloy; this policy idea served as the basis for President Kennedy's famous "Sword of Damocles" speech (about the threat of nuclear war) before the UN's General Assembly on 25 September 1961; Chairman, Arms Control Disarmament Agency Research Council (1962-1966); National War College (1964-1965); Senior Advisor and Director of Research Staff, Arms Control Disarmament Administration (1965-1967); Director, Office of Civilian Affairs, II Corps, Vietnam (1967); Deputy Head of Civil Operations, Revolutionary Development Support Command, II Corps, Vietnam (1967-1968); Director, Agency for International Development International Training Program (1968-1971); Director, Foreign Affairs Executive Seminar (1970-1972).

In June 1972, after opposing the Nixon administration's invasion of Cambodia and continuation of the Vietnam War (Nixon's advisers John Ehrlichman and Bob Haldeman told Matteson that he "was not to the proper degree" a supporter of the Nixon administration and wondered why he had a picture of John F. Kennedy over his desk, he later quietly told us—Sumner and Rick), Matteson left Washington, D.C., to begin a new chapter of his life, teaming up with renowned environmentalist and fellow canoe adventurer and naturalist Sigurd F. Olson to become Northland College's first director of the Sigurd Olson Environmental Institute (1972-1974). He also served from 1974 to 1975 as a trustee of Northland College. Finally, in 1976 and 1977, while living in retirement on northern Wisconsin's Lake Namekagon with incandescent, steadfast partner, Jane Matteson (they were married in 1940), he served as chairman of President Ford's Quetico-Superior Advisory Committee.

Regarding his passions—beyond his family—Matteson loved canoeing and devised the idea of retracing historic routes of voyageurs across Canada and Alaska to the Bering Sea, 1958–1972. He recruited all five of his children at different times for what amounted to seven trips in the far north, including in 1970 a 425-mile trip (with friends John Lentz and Bob O'Hara) down the Coppermine River to Coronation Gulf on the Arctic Ocean—the eighth party ever to go down the river at that time. A college champion boxer, master tennis and squash player, he was, unknown to many, also an accomplished mountaineer who climbed in his mid-40s the Matterhorn and Mont Blanc, located in the western Alps.

"Aristotle taught us that life is a circle—that life is a journey that should end at its beginning—that at the end one should return home where it all started and share with youth what one has learned on the journey."

—Robert E. Matteson

Matteson passed away in 1994 from complications due to Parkinson's disease. Four months before he died, however, at an awards recognition dinner, he humbly repeated advice originally given to the 1969 St. Paul Academy graduating class:

First: Know yourself, your limitations, and your strengths. Second: Be adventuresome. If opportunities don't exist, make your opportunities. Choose an occupation in which you can make a meaningful contribution—not one just for the money, prestige, and status purposes. Then relate your field of interest—your occupation—to the rest of life. For happiness, as Aristotle said, is the realization of the whole self in relationship to all of life. Third: Don't neglect your health—your physical or your mental health. Fourth: Learn to think—take time to think. Fifth: As you know from the current songs of the period and also the Bible, there is a time for everything. There is a time to be silent and a time to speak, a time to rebel, a time to hold steady.

Above all, don't be discouraged.... Any person today may be discouraged, believing there is nothing one man or one woman can do to make a meaningful contribution in resolving the frustrating problems he or she sees. Some, for that reason, do nothing.

But remember ... each person can work to change a small portion of events.... Tiny ripples become waves that break down the greatest walls of convention, hypocrisy, and oppression.[137]

Matteson was 79 when he passed away on 24 January 1994, surrounded at the bedside by his family and, as if summoned to bear witness, two deer that appeared suddenly outside the large picture window at the far end of his bedroom.

Robert Matteson with his three sons (left to right Fredric, Rob, and Sumner) about to start up to the Wildensee to reenact the capture of Kaltenbrunner; summer, 1960.
Photo by Jane Matteson.

NOTES

Foreword

1. Peter Black (pers. comm. to S. Matteson, 24 January 2024), author of *Ernst Kaltenbrunner, Ideological Soldier of the Third Reich* (Princeton University Press, 1984), commented: "The RSHA was responsible for sending prisoners to concentration camps and for the length of time of incarceration (as well as for ordering official executions). It was also responsible for deportation from Central and Western Europe of Jews and Roma to killing centers as well as some of the mass shooting operations in the occupied Soviet Union and Serbia. It did have jurisdiction over so-called Security Police 'Labor Education Camps' as well as treatment of foreign forced laborers in the so-called Greater German Reich. The Concentration Camp system was subordinate to the Inspectorate of the Concentration Camps, which after a short period of direct subordination to Himmler in the 1940s came under the jurisdiction successively of the SS Main Office, the SS Operations Main Office, and the SS Economic-Administration Main Office. Auschwitz was considered a concentration camp that had a killing center function. The RSHA had the responsibility of sending most of those who died at Auschwitz to that facility. The killing centers of Operation Reinhard (Belzec, Sobibor & Treblinka) were under the jurisdiction of the SS and Police Leader in Lublin District, while that at Chełmno was directly under the command of Reich Governor Artur Greiser, who was also an SS general."

   In Robert Matteson's inscription (9 June 1984) to family members inside Peter Black's original 1984 book copy, Matteson wrote: "This is the first book I know of on Kaltenbrunner—a person you have heard about all of your lives. It is the expansion of a PhD thesis by Peter Black, now [at the time] with the Department of Justice. There is a brief reference to the capture in 1945.... The book gives more detail on his career than any other source."

2. Robert E. Matteson, *A Search for Adventure and Service: A Matteson Family Chronicle, Part I—The Early Years 1914-1940; Part II—The War Years 1940-1946; Part III—The Post War Years 1946-1952*. Self-published 3 December 1990; material referenced from reprints of self-published Part I (1979) and Part II (1980). Written for Matteson's children and grandchildren "in the hope that they will, in time, add to this family chronicle."

3. Peter Black (pers. comm. to S. Matteson, 24 January 2024) commented: "Kaltenbrunner's name was no more secret than that of Heydrich, at least within Nazi leadership circles. His appointment [in January 1943] was announced in all of the appropriate agency journals and newsletters."

Preface

4. Robert Eliot Matteson, *A Search for Adventure and Service: A Matteson Family Chronicle, Part I—The Early Years 1914-1940; Part II—The War Years 1940-1946; Part III—The Post War Years 1946-1952*. Self-published 3 December 1990; material referenced from reprints of self-published Part I (1979) and Part II (1980).

5   Bishop Douglas Atwill, March 21, 1936. Eulogy for Adelaide and Charles Matteson. *St. Clement's Chimes*. Newsletter of St. Clement's Episcopal Church, 901 Portland Avenue, St. Paul, Minnesota.

6   For details on the plot to take Hitler's life, see relevant chapters of R. J. Evans, *The Third Reich at War: How the Nazis Led Germany from Conquest to Disaster*, London: Penguin, 2009. Ian Kershaw, *Hitler: 1936-1945 Nemesis*, New York: Norton, 2000). Völker *Ullrich, Hitler: 1936-1945 Nemesis* (New York: Knopf, 2020).

7   Peter Black (pers. comm. to S. Matteson, 24 January 2024) commented: "Kaltenbrunner's influence increased after July 20, 1944—mostly due to his connections with Bormann and with Himmler's liaison to Hitler's headquarters, SS General Hermann Fegelein. Himmler remained firmly in the saddle as Reichsführer SS until almost the very end. Tension between Kaltenbrunner and Himmler has been greatly exaggerated since the war, in part due to [writings by] Höttl and in part due to Kaltenbrunner's own self-serving statements after the war."

8   Desmond Flower and James Reeves, Eds., *The Taste of Courage: The War, 1939-1945* (New York: Harper, 1960).

Introduction

9   Peter Black (pers. comm. to S. Matteson, 24 January 2024) commented: "This is a complex issue. While the RSHA and Eichmann played a significant role in the deportation of Jews from most of Europe to killing centers, the exceptions are important. They include Poland and, in part, the Soviet Union. Much to Heydrich's dismay, other agencies took control of the annihilation process. In the Government General, where the Security Police acted primarily as advisors, the SS and Police Leader in Lublin District and his staff managed "final solution policy." While the Einsatzgruppen of the Security Police and SD played a more direct role in shooting the Jews of the occupied Soviet Union, at least half, if not more, of the Soviet Jews were killed under the auspices of the Higher SS and Police Leaders, who controlled the police battalions, and the Waffen SS units, who engaged in shooting operations, and the German army commanders, who also participated directly in shooting operations. As for Eichmann, although he was the RSHA numbers cruncher for the Final Solution, his direct role in Final Solution policy did not extend to Poland and the occupied Soviet Union, where 80% of the Jews who would die in the Holocaust lived."

10 See items under Footnote 6 above.

11 Peter Black, *Ernst Kaltenbrunner, Ideological Soldier of the Third Reich* (Princeton University Press, 1984).

12 A 15 May 1945 *Stars and Stripes* article, in fact, mistakenly used a photo of H. V. Kaltenborn, a famous radio announcer during the war.

1   Peter Black (pers. comm. to S. Matteson, 24 January 2024) commented: "This may have been due as much to the fact that Kaltenbrunner, having held positions only in Austria prior to 1943, was rarely in Berlin and even more rarely in Hitler's presence—

this would explain the lack of pictures in Hoffmann's collection. Kaltenbrunner, even though in the underground Nazi movement in 1938, was well-known in Linz and later in Vienna, his appointment as Higher SS and Police Leader in Vienna was reported in the Viennese press. Heydrich was much better known, even to Brits and Americans, due to the memoir literature of rivals (for control of the Gestapo in the early years), such as Rudolf Diels."

Parenthetically, Heinrich Hoffmann, Hitler's official photographer, was at Nuremberg to help identify people in the Nazi hierarchy. He gave Matteson a photo of Kaltenbrunner and Franz Ziereis, SS commandant of Mauthausen, together at the infamous concentration camp—used to help prove Kaltenbrunner's visit to a concentration camp.

14 Summation for Prosecution by Justice Robert Jackson, July 26, 1946. Famous Trials (https://www.famous-trials.com). U.S. Chief of Counsel Justice Jackson's closing summary statement on 26 July 1946 at the Nuremberg trial before the International Military Tribunal.

15 Count Folke Bernadotte, *The Curtain Falls, a Unique Eyewitness Story of the Last Days of the Third Reich as Seen by a Neutral Observer Inside Germany* (Knopf, 1945). See also the relevant chapter(s) of Peter Longerich, *Heinrich Himmler*, New York: Oxford University Press, 2013.

Chapter One. Gathering Intelligence

16 The National Redoubt is the same as the Alpine Redoubt (or *Alpenfestung*). Peter Black, *Ernst Kaltenbrunner: Ideological Soldier of the Third Reich* (Princeton University Press, 1984), pp. 235-237.

17 The discovery and recovery of these art treasures are explored in the major motion picture, *The Monuments Men*, and the book by Robert M. Edsel and Bret Witter, (Center Street, 2010).

18 Peter Black (pers. comm. to S. Matteson, 24 Janaury 2024) commented: "While the Allies, and the Americans in particular, believed in it--as did many Germans--the Alpine Redoubt was largely a figment of popular imagination fueled by Goebbels's propaganda, the movement of German units into the Alps at the end of the war, and the presence of many underground factories built in 1943 and 1944 for the construction of aircraft and other military equipment in locations less vulnerable to Allied bombardment. The Alpine fortress was truly the fortress that never was, as the Americans and British found out when they arrived there in April and May 1945.

19 Königssee is a lake in the German state of Bavaria, near the Austrian border.

20 Samuel Goetz, *I Never Saw My Face* (Rutledge Books, Inc., 2001). In 2009, Mr. Goetz corresponded with Sumner Matteson regarding his personal travails at the Ebensee concentration camp (see Appendix F). See also Florian Freund, *Konzentrationslager Ebensee: KZ-System Mauthausen - Raketenrüstung – Lagergeschehen*, New Academic Press, 2016.

21 Robert Eliot Matteson, *A Search for Adventure and Service: A Matteson Family Chronicle, Part*

II—*The War Years 1940–1946* (self-published, 1980).

22. Peter Black (pers. comm. to S. Matteson, 24 January 2024) commented: "Kaltenbrunner and Seyss-Inquart agreed that the Nazi radicals needed to be restrained until the opportunity arose to topple the Schuschnigg regime. They understood that July 25, 1934, could not be repeated without major international consequences. Himmler and Heydrich also pursued this tactical line. Hence, Kaltenbrunner's role (like that of his allies in the underground Party and SS--Anton Reinthaller, Friedrich Rainer, Odilo Globocnik, and Hubert Klausener) was to restrain Nazi radicalism until that opportunity rose. The hoped for opportunity came sooner than anyone suspected when Schuschnigg called for a plebiscite on Austrian independence on March 9, 1938."

23. Peter Black (pers. comm. to S. Matteson, 24 January 2024) commented: "This is an accurate representation of Schellenberg's testimony, but equally clear is its self-serving purpose for Himmler's confidant during the last years of the war – a man who sought to conceal or downplay his earlier activity in the Gestapo and his involvement in planning the activities of the Einsatzgruppen in Poland and the Soviet Union. "

24. See David Ceserani, *Becoming Eichmann: Rethinking the Life, Crimes, and Trial of a "Desk Murderer"*, DeCapo Press, 2006. Also Michael Wildt, *An Uncompromising Generation: The Nazi Leadership of the Reich Security Main Office*, Madison, Wisconsin: University of Wisconsin Press, 2010; Helmuth Krausnick et al. *Anatomy of the SS State*, New York, Walker, 1968; Robert Gellately, *The Gestapo and German Society: Enforcing Racial Policy 1933-1945*, New York: Clarendon Press, 1992; Klaus Hesse et al., *Topography of Terror Gestapo, SS and Reich Security Main Office on Wilhelm-and Prinz-Albrecht-Strasse*, Topography of Terror Foundation, 2010.

25. For more on Skorzeny's daring rescue of Mussolini, see Gerald Reitlinger, *The SS: Alibi of a Nation, 1922–1945* (New York: The Viking Press, Inc., 1957), p. 246. Skorzeny greeted Mussolini with the words: "The Führer has sent me." Heinz Zollin Höhne's *The Order of the Death's Head: The Story of Hitler's SS* (Penguin Books, 2000), p. 546.

26. In attendance: Hermann Neubacher, former mayor of Vienna; General Edmund Glaise-Horstenau, the last vice-chancellor of independent Austria; Gauleiter Friedrich Rainer of Salzburg; RSHA foreign intelligence chiefs Wilhelm Waneck and Wilhelm Höttl; art historian Kajetan Mühlmann, the man chiefly responsible for confiscating art treasures for the Reich; and Otto Skorzeny.

27. Gerald Reitlinger, *The SS: Alibi of a Nation, 1922–1945* (New York: The Viking Press, Inc., 1957), pp. 137–138.

28. Also known as the Ahnenerbe and created by Heinrich Himmler as an SS appendage devoted to the task of promoting the racial doctrines espoused by Adolf Hitler and the Nazi Party. Heather Pringle, *The Master Plan: Himmler's Scholars and the Holocaust* (New York: Hyperion, 2006).

29. Peter Black (pers. comm. to S. Matteson, 27 January 2024) commented: "As far as I know, there was no effort at all to rewrite Nazi ideology in Office VII of the RSHA. This

was more of a group of like-minded individuals, who like Schellenberg, had come to doubt that Germany would win the war and started to make contingency plans for a post-Hitler Austria, if the German Reich as a whole could not be saved. It was by no means a serious effort, nor did it involve as much personal risk as the participants sought later to claim. Kaltenbrunner would listen at times—in the spring of 1945 with more interest—in the same way Himmler would listen to Schellenberg."

30 SS Havelinstitut—the cover name of the RSHA—the Nazi Party's intelligence and security services, which in 1939 absorbed the SD—the Nazi Party's security service—all under Himmler and his subordinate, first Reinhard Heydrich, then after his assassination, Kaltenbrunner. See www.cryptomuseum.com/intel/rsha/.

31 Peter Black, *Ernst Kaltenbrunner, Ideological Soldier of the Third Reich* (Princeton University Press, 1984); Frederic Spotts, *Hitler and the Power of Aesthetics* (Woodstock and New York: The Overlook Press, 2003). When Kaltenbrunner (urged on by Höttl) appeared at Hitler's Berlin bunker on 13 February 1945 to persuade Hitler to negotiate a truce with the Americans and British, he was ushered into a room where Hitler's valet Heinz Linge and architect Hermann Geisler were also present. Black (p. 238) describes what happened next: "When Kaltenbrunner entered Hitler's private quarters, he found the Führer bent over a large-scale model of Linz, where both men had spent much of their childhood and adolescence. Before his guest could speak, Hitler launched into a monologue on the post-war transformation of Linz into a European cultural center … and [then], summoning all the charisma and sentimentality that he could, announced, 'I know, Kaltenbrunner, what you want to say to me. But believe me, if I were not convinced that one day you and I will rebuild the city of Linz according to these plans, I would put a bullet through my head this very day. You need do nothing more than believe! I still have ways and means to conclude the war victoriously!'

32 Peter Black (pers. comm. to S. Matteson, 24 January 2024 commented: "Though this may have been reported in the SHAEF document, it was not true, nor was there anywhere near the organization that this account of the contents of the referenced report supposes."

33 Peter Black (pers. comm. to S. Matteson 24 January 2024) commented: "Although Kaltenbrunner sometimes signed these 'orders for protective custody' (Schützhaftbefehle) or 'preventative arrest warrants' (Vorbeugungshaftbefehle), most were signed by Gestapo chief Heinrich Müller or Kripo chief Artur Nebe, or subordinates delegated by them respectively."

34 Peter Black (pers. comm. to S. Matteson, 2 February 2024) commented: "Although Nebe (who flirted with the 20 July conspirators, for which he was executed in March 1945 pursuant to a People's Court death sentence) harbored doubts about the regime perhaps as early as 1934 and certainly after 1941, he also commanded an Einsatzgruppe in 1941 and was an aggressive persecutor and planner for the annihilation of Roma and people with disabilities. Finally, the Kripo hierarchy, less well known that the Gestapo or SD leadership, managed to invent a 'clean hands'

image after the war, which certainly fooled the Western Allies."

35 Peter Black (pers. comm. to S. Matteson, 11 March 2024) commented: "Yet the fact remains that the major concentration camps in the south of the Reich *were not* evacuated, while the major camps in the northern half *were* evacuated after the Allies publicized what they found at Buchenwald in mid-April."

36 Peter Black (pers. comm. to S. Matteson, 12 March 2024) commented: "But in his book about these negotiations, Dulles made it clear that he would say anything in order to weaken the resolve of Nazi leaders to keep on fighting. The interest in Kaltenbrunner's attitude was unlikely to have been genuine."

37 Peter Black (pers. comm. to S. Matteson, 2 February 2024) commented: "Perhaps Höttl, Waneck, and Göttsch talked about this possibility (though I never saw any reliable evidence that this was ever tabled). But if so, it was not a suggestion to be taken seriously. Kaltenbrunner's attitude towards negotiations along these lines was hostile."

38 Peter Black (pers. comm. to S. Matteson, 2 February 2024) commented: "Schellenberg and Sandberger may have said this, but neither was in a position to know much about Kaltenbrunner's thought after mid-April 1945. Kaltenbrunner does appear to have given up, but only after the surrender in Italy and the death of Hitler in late April 1945."

Chapter Two. Closing In

39 The first meeting with a Dulles representative occurred on 28 February 1945 according to Peter Black, *Ernst Kaltenbrunner, Ideological Soldier of the Third Reich* (Princeton University Press, 1984), p. 242. The second meeting occurred on 15 April 1945 (p. 244). A last attempt to contact Dulles occurred on or about 25 April 1945 (p. 245), with Höttl reporting 27 April 1945 as the date "when capitulation was signed at Caserta" in Italy (pp. 294-299 in Wilhelm Höttl, *The Secret Front: The Inside Story of Nazi Political Espionage* (Weidenfeld & Nicolson, 1953; referenced paperback edition published 2000 by Phoenix Press, London). Peter Black (pers. comm. to S. Matteson, 2 February 2024) commented on Höttl's account: "At times inaccurate. See Bradley Smith and Elena Agarossi, *Operation Sunrise: The Secret Surrender*, New York: Basic Books, 1979."

Chapter Three. Capture and Interrogation

40 About four months before Robert E. Matteson passed away, the CIA Historical Review Program approved for release on 22 September 1993 his confidential post-war CIA report titled "The Last Days of Ernst Kaltenbrunner," which the CIA described (without ascribing authorship to) as "Personal recollections of the capture and show trial of an intelligence chief." Matteson used this report, his self-published 1980 booklet, and his personal recollections, to shape the self-published 1993 booklet that we have edited and supplemented with appendices to present the current manuscript here as indicated at the beginning of this book.

41 In 2001, Ernst Kaltenbrunner's personal Nazi security seal was retrieved from an

Alpine lake by a Dutch citizen on vacation, 56 years after Kaltenbrunner threw it away in an effort to hide his identity. The seal has the words *Chef der Sicherheitspolizei und des SD* (Chief of the Security Police and SD) engraved on it. Experts at Vienna University have examined the seal and believe it was discarded in the final days of the war in May 1945.

42 Peter Black (pers. comm. to S. Matteson, 2 February 2024).

43 In a 9 April 1997 interview with the University of Southern California Shoah Foundation, Sydney Bruskin, directed by Matteson to keep Gisela von Westarp and Iris Scheidler under guard, disputed Matteson's original account that both Iris and Gisela broke free to run up and embrace their men, saying only Iris broke free. And Matteson's 26 May 1945 letter to wife, Jane (see Appendix C), mentioned only Iris as publicly embracing her husband. We have made the edits here to make the record clear. The only commercially published book that detailed Matteson's capture of Kaltenbrunner and the party's return to Altaussee was: Guy Walters, *Hunting Evil, The Nazi War Criminals who Escaped and the Hunt to Bring Them to Justice* (Bantam Press 2009). Walters relied on Matteson's 1993 confidential post-war CIA report titled "The Last Days of Ernst Kaltenbrunner," to which the CIA did not ascribe authorship. The book by Walters (that begins with Kaltenbrunner's capture) did an excellent job for the most part in describing events but unfortunately incorrectly repeated the same scene involving Gisela and Iris: "As Matteson took his charges into custody, Iris and Gisela leaped from the crowd and kissed and hugged their men." pp. 17–18.

44 Höttl expands on Kaltenbrunner's personna and roles in: Wilhelm Höttl, *The Secret Front: The Inside Story of Nazi Political Espionage* (Weidenfeld & Nicolson, 1953; referenced paperback edition published 2000 by Phoenix Press, London). And perhaps the definitive source on Kaltenbrunner's psychological and political profile: Peter Black, *Ernst Kaltenbrunner, Ideological Soldier of the Third Reich* (Princeton University Press, 1984).

Chapter Four. Testing Security

45 There's no doubt Kaltenbrunner's physical appearance made a formidable impression, as noted by Michael Selzer in *The Nuremberg Mind: The Psychology of the Nazi Leaders* (Quadrangle, 1977). Jacques Delarue, *The Gestapo: A History of Horro* (Frontline Books, 2008); originally published in French: *Histoire de la Gestapo* – Librarie Artheme Fayard 1962) presented perhaps the most graphic description: "The man who arrived in Berlin at the end of January 1943 as successor to Heydrich was a veritable giant. Kaltenbrunner was nearly seven feet tall, equipped with massive broad shoulders. At the end of his huge arms were two relatively small and strangely delicate hands (nonetheless capable of immense feats of strength). On the top of this vast body sat a long, harsh, heavy, massive face. A face cut with a billhook in a piece of badly hewn wood. A great flat forehead had nothing intellectual about it; a pair of small brown hard eyes, glittering and deep-set and half covered by heavy lids; a big straight mouth like a slash, thin lips, and a huge thick square chin, stressing the massive and bestial aspect of the person—such was Kaltenbrunner at this period.... He had no fear of

treachery.... Kaltenbrunner had recourse to the most brutal repressions. He did not hesitate to check in person the methods used in camps to exterminate the prisoners. While still active in Austria in the autumn of 1942, he inspected Mauthausen and, accompanied by the camp commandant, Ziereis, insisted upon seeing the transit to the gas chamber of a group of prisoners, watching their death agonies through a spyhole. At the beginning of 1943, he returned to Mauthausen, and some prisoners were executed by way of experiment in his presence, using three different methods: by hanging, by a bullet in the neck, and finally by the gas chamber. The prisoners and employees of the camp have related that Kaltenbrunner arrived in excellent humor, laughing and joking all the way to the gas chamber where these experiments took place and while waiting for the victims to be brought in."

46 Joseph E. Persico, *Nuremberg: Infamy on Trial* (Penguin Books, 1994), pp. 398, 426-427. "After Streicher disappeared through the [hangman's] trapdoor," wrote Persico, "an eerie moan persisted. [The hangman – Master Sergeant John C.] Woods descended the steps and vanished behind the curtain. Soon the moaning stopped." After the hangings of Nazi war criminals, Woods held his first press conference. Pp. 429-430: "The coarse red face beamed. 'I hanged those ten Nazis, and I'm proud of it,' he said. 'I did a good job of it too. Everything clicked. I [have] hanged 347 people, and I never saw one go off better.' ... What had he done immediately after the executions, a reporter asked. 'Had me and the boys a stiff drink.' He smiled. 'We earned it.' ...

"Cecil Catling, a veteran crime reporter for the *London Star*, asked Woods about reports that an unconscionable amount of time had elapsed before some of the men were pronounced dead—seventeen minutes for Ribbentrop, eighteen minutes for Jodl, a startling twenty-eight minutes for Keitel [13 minutes for Kaltenbrunner]. He further had it on good authority, Catling said, 'that some of the men's faces were smashed.' Woods looked briefly uncomfortable. 'Any noises heard from hanged men were reflex reactions, as any doctor could confirm,' he said....

"What did Catling think of Woods's performance? his colleagues asked later. 'Rubbish,' Catling said later. The men had not been properly tied, nor had they been dropped from a sufficient height. He had witnessed enough hangings to know that they had not experienced the instant unconsciousness of a broken neck but death by strangulation. Catling had it right. The army never used Master Sergeant Woods as a hangman again."

47 Diane Marie Amann, "Portraits of Women at Nuremberg," American Society of International Law, Forthcoming Third International Humanitarian Dialogs, UC Davis Legal Studies Research Paper No. 225, (August 6, 2010), pp. 31-54, https://papers.ssrn.com/sol3/papers.cfm?abstract_id=1654732.

Chapter Five. War Crimes and the Trial of the Century

48 For more information on Robert Kempner, see "Reversal of Fortune: Robert Kempner," Holocaust Encyclopedia (United States Holocaust Museum), https://encyclopedia.ushmm.org.

49 Peter Black (pers. comm. to S. Matteson, 2 February 2024) commented: "While this

may have been done on occasion after the shootings were over, it was not common; nor were the logistics around the mass graves conducive to such a grisly task."

50 Peter Black (pers. comm. to S. Matteson, 2 February 2024) commented: "Most of the shooting operations referred to here took place before Kaltenbrunner came to Berlin. This evidence helped to convict Kaltenbrunner, but was much more relevant to the criminal cases against the SS, the Gestapo and the SD."

51 Peter Black (pers. comm. to S. Matteson, 2 February 2024) commented: "What Ohlendorf was explaining was the practice of having at least two shooters shoot at one individual to reduce the burden of responsibility. This was practiced frequently in smaller-scale shootings. Whether the logistics of larger shooting operations permitted such "care" is dubious. In these cases, the actual shooters—usually volunteers—stood at the edge of the pit or even inside the pit with automatic weapons."

52 Peter Black (pers. comm. to S. Matteson, 2 February 2024) commented: "There is no record of such an estimate made during the war. Moreover, Eichmann, who was keeping track of the reported numbers of Jewish deaths would have known this to be an exaggeration.

"It is now estimated that the number of Soviet Jews killed in 1941/1942 was between 1.3 and 1.5 million. The perpetrators, under the overall command of the Higher SS and Police Leaders and the High Command of the Armed Forces, depending on their affiliation, included the Einsatzgruppen, but also numerous Order Police Battalions, Waffen SS units, and various military units (army, air force, and navy), as well as individual members of the civilian occupation authorities. All were backed up by numerous armed and organized auxiliaries recruited locally."

53 Peter Black (pers. comm. to S. Matteson, 2 February 2024) commented: "The use of poison gas to kill large numbers of persons was primarily an invention and concept involving the concentration camp commanders and the Technical Institute of the RSHA, which was a part of the Criminal Police. But all of this happened before Kaltenbrunner came to Berlin. As noted previously, Kaltenbrunner's responsibility for Mauthausen was supervisory, but as Higher SS and Police Leader, he would only take direct command of the facility and what happened therein in an emergency. Once he came to the RSHA, he did exercise authority to approve incarceration or release of prisoners, as well as shooting prisoners upon application of the Camp Commandants and the Security Police officers stationed in the camps."

54 Peter Black (pers. comm. to S. Matteson, 2 February 2024) commented: "The RSHA was not responsible for ordering deportations for forced labor in the Reich, though on occasion, local security police and criminal officials supervised or assisted in these roundups, particularly if they occurred in connection with anti-partisan operations. Authority for the roundups lay with the General Plenipotentiary for Mobilization of Labor, Fritz Sauckel—also a defendant at Nuremberg. Deployment—insofar as it was not from a concentration camp or an AEL—was increasingly the responsibility of the Ministry of Armaments Production, Albert Speer—another defendant at the trial of

the major war criminals in Nuremberg. RSHA responsibility began with imposing discipline on the workers, gathering intelligence on their activities, and general surveillance on their work, social, and even sexual activity. Sexual relations between Germans and Poles or Soviet civilians were prohibited, and could bring the death penalty to the male non-German partner."

55 Peter Black (pers. comm. to S. Matteson, 2 February 2024) commented: "While Gerdes did testify to a plan to annihilate the Dachau prisoners and attributed it to Kaltenbrunner's orders, perhaps to protect his former boss in the civilian administration, Gauleiter Paul Giesler (who seems likely to have been the actual originator of this plan), the fact remains that there was no final massacre of prisoners at Dachau, nor were orders issued to evacuate the camp, which was liberated by U.S. troops on April 27, 1945. Moreover, in April 1945, there was no Luftwaffe left to deploy in killing prisoners by bombing."

56 Höttl's testimony is thought to be the source of the much-cited figure of six million Jews exterminated by Nazis in World War II. Lucy Dawidowicz, in her book *The War Against the Jews, 1933–1945* (New York: Holt, Rinehart and Winston, 1975), used prewar birth and death records to come up with a more precise figure of 5,933,900. Wolfgang Benz, an authoritative German scholar on the subject, cited a range of 5.3 to 6.2 million.

Peter Black (pers. comm. to S. Matteson, 2 February 2024) commented: "As I understand it, this went as follows: 1) Höttl's testimony was that Eichmann dropped a flippant remark about having killed 5 million Jews. This was a gross inflation of Eichmann's responsibilities, impact on Nazi Final Solution policy, and actual number of deaths for which he was directly responsible. For the extent and limits of Eichmann's responsibilities, see my previous comments. 2) Rudolf Höss, the commandant of Auschwitz, testified at Nuremberg that in his estimation, some four million Jews died in the gas chambers at Auschwitz, another gross inflation. The actual figure is about one million Jewish deaths at Auschwitz—and not all in the gas chambers. 3) In 1945, based on reports from Jewish communities around the world the World Jewish Congress calculated the European loss at approximately six million Jews, a remarkably accurate figure. 4) The Nuremberg prosecutors took the five million figure in Höttl's testimony and the total figure from the Jewish demographic figures in their indictment for the major Nuremberg Trial. 5) Consequently, the prosecutors in the Einsatzgruppe trial at Nuremberg had to limit themselves to one million murdered by the Einsatzgruppen to make the math work. This turned out to be somewhat of a lowball estimate, as indicated earlier, about 1.3-1.5 million Jews were killed by the Germans in the occupied Soviet Union, though not all—or even a majority--by the personnel of the Einsatzgruppen."

57 See Peter Black, *Ernst Kaltenbrunner, Ideological Soldier of the Third Reich* (Princeton University Press, 1984), p. 232, regarding Himmler's view of Kaltenbrunner's power and Kaltenbrunner's reluctance to release concentration-camp prisoners. Heinz Höhne wrote in *The Order of the Death's Head: The Story of Hitler's SS* (Penguin Books, 2000), p. 553, "By 1944, he [Kaltenbrunner] was considered the second most powerful man in

the SS: even Himmler sometimes shuddered, as had Canaris the head of the Abwehr, at the sight of Kaltenbrunner's coarse, unmanicured hands.... Kaltenbrunner [had] a privilege which even Heydrich had not enjoyed. He became a constant visitor to the Führer's Headquarters, and Hitler gave him orders direct—not through Himmler. This was something entirely new—Kaltenbrunner acted as if he was responsible to his Führer alone in matters of RSHA policy."

58 Peter Black (pers. comm. to S. Matteson, 5 February 2024) commented: "As we now know, the order to destroy the Warsaw ghetto went from Himmler to the SS and Police Leader, von Sammern-Frankenegg and then his replacement, Jürgen Stroop. The office of the local commander of Security Police and SD for Warsaw, Ludwig Hahn, was involved, however, and though subordinated to the SSPF during the course of the operation, he also reported to Kaltenbrunner via the BdS for the Government General."

59 Joseph E. Persico, *Nuremberg: Infamy on Trial* (Penguin Books, 1994), pp. 143, 193).

60 Peter Black, *Ernst Kaltenbrunner, Ideological Soldier of the Third Reich* (Princeton University Press, 1984).

61 Peter Black, *Ernst Kaltenbrunner, Ideological Soldier of the Third Reich* (Princeton University Press, 1984), p. 276. "Ninety-six minutes after midnight on the night of 15-16 October 1946, he [Kaltenbrunner] ascended the scaffold. Reportedly, he took thirteen minutes to die."

62 Ann Tusa and John Tusa, *The Nuremberg Trial* (New York: Atheneum, 1984), pp. 482-492. Of those sentenced to death, Göring killed himself via a hidden cyanide capsule, and Bormann was presumed (but not proven) dead before the trial, having been tried in absentia.

63 Peter Black (pers. comm. to S. Matteson, 5 February 2024) commented: "I believe that we now know that one of the prison guards passed Göring the poison."

64 Ann Tusa and John Tusa, *The Nuremberg Trial* (New York: Atheneum, 1984), p. 485. "As each man stood under the gallows, his handcuffs were removed and replaced with what looked like knotted black shoelaces; his ankles were buckled with an Army webbing belt. A black hood was slipped over the head, tied around the neck, and followed by the noose. Then the lever was pulled, the trap sprung." Regarding Kaltenbrunner's final words: "The man who used to weep, who was described as dying of fear in the early days of his trial said in a steady, mild voice: 'I have served my German people and my Fatherland with a willing heart. I have done my duty in accordance with the laws of the Fatherland. I regret that crimes were committed in which I had no part. Good luck Germany.'"

65 Eugene Davidson, *The Trial of the Germans: An Account of the Twenty-Two Defendants Before the International Military Tribunal at Nuremberg* (New York: Collier Books, 1966), see footnote on p. 587. As noted, Senator Taft remarked: "My objection to the Nuremberg

trials is that while clothed with the forms of justice, they were in fact an instrument of government policy determined months before at Yalta and Teheran."

66 Kaltenbrunner did not have advice for Eichmann as to what to do next by late May 1945 except apparently to make himself scarce. Peter Black, *Ernst Kaltenbrunner, Ideological Soldier of the Third Reich* (Princeton University Press, 1984), p. 257.

Chapter Six. Perspectives

NOTE: Kalternbrunner biographer Peter Black (pers. comm. to S. Matteson) suggests that the reader should consult the following texts to provide a thorough modern-day perspective on Nazi leaders and acts, the Himmler-Heydrich relationship, Himmler-Kaltenbrunner relationship; Kaltenbrunner-Hitler relationship, implementation of the Final Solution, concentration camps, and Eichmann's role:

Michael Wildt, *An Uncompromising Generation: The Nazi Leadership of the Reich Security Main Office*, Madison, Wisconsin: University of Wisconsin Press, 2010;

Ulrich Herbert, *Best: Biographische Studien über Radikalismus, Weltanschauung und Vernunft, 1903-1989*, Berlin: J. H. W. Dietz, 1996;

Robert Gerwarth, *Hitler's Hangman: The Life of Heydrich*, New Haven: Yale University Press, 2012;

Reinhard Doerries, *Hitler's Intelligence Chief: Walter Schellenberg*, Enigma Books, 2009.

Katrin Paehler, *The Third Reich's Intelligence Services: The Career of Walter Schellenberg*, Cambridge University Press, 2019;

David Cesarani, *Becoming Eichmann: Rethinking the Life, Crimes, and Trial of a "Desk Murderer"*, DeCapo Press, 2006.

On the Einsatzgruppen (and especially Eichmann's absence from the chain of command):

Andrej Angrick & Peter Klein, *The Final Solution in Riga: Exploitation and Annihilation, 1941-1945*, New York: Berghahn, 2012.

Christian Gerlach, *Kalkulierte Morde: Die deutsche Wirtschafts- und Vernichtungspolitik in Weißrußland 1941 bis 1944* Hamburg: Hamburger Edition, 2013.

Andrej Angrick, *Besatzungspolitik und Massenmord: Der Einsatzgruppe D in der südlichen Sowjetunion, 1941-1943*, Hamburg: Hamburger Edition, 2003

Ronald Headland, *Messages of Murder: A Study of the Reports of the Einsatzgruppen of the Security Police and the Security Service, 1941-1943*, Farleigh Dickensen University Press, 1992.

Peter Black, "Holocaust by Bullets; Hitler's Hidden Holocaust?" in *The Holocaust:*

Memories and History, Victoria Khiterer, ed., Newcastle upon Tyne: Cambridge Scholars Publishing, 2014, pp. 1-42.

On the annihilation of the Jews in German occupied Poland (Government General) and Eichmann's absence in the chain of command:

Christopher Browning, *Ordinary Men: Police Battalion 101 and the Final Solution in Poland*, New York: Harper Perennial, 1993.

On *Odessa* - the U.S. military's codename for the SS plan to assist the post-war escape of SS officers to Argentina:

Gerald Steinacher, *Nazis on the Run: How Hitler's Henchmen Fled Justice*, New York: Oxford University Press, 2011; Uki Goni, *The Real Odessa: Smuggling the Nazis to Peron's Argentina*, Granta Books, 2002.

On Operation Reinhard:

Yitzhak Arad, *Belzec, Sobibor, Treblinka: The Operation Reinhard Death Camps*, Revised Ed., Indianapolis: University of Indiana Press, 2018.

Jules Schelvis, *Sobibor: A History of a Nazi Death Camp*, New York: Berg, 2007.

Peter Black, "Footsoldiers of the Final Solution: The Trawniki Training Camp and Operation Reinhard," *Holocaust and Genocide Studies*, vol. 25, no. 1 (Spring 2011), p. 1-99.

On the shooting operations conducted by Waffen SS units and Eichmann's absence in this chain of command:

Martin Cüppers, *Wegbereiter der Shoah: Die Waffen SS, der Kommandostab Reichsführer-SS und die Judenvernichtung, 1939-1945*, Darmstadt: Wissenschaftliche Buchgesellschaft, 2005)

On the destruction of the Jews in German-annexed Poland (and Eichmann's absence in this chain of command):

Peter Klein, *Die "Gettoverwaltung Litzmannstadt", 1940-1944: Eine Dienststelle im Spannungsfeld von Kommunalbürokratie und staatlicher Verfolgungspolitik*, Hamburg: Hamburger Edition, 2009;

Patrick Montague, *Chelmno and the Holocaust: The History of Hitler's First Death Camp*, Chapel Hill: University of North Carolina, 2012;

Catherine Epstein, *Model Nazi: Arthur Greiser and the Occupation of Western Poland*, New York: Oxford University Press, 2010.

On the Wehrmacht's role in implementation of the annihilation of the Jews:

Dieter Pohl, *Die Herrschaft der Wehrmacht: Deutsche Militärbesatzung und einheimische Bevölkerung in der Sowjetunion, 1941-1944*, Munich: R. Oldenbourg, 2008.

On the concentration camp system:

Nikolaus Wachsmann, *kl: A History of the Nazi Concentration Camps*, New York: Farrar, Straus & Giroux, 2015.

Stefan Hördler, *Ordnung und Inferno: Das KZ-System im letzten Kriegsjahr*, Göttingen, 2015.

On Operation Bernhard and the forgery of British currency:

Peter Bower, "Operation Bernhard: The German Forgery of British Paper Currency in World War II," *The Exeter Papers:* Proceedings of the British Association of Paper Historians Fifth Annual Conference (Studies in British Paper History), Plough Press, The British Association of Paper Historians, 2001, pp. 43-65.

67 "Gas Chamber Atrocity Boss Taken in Chalet," *Stars and Stripes*, May 15, 1945.

68 William Stevenson, *A Man Called Intrepid* (Rowman & Littlefield, 1976), p. 189.

69 Desmond Flowers and James Reeves, eds., *The War, 1939-1945* (New York: Da Capo Press, 1997; originally published in London in 1960 by Cassell & Company Ltd.), p. 1. "Poland, An Act of Aggression is Arranged: 26 August 1939. [Georg Herbert] Mehlhorn's [Mehlhorn was an SS Oberführer, Nazi legal expert, and Gestapo official – *Wikipedia*: Herbert Mehlhorn] voice grew more excited as he told me that Heydrich had asked him to come to his office and, surprisingly, had confided to him one of Hitler's secret orders. Before 1 September, if possible, an absolutely irreproachable cause for war had to be created, one that would stand in history as a complete justification and would brand Poland in the eyes of the world as the aggressor against Germany. It had therefore been planned to dress troops in Polish uniforms and attack the Gleiwitz radio transmitter. Hitler had assigned Heydrich and Admiral Canaris, Chief of Army Intelligence, to carry out this operation. However, Canaris was so repelled by the order that he had managed to withdraw, and Heydrich alone was in charge of it. Heydrich had explained to Mehlhorn the details of the plan. The Polish uniforms were to be supplied by the O.K.W.—the Supreme Command of the Armed Forces. I asked Mehlhorn where they would get the Poles who were to wear these uniforms. 'That's just it,' Mehlhorn replied. 'That's the devilish thing about this plan: the "Poles" will be convicts from the concentration camps. They're going to be armed with proper Polish weapons, but most of them will just be mown down, of course. They've been promised that any who get away with it will have their freedom immediately. But who's going to believe such a promise?'"—Walter Schellenberg, German Foreign Intelligence Service.

70 William Stevenson, *A Man Called Intrepid* (Rowman & Littlefield, 1976), p. 38.

71 Peter Black (pers. comm. to S. Matteson, 5 February 2024) commented: "Recent

scholarship has shown that while it had some impact, the Soviet purges did not weaken the Soviet armed forces as much as was supposed at the time, not least by the Germans."

72 William Stevenson, *A Man Called Intrepid* (Rowman & Littlefield, 1976), p. 37.

73 Peter Black (pers. comm. to S. Matteson, 5 February 2024) commented: "The reason for selecting Heydrich as a target had less to do with his role as chief of the RSHA than with his recent appointment as Acting Reich Protector for Bohemia and Moravia along with a certain recklessness he displayed with his own security at times when he was in Prague. One of the strongest advocates of an assassination attempt on Heydrich was the head of the Czechoslovak exile government in London, Beneš, who feared that the relative calm in the Czech lands, fostered in part by significant concessions to Czech workers and farmers by Heydrich's administration, would undermine Czechoslovak claims to resurrection of the interwar state after the German defeat. After all, for the British, the Munich Pact remained a valid document. Beneš wanted a spectacular gesture to demonstrate Czech commitment to their own independent state."

74 Peter Black (pers. comm. to S. Matteson, 5 February 2024).

75 Walter Schellenberg, *Memoiren*, Verlag fur Politik und Wirtschaft, Koln 1956; *The Schellenberg Memoirs*, introduction by Alan Bullock, translated by Louis Hagen (London: Andre Deutsch, 1961), p. 30.Peter Black (pers. comm. to S. Matteson, 5 February 2024) commented on Schellenberg's memoirs: "Inaccurate, self-serving, obsolete. See Reinhard Doerries, *Hitler's Intelligence Chief: Walter Schellenberg*, Enigma Books, 2009; Katrin Paehler, *The Third Reich's Intelligence Services: The Career of Walter Schellenberg*, Cambridge University Press, 2019."

76 Peter Black, *Ernst Kaltenbrunner, Ideological Soldier of the Third Reich* (Princeton University Press, 1984), p. 123; and Eugene Davidson, *The Trial of the Germans: An Account of the Twenty-Two Defendants Before the International Military Tribunal at Nuremberg* (New York: Collier Books, 1966), p. 318.

77 Peter Black (pers. comm. to S. Matteson, 5 February 2024) commented: "Tension did exist between Heydrich and Kaltenbrunner. It stemmed from Heydrich's successful efforts to exclude Kaltenbrunner—first as State Secretary for Security and then as Higher SS and Police Leader in Vienna (particularly in 1938-1939)—from direct control over Security Police operations on Austrian territory. Moreover, Schellenberg quite willingly cooperated with Kaltenbrunner and Müller in taking down the Abwehr in 1943-1944. Here their interests and ambitions coincided. The fact that Schellenberg hated Kaltenbrunner and might himself have hoped either for the RSHA job or to hive off the intelligence apparatus and place it directly under himself with direct access to Himmler should be calculated into any assessment of the reliability of his statements."

78 Walter Schellenberg, *Memoiren*, Verlag fur Politik und Wirtschaft, Koln 1956; *The Schellenberg Memoirs*, introduction by Alan Bullock, translated by Louis Hagen

(London: Andre Deutsch, 1961), pp. 374–375, 400, 412. Peter Black (pers. comm. to S. Matteson, 5 February 2024) commented again on Schellenberg's memoirs: "Obsolete, inaccurate, self-serving. Regarding Canaris, suggest adding Heinz Höhne, *Canaris: Hitler's Master Spy*, New York: Doubleday, 1993; Michael Mueller, *Nazi Spymaster: The Life and Death of Admiral Wilhelm Canaris*, Skyhorse, 2017."

79 Peter Black (pers. comm. to S. Matteson, 5 February 2024) commented: "The assignment of the investigation following July 20, 1944 would naturally have devolved to the RSHA and via Himmler—as it in fact did. Bormann requested and received daily reports from Kaltenbrunner, a venue of communication that strengthened the connection between the two men. Canaris's support of the German opposition was at best lukewarm throughout the war until his house arrest in February 1944 made it difficult for him to do much. As Heinz Höhne's biography showed already in the 1970s, Canaris had great difficulty distancing himself from the military, political, and even population policy aims of Nazi Germany."

80 Wilhelm Höttl, *The Secret Front: The Inside Story of Nazi Political Espionage* (Weidenfeld & Nicolson, 1953; referenced paperback edition published 2000 by Phoenix Press, London).

81 Ibid., pp. 32–33.

82 Niccolo Machiavelli, *The Prince*, Second Edition (W.W. Norton & Company, 1992).

83 Peter Black (pers.comm. to S. Mattesson, 5 February 2024) commented: "Höttl consistently underestimated the element of Nazi ideology as a driving force in Heydrich's actions. I cannot say whether this was deliberate or simply how he remembered Heydrich."

84 Peter Black (pers. comm. to S. Matteson, 5 February 2024) commented: "Another exaggeration [by Höttl]. Heydrich was a key figure of course, but many others, in the concentration camp system, at the headquarters of the SS and Police Leader in Lublin District and of the Reich Governor in German annexed Poznań were involved in the planning process as well as the implementation."

85 Peter Black (pers. comm. to S. Matteson, 5 February 2024) commented: "Höttl dramatically underestimated Heydrich's loyalty to both Hitler and Himmler."

86 Wilhelm Höttl, *The Secret Front: The Inside Story of Nazi Political Espionage* (Weidenfeld & Nicolson, 1953; referenced paperback edition published 2000 by Phoenix Press, London), p. 305. Peter Black (pers. comm. to S. Matteson, 5 February 2024) commented: "Inaccurate, self-serving, obsolete. See Reinhard Doerries, *Hitler's Intelligence Chief: Walter Schellenberg*, Enigma Books, 2009. Katrin Paehler, *The Third Reich's Intelligence Services: The Career of Walter Schellenberg*, Cambridge University Press, 2019."

87 Wilhelm Höttl, *The Secret Front: The Inside Story of Nazi Political Espionage* (Weidenfeld & Nicolson, 1953; referenced paperback edition published 2000 by Phoenix Press, London), pp. 290–291. Peter Black (pers. comm. to S. Matteson, 5 February 2024) commented: "See earlier comment about the alleged reduction of Kaltenbrunner's

responsibilities. Bradley Smith's Operation Sunrise reveals that Wolff, Kaltenbrunner, Himmler, and even Hitler were much more in contact about negotiations through Dulles than Höttl cared to admit."

88 Wilhelm Höttl, *The Secret Front: The Inside Story of Nazi Political Espionage* (Weidenfeld & Nicolson, 1953; referenced paperback edition published 2000 by Phoenix Press, London), p. 296.

89 Ibid., p. 316.

90 Ibid., pp. 320–321.

91 Robert E. Matteson, "The Last Days of Ernst Kaltenbrunner," *Studies In Intelligence*, Spring 1959: A11–A29 and 4 (2), Spring 1960 Freedom of Information Act Electronic Reading Room, Historical Collections, https://www.cia.gov.

92 Ibid.

93 Wilhelm Höttl, *The Secret Front: The Inside Story of Nazi Political Espionage* (Weidenfeld & Nicolson, 1953; referenced paperback edition published 2000 by Phoenix Press, London), p. 305.

94 Ibid., p. 326.

95 Peter Black (pers. comm. to S. Matteson, 31 January 2024) commented: "This seems unlikely. Kaltenbrunner and Bormann cooperated closely even before the July 20, 1944 plot; Bormann had also supported Kaltenbrunner's appointment as chief of the RSHA. If it was indeed Kaltenbrunner who sent this agent, I'm guessing something got lost in the translation on the way to Allen Dulles. Karl Wolff, on the other hand, did not care so much for Bormann and might have briefed this agent."

96 Allen Dulles, *The Secret Surrender* (New York: Harper and Row, 1966), p. 50. Peter Black (pers. comm. to S. Matteson, 5 February 2024) commented on the Dulles account: "Obsolete, inaccurate, self-serving, sensationalized. See Jochen Lang, *Top Nazi SS General Karl Wolff: The Man Between Hitler and Himmler*, New York: Enigma, 2005; Bradley Smith and Elena Agarossi, *Operation Sunrise: The Secret Surrender*, New York: Basic Books, 1979."

97 Peter Black (pers. comm. to S. Matteson, 5 February 2024) commented: "This is belied by correspondence between Kaltenbrunner and Wolff in Kaltenbrunner's SS officer's file. It is likely that Wolff, who was close to Himmler, favored and supported Kaltenbrunner's appointment as chief of the RSHA. See also earlier note about the communications between Wolff, Himmler and Kaltenbrunner during the negotiations in Italy."

98 Allen Dulles, *The Secret Surrender* (New York: Harper and Row, 1966), p. 132.

99 Peter Black (pers. comm. to S. Matteson, 5 February 2024) commented: "Wolff played a larger role in pushing Himmler and Kaltenbrunner to bring the matter to Hitler than Wolff would admit after the war, when he was seeking to avoid prosecution. Nor

did Hitler forbid negotiations with the West; he simply doubted they would lead to anything that would enable the Nazi regime to survive."

100 Allen Dulles, *The Secret Surrender* (New York: Harper and Row, 1966), p. 152.

101 Ibid., p. 179.

102 Ibid., pp. 22-23.

103 Walter Schellenberg, *Memoiren*, Verlag fur Politik und Wirtschaft, Koln 1956; *The Schellenberg Memoirs*, introduction by Alan Bullock, translated by Louis Hagen (London: Andre Deutsch, 1961), pp. 437-440. Peter Black (pers. comm. to S. Matteson, 5 February 2024) commented on Schellenberg's account: "Self-serving, inaccurate, obsolete. See Peter Longerich, *Heinrich Himmler*, New York: Oxford University Press, 2013."

104 Count Folke Bernadotte, *The Curtain Falls: Last Days of the Third Reich*, (Literary Licensing, LLC, 2011), pp. 91, 133.

105 Ibid., p. 91.

106 Ibid., p. 133.

107 Walter Schellenberg, *Memoiren*, Verlag fur Politik und Wirtschaft, Koln 1956; *The Schellenberg Memoirs*, introduction by Alan Bullock, translated by Louis Hagen (London: Andre Deutsch, 1961), pp. 241-242. Peter Black (pers. comm. to S. Matteson, 5 February 2024) commented: "See previous footnotes on Schellenberg."

108 G. M. Gilbert, *Nuremberg Diary* (Farrar, Straus and Company, 1947).

109 Eugene Davidson, *The Trial of the Germans: An Account of the Twenty-Two Defendants Before the International Military Tribunal at Nuremberg* (New York: Collier Books, 1966), p. 318.

Chapter Seven: Coda

110 Heather Cox Richardson, *Democracy Awakening: Notes on the State of America* (Random House, 2023).

111 Adolf Hitler, *Mein Kampf* (8th edition, Reynal & Hitchcock, 1939).

112 Opening Statement before the International Military Tribunal (Robert H. and Jackson Center, https://www.roberthjackson.org). At the Nuremberg trial, Justice Robert H. Jackson, U.S. Chief of Counsel, made his opening statement to the International Military Tribunal on 21 November 1945 in the Palace of Justice, Nuremberg, Germany.

113 Summation for Prosecution by Justice Robert Jackson, July 26, 1946. Famous Trials (https://www.famous-trials.com). U.S. Chief of Counsel Justice Jackson's closing summary statement on 26 July 1946 at the Nuremberg trial before the International Military Tribunal.

114 General Order-140, 29 May 1945.

Appendix A. Excerpts from the *Last Valhalla of the Nazis* by Geoffrey Bocca

115 Geoffrey Bocca, excerpts from the *Last Valhalla of the Nazis*, *True* magazine, February 1964.

116 Peter Black (pers. comm. to S. Matteson, 5 February 2024) commented: "Alt Aussee was in Upper Austria during the Nazi period and today is in Styria. It was never part of Tyrol."

Appendix B. Testimony of Ernst Kaltenbrunner, 12 October, 9–10 November 1945

117 Excerpts from three transcripts of Kaltenbrunner's testimony (obtained by REM from the National Archives and Records Service, 3 July 1979) taken at Nuremberg, Germany, by U.S. Army Lieutenant Colonel Smith W. Brookhart. Also present: (12 October 1945) Captain Jesse F. Landrum, court reporter and Captain Mark Priceman, interpreter; (9 November 1945) Captain H.W. Frank, interpreter, and Private Clair Van Vleck, court reporter; (10 November 1945) John Albert, interpreter and Frances Karr, court reporter. In brackets, we have provided clarifying comments, as well as supplementary information from *Wikipedia* (largely) and *Euromaidan Press* about persons or places mentioned.

118 See Winkelmann's role as SS police leader in Hungary described in Gerald Reitlinger's *The SS: Alibi of a Nation, 1922–1945* (New York: The Viking Press, Inc., 1957). For his avoiding a war crimes trial, see Max Williams, *SS Elite: The Senior Leaders of Hitler's Praetorian Guard* (Fonthill Media LLC, 2018, Volume 3).

119 See Jewish Telegraphic Agency's historical archive titled "Hungary Appoints Commissioner for Jewish Affairs; Orders More Jews to Vacate Homes," 12 April 1944. Summary of German-controlled Budapest radio broadcast.

120 Learn more about Horthy and his relationship to Nazi Germany through Joseph E. Persico's *Nuremberg: Infamy on Trial* (Viking Penguin, 1994); and through Eugene Davidson, *The Trial of the Germans: An Account of the Twenty-Two Defendants Before the International Military Tribunal at Nuremberg* (New York: Collier Books, 1966). For a contemporary perspective, see Randolph Braham, *The Politics of Genocide: A History of the Holocaust in Hungary*, 2 vols. Boulder, Colorado: Distributed by Columbia University Press, 2016.

121 Hitler's plenipotentiary, Edmund Veesenmayer, was the one who carried out Otto Winkelmann's monstrous charge of exterminating Hungarian Jews as directed by Adolf Eichmann. See Randolph Braham, *The Politics of Genocide: A History of the Holocaust in Hungary*, 2 vols. Boulder, Colorado: Distributed by Columbia University Press, 2016.

122 Description in *Wikipedia* is the source of 76,000 individuals. See also Eugene Davidson, *The Trial of the Germans: An Account of the Twenty-Two Defendants Before the International Military Tribunal at Nuremberg* (New York: Collier Books, 1966).

123 Two sources on Artur (Arthur) Seyss-Inquart: Eugene Davidson, *The Trial of the Germans: An Account of the Twenty-Two Defendants Before the International Military Tribunal at Nuremberg* (New York: Collier Books, 1966); and Joseph E. Persico, *Nuremberg: Infamy on Trial* (Viking Penguin, 1994).

124 Dr. Morgen's investigations of Nazi concentration camp atrocities proved too much for Himmler, who eventually shut them down when Morgen began to investigate the Auschwitz mass killings. The best account of Morgen's role and actions is provided by Heinz Höhne, *The Order of the Death's Head: The Story of Hitler's SS* (Penguin Books, 2000).

125 "The Vengeful Execution of Erich Muhsfeldt," YouTube, May 12, 2022, https://www.youtube.com/watch?v=Ide-uFRs9aI&ab_channel=TheUntoldPast.

126 For additional detail on Oswald Pohl, see Heinz Höhne, *The Order under the Death's Head: History of the SS*, Secker and Warburg, 1969; Jan Erik Schulte, *Zwangsarbeit und Vernichtung: Das Wirtschaftsimperium der SS. Oswald Pohl und das SS-Wirtschaftswaltungshauptamt*, Paderborn: Schöningh, 2001.

127 SS Sturmbannführer Georg Wippern was responsible for smelting precious metal items taken from Jewish Holocaust victims, and these, along with other valuables, were sent to Berlin and Krakow. "Georg Wippern," Holocaust Historical Society, 20 June 2023, https://www.holocausthistoricalsociety.org.uk/contents/aktionreinhardt/georgwippern.html.

128 See Albert Speer, *Inside the Third Reich* (London: Weidenfeld & Nicolson, 1995); and Martin Kitchen, *Speer: Hitler's Architect*, New Haven: Yale University Press, 2015.

129 See Froliak-Eliashevsky, *Ravensbrück – The Largest Women's Concentration Camp in Germany*. Translated by Christine Eliashevsky-Chraibi. Edited by Lydia Eliashevsky-Replansky. (Euromaidan Press, 2020).

130 Eugene Davidson, *The Trial of the Germans: An Account of the Twenty-Two Defendants Before the International Military Tribunal at Nuremberg* (New York: Collier Books, 1966). About 5,000 Dutch Jews were sent to the Theresienstadt concentration camp; only 1,300 survived. (33,000 died in total at the camp—*Theresienstadt Ghetto*, Wikipedia.)

Appendix C. War Letters, July 1944 – October 1945

131 V-mail (Victory Mail) was instituted on 15 June 1942 until November 1945 and consisted of microfilmed letters to and from military personnel, with the letters reproduced and delivered to save shipping and airplane space. "Mail Call: V-mail, Between June 1942 and November 1945, Over 1 Billion V-mails Were Processed," The National WWII Museum, December 7, 2019, https://www.nationalww2museum.org/war/articles/mail-call-v-mail.

132 Max Lincoln Schuster, ed., *A Treasury of the World's Great Letters*, (Simon & Schuster, 1940).

133 Aldous Huxley, *Point Counterpoint* (Doubleday, 1928).

134 Lord Byron, *The Prisoner of Chillon, and Other Poems* (London: John Murray, 1816). The castle referred to in the poem's title is situated near Montreux, Switzerland—*The Prisoner of Chillon*, Wikipedia.

135 "IG Farben," *Wikipedia*, https://en.wikipedia.org/wiki/IG_Farben#:~:text=IG%20 Farben%20has%20been%20described,and%20the%20largest%20in%20Europe.

Appendix E. Robert B. Persinger on 6 May 1945 Liberation of Ebensee Concentration Camp – 6 October 2009 Email to Sumner Matteson

136 Listen to "Oral History Interview with Robert Persinger," United States Holocaust Memorial Museum, as he discusses his experience as a 21-year-old staff sergeant in the 3rd Calvary Reconnaissance Squadron of the Third Army's XX Corps; he drove his tank through the open gates of the Austrian Ebensee concentration camp and liberated the camp. He mentions that the SS guards had vacated the camp the day before, which is why the gates were open. He had arrived at midday with another tank and crew. Oral History/Accession Number: 2014.51.99/RG Number: RG-50.759.0099, https://collections.ushmm.org.

About the Author

137 Based on/taken from (but not limited to) Robert Eliot Matteson's self-published pamphlets—*A Matteson Family Chronicle* (1978) and *The September 30, 1993, St. Paul Academy and Summit School Award Dinner Honoring Virginia McKnight Binger, Class of '34, and Robert Eliot Matteson, Class of '33, Recipients of the 1993 Distinguished Alumni Award* (December 1993).

Photo from Matteson's WWII scrapbook,"Kaltenbrunner + World War II + Nuremberg Trial," courtesy of Wisconsin Veterans Museum.

Index

Note: Page numbers followed by *i* refer to photos and illustrations; page numbers followed by *n* and a number refer to Notes.

Numbers

2nd French Armored, 23
4th Armored Division (U.S.), 27, 28
5th Panzer Army, 27
80th Counter Intelligence Corps (CIC), 24, 189–190. *See also* CIC (80th Division Counter Intelligence Corps)
80th Infantry Division, 20–21, 27
318th Infantry Regiment, 24, 27
VIII Corps, 1st Army (U.S.), 26

A

Abwehr, 61, 118
action groups (Einsatzgruppen), 104–5, 283*n*
Ahnenerbe, 274*n*28
Alpine [National] Redoubt
    description in *Last Valhalla of the Nazis*, 146–48
    fortification near war's end, 39–40, 109, 121, 147
    high-ranking Nazis retreating to, 40, 41, 122, 147–48
    Höttl's account in *The Secret Front*, 121–24
    Peter Black's observations about, 273*n*18
Alt Aussee. *See also* Alpine [National] Redoubt
    celebrities in, 212, 214, 216
    as center of Alpine Redoubt, 48
    Höttl's account in *The Secret Front*, 121–24
    Jandl painting, 38*i*
    places of interest to CIC, 68*i*
    scenic impressions, 48*i*, 49*i*, 49–51, 135, 212

Andrus, Burton C. (Colonel), 87, 89, 91, 93
anti-aircraft training, 18–19
Arbeitserziehungslager (AEL), 106
Ardennes offensive, 26–28
Argentan campaign, 23
art treasures, 48, 57–58, 123
Atwill, Douglas, 15, 16–17
Auschwitz concentration camp, 53, 270*n*1
Austrian Freedom Movement, 43, 48, 55
Austrian political murders, 157

B

"B" Company, 318th Regiment, 80th Division, 21, 26
Bachman, Charlie, 19, 26
Bad Ischl, 43
Baillie-Stewart, Norman, 228
Bastogne, 28
Battle of the Bulge, 26–28
Bausher, Phyllis, 250
Bernadotte, Folke (Count), 84, 128–131, 235
Black, Peter, 270*n*1
Blank (Hauptscharführer), 156–57
booby traps, 22–23
Borgia, Cesare, 119
Bormann, Martin
    Kaltenbrunner's relationship with, 22, 287*n*79, 288*n*95
    trial *in absentia*, 97
    Westarp's opinion of, 84, 235
Brandauer, Johann, 52, 70
Braun, Eva, 34
Braunau, 34
British casualties, 34
British Interrogation Center 020, 83
Brookhart, Smith (Lt. Colonel), 88
Brunner, Karl, 162, 163
Bruskin, Sam, 251–52
Bruskin, Sydney
    in initial pursuit of Kaltenbrunner, 41, 49
    life after war, 250–52
    role in Kaltenbrunner arrest operation, 72, 252*i*, 260–62

C

Camp 020, 90
Camp Callan, 18–19
Camp Marcus W. Orr, 236
Camp Owakonze, 12
Camp Ritchie intelligence school, 21
Canaris, Wilhelm, 46, 61, 118–19
casualties in Europe (total), 34
casualties in Europe (U.S.), 34
casualties in U.S. advance, 26
catacombs at Nuremberg, 94, 208–9, 210
Catling, Cecil, 278n46
Chandler, Porter, 21
Chemical and Physical Experimental Laboratory for Rockets, 242
Christmas carols, 191
CIC (80th Division Counter Intelligence Corps)
   automatic arrest list, 38, 44
   friction with military government, 220, 232–33
   Gisela von Westarp and Iris Scheidler in custody of, 84–85
   Matteson's enjoyment of work, 219–220, 221
   Matteson's transfer to, 24, 141, 189–190
   operational confidentiality, 71
   secret 8 June 1945 report, 240–42
   white list, 52
CIC Automatic List, 38, 44
Cochran, Mabel Taylor, 52
Commission to Slovakia, 106
concentration camps
   Auschwitz, 53, 270n1, 280–81n56
   civilians forced to witness, 207–8
   Dachau, 167, 280n55
   Ebensee. See Ebensee concentration camp
   Eichmann's role, 53
   evacuations, 275n35
   executions in, 106–7, 108, 158–161, 278n45
   as Gestapo enforcement tool, 62
   inmate affidavits, 88, 100
   inmate photos, 42i
   inmate recollections, 41, 245–48
   Kaltenbrunner's contributions to system, 106, 147
   Kaltenbrunner's denial of responsibility, 83, 108, 112–13, 164–65, 166
   Kaltenbrunner's execution orders to, 106–7
   Kaltenbrunner's oversight, 35, 37, 42, 106, 279–280n53
   Matteson's physical impressions, 22, 41–43
   Mauthausen. See Mauthausen concentration camp
   medical experiments on inmates, 162–65
   RSHA oversight, 35, 63–64, 270n1
   SS investigations of crimes in, 158
   Swedish attempts to secure inmate release, 128–29
   system, 284n
Coppermine River canoe trip, 268
counterfeiting operations, 40, 131i, 131–32, 147, 241–42
crimes against peace, 110
The Curtain Falls (Bernadotte), 129

D

Dachau concentration camp, 167, 280n55
Dachstein Mountains, 50i
De Luce, Daniel, 103, 109
death marches, 247
Determann, Hermann, 242
Dollfuss, Engelbert, 44–45
Doppler, Karl, 64
Dulles, Allen
   German knowledge of, 121
   Gisevius as informant for, 108
   Höttl's attempt to contact, 65
   Operation Sunrise, 125–28
   The Secret Surrender, 125
   Wolff's surrender to, 112, 121–22

E

Ebensee concentration camp
  counterfeiting operation, 39
  creation of, 147
  inmate recollections, 41, 245-48
  liberation, 243-44
  Matteson's physical impressions, 22, 42-43
Eichmann, Adolf
  Final Solution role, 271-72n9
  under Kaltenbrunner, 35, 39, 112-13, 154-56
  last meeting with Kaltenbrunner, 122
  rise to power, 52i, 52-53
  RSHA unit responsibilities, 44
Eigruber, August (Gauleiter), 41, 173
Einsatzgruppen (action groups), 104-5, 283n
Eisenhower, Dwight (General), 40, 109
Endre, Ladislaus, 150-51
Enigma coding machines, 116
Enns River bridge, 34
Etcheverry, Alfred "Etch"
  CIC assignment, 26, 27
  circumstances of death, 2-3, 30-31, 221
  last letter to wife Marion, 3-5, 31-33
  Luxembourg memorial, 5
  McMillen and Matteson's letters to Marion, 256-59
  New Year's 1945 letter to Marion, 28-29
Etcheverry, Nicholas, 3, 4
executions
  in concentration camps, 106-7, 108, 158-161, 278n45
  of Eichmann, 53
  by Einsatzgruppen, 104-5
  following Nuremberg convictions, 111-12, 278n46
  of prisoners of war, 106, 174-75

F

Falaise Gap, 201-2
Fegelein, Hermann, 59, 63, 127
Fickett, Edward, 89, 91
Finch, Roscoe, Jr., 8i, 8-12
Fleischer, Richard (Colonel), 21, 22
Foley, Betty, 9
Foley, Frederick, 9
Foley, Jessie Ann, 9-10
forged pound notes, 130, 131-32, 147
Fort Snelling, 17-18
Free Austria Movement, 57, 64-66
Free French (FFI), 23-24
French casualties, 34
French resistance forces, 25, 55

G

Gabcik, Josef, 117
Gaiswinkler, Albrecht, 48, 55, 227
gas chambers, 106, 215, 278n45, 281n56
gas wagons, 105
Gauleiters, 41, 51
Gaza conflict, 6
Gebhardt, Karl, 162-63
Gerdes, Bertus, 107
German casualties, 34
German civilians
  at Alt Aussee, 50-52
  as cause of Nuremberg security concerns, 93-94
  common views of Hitler, 196, 197, 198, 202, 203
  fear of Russian army, 204, 206, 210, 212
  immediate postwar privations, 230
  Matteson's observations about, 196-97, 203-4, 205-8
Gestapo
  Eichmann's role, 52-53
  Kaltenbrunner's rank, 1, 2, 79
  Nuremberg member list, 34
  organization and activities, 62
  POW executions by, 174-75
Gilbert, G. M., 132
Girbl, Hans, 47
Gisevius, Hans Bernd, 108-9, 133
Goebbels, Joseph, 34
Goesdorf interrogation trips, 29-30
Goetz, Bernard, 246i
Goetz, Samuel, 41-42, 245-49, 246i
gold buried at Alt Aussee, 122-23

Göring, Hermann (Reich Marshal), 91, 96i, 101i, 110, 111
Göttsch, Werner, 56–57, 64–65, 241
"Great Hitler Museum," 58
Griebenow, George, 254–55

H

Halloween pranks, 11–12
Hamm, 33
Hannah (stenographer), 228–230
Harris, Whitney Robson (Lieutenant), 87–88, 100, 110
Harster, Wilhelm (General), 125
Hegewald, Ursula, 57
Heiderscheider Grund, 29
Hensel, Carl, 8i, 8–9
Hess, Rudolph, 98–99, 101i
Heydrich, Lina, 116
Heydrich, Reinhard
  assassination, 5, 23, 117, 285–86n73
  files on Reich leadership, 62
  as first RSHA head, 36, 46
  Höttl's description in *The Secret Front*, 119–120
  Kaltenbrunner's relationship with, 118, 286n77
  photo with Himmler, 37i
  RSHA's role under, 116–17
Himmler, Heinrich
  contacts with Bernadotte, 128
  fear of Kaltenbrunner, 47, 107–8, 118
  Höttl's description in *The Secret Front*, 120, 121
  illegitimate children, 165
  interest in occult, 56
  Mauthausen camp photo, 36i
  photo with Heydrich, 37i
  pursuit of negotiated peace, 81
  selection of Kaltenbrunner, 5
  Westarp's opinion of, 84, 235
  Wolff's connection to, 121, 125–26
Hitler, Adolf
  bomb plot against, 21–22, 82, 108
  common Germans' views of, 196, 197, 198, 202, 203
  Kaltenbrunner's last message to, 63–64
  Kaltenbrunner's relationship with, 82, 118, 120
  Matteson's early views, 140
  meetings on Wolff's talks with Dulles, 127
  Mussolini rescue, 53–54, 54i
  order on POW treatment, 170–71, 175–76
  plans for Linz, 275n31
  suicide, 34
Hitler's Paper Weapon (Höttl), 131
Hodges, Tom (Lieutenant), 99
Hoffmann, Heinrich, 36i, 37, 59, 99–100, 211
Hohenlohe, Chlodwig (Prince), 51i, 51–52
Hohenlychen Hospital, 162–65
Horthy, Miklos, 151
hospitalization during basic training (Matteson), 19
Höttl, Wilhelm
  arrest reported, 241
  attempt to negotiate with Dulles, 65, 69, 126–27
  book describing RSHA and Kaltenbrunner, 119–125
  counterfeiting operation, 131
  on Kaltenbrunner's fascination for Hitler, 82, 120
  as Nuremberg trial witness, 46i, 47, 66

I

I Never Saw My Face (Goetz), 246i, 249
IG Farben, 226
intelligence school, 21
international law, Matteson's closing thoughts, 141–42
International Military Tribunal. *See* Nuremberg trials
Interrogators of Prisoners of War, 191
IQs of Nazi leaders, 132

J

Jackson, Robert, 37, 142
Jacoby, Elise, 28
Jacoby, Josel, 28
Jodl, Alfred, 110

K

Kaltenborn, H. V., 104, 115
Kaltenbrunner, Ernst
  1938 portrait, 76i
  absence from trial opening day, 98
  Alpine Redoubt oversight, 39, 40, 147–48
  arrest, 77–80, 143–44, 216–18
  attempted alibi, 65–66, 78, 81, 90–91, 109–10
  charges against, 98, 104–8
  concentration camp oversight, 35, 37, 42, 147
  contacts with Bernadotte, 128–131
  conviction and execution, 109–13, 281n61, 282n64
  denial of concentration camp role, 83, 108, 112–13
  first appearance at trial, 101–3
  Höttl's account in *The Secret Front*, 120–25
  initial interrogations, 81–83
  initial pursuit of, 41–43
  intelligence services, 55–56, 60–63
  investigation of Hitler's attempted assassination, 22, 82, 118
  Kerry Villa headquarters, 55–57
  last message to Hitler, 63–64
  letter to wife, 81–82, 111
  Mauthausen camp photo, 36i, 99–100
  Nuremberg questioning of, 149–178
  Nuremberg trial photos, 86i, 96i, 101i, 102i
  Operation Sunrise and, 125–28
  opposition to Wolff's surrender, 112, 121, 126
  personality described, 129, 132–34
  physical descriptions, 48, 89–90, 117–18, 132, 277–78n45
  plan to lead new Austrian government, 65–66, 125
  press coverage of capture, 115–16
  rank kept secret, 2, 5, 100
  relationship with Hitler, 82, 118, 120
  retreat to Wildensee hideout, 68i, 69–74
  rise to power, 44–47, 271n7
  role in Nazi crimes, 35–37
  RSHA leadership, 35–36, 45–47, 61–63, 66, 178
  Schellenberg's relationship with, 117–18
  speculation on surrender, 134
  Sydney Bruskin's recollections about, 260–62
  testimony against, 108–9
  transport and imprisonment at Nuremberg, 87–88, 89–91
Kaltenbrunner, Liesl, 47–48, 81–82, 111
Kaltenbrunner, Ursula, 84
Kaltenbrunner, Wolfgang, 84
Kauffmann, Kurt, 98
Keitel, Wilhelm, 101i, 110, 111
Kempner, Robert, 99
Kennedy, John F., 267
Kerr, Coe (Captain), 21, 23
Kerry Villa, 55–57
Kersten, Felix, 118
Kesselring, Albert (Field Marshal), 40
Klimek, John, 24, 27, 30, 31
Kreuder, Peter, 227
Kripo, 62, 79
Kubris, Jan, 117
Kugel Erlass (Bullet Decree), 106

L

Labor Education Camps, 106
Lake Toplitz, 147
landmines, 22–23
"The Last Days of Ernst Kaltenbrunner," 276n40
Last Valhalla of the Nazis (Bocca), 146–48
Lehár, Franz, 224–25, 226
Ley, Robert, 41, 84, 89, 235
Lidice massacres, 23, 117
Lieffers (Dr.), 232–33
Lublin massacre, 158–161

M

M&F game, 9
A Man Called Intrepid (Stevenson), 116, 119
Manteuffel, Hasso von (General), 27
Maquis, 25
Marcus W. Orr POW camp, 85
Marks, David, 87
Masaryk, Jan, 117
Matteson, Adelaide H., 12–17, 13i
Matteson, Charles D., 12–17, 13i
Matteson, Frederic, 269i
Matteson, Jane
    arrival at La Jolla during basic training, 19
    Bob's wartime letters to, 181–238
    Lloyd Roach letter to, 253
    reunion with Bob in 1946, 140
    wedding photo, 180i
Matteson, Rob Jr., 269i
Matteson, Robert E.
    arrest and interrogation of Frau Kaltenbrunner, 47–48
    arrest of Kaltenbrunner, 77–80, 143–44, 216–18
    ascent to Wildensee hideout, 70–74, 216–17
    attendance at opening of Nuremberg trials, 97–100
    basic training at Camp Callan, 18–19, 140
    childhood memories, 8–12
    concentration camp reactions, 22, 41–43
    continued early 1945 advance into Germany, 33–34
    correspondence with Etcheverry children, 6
    correspondence with Kaltenbrunner children, 6
    drafted into service, 17–18
    early CIC assignments, 24–26
    Goesdorf trips and loss of Etch, 29–31
    initial pursuit of Kaltenbrunner, 41–43
    with Kaltenbrunner's Gestapo badge, 79i
    letter from George Griebenow, 254–55
    letter to Jane after Nuremberg trial day 1, 98–99
    letter to Marion Etcheverry, 257–58
    location of Nazi intelligence headquarters, 55–57
    loss of family members, 2, 12–17
    mission with Alt Aussee task force, 48–52
    photo of 1945 mountain hike, 136i
    postwar career and later life, 266–69
    promotions, 27, 29, 184
    return home and final thoughts on war, 103–4, 139–143
    security mission at Nuremberg trials, 87–95, 100, 237–38
    self-published works, 1–2
    Silver Star award, 143–44, 223–24
    striking interrogation subject, 225
    transfer to 80th Counter Intelligence Corps (CIC), 24, 141, 189–190
    transfer to 80th Infantry Division and G-2 role, 20–24, 140–41
    transport to European theatre, 21–22
    wartime letters to Jane, 181–238
    wedding photo, 180i
Matteson, Sumner III, 10, 14
Matteson, Sumner W., 269i
Mauthausen concentration camp
    executions, 106, 108, 278n45
    Goetz's recollections, 247
    interrogation of Kaltenbrunner on, 166, 173
    Kaltenbrunner photo, 36i, 99–100
    Kaltenbrunner's oversight, 106, 278n45, 279–280n53
McLaughlin, Kathleen, 109
McMillen, Thomas (Captain)
    as 80th Division CIC head, 21, 220
    Kaltenbrunner interrogation, 81
    letters to Marion Etcheverry, 256–57, 258–59
    provisions for team in Heiderscheider Grund, 30

request for Matteson to transfer to CIC, 24, 24i, 189-190
return of Kaltenbrunner badge to Matteson, 79-80
secret 8 June 1945 report, 240-42
medical experiments, 162-65
Mendel, Sammy, 12
Merlebach, 26
Merry Widow (Lehár), 224-25
military government, 220, 232-33
Military Intelligence (G-2), 21
mistresses in SS, 84, 235
Morgen, Konrad, 158, 160, 161, 291n124
Morton, Joseph, 106
Moscow trials, 116
Moser, Karl, 70
Moyzisch, C. L., 130, 132
Muhsfeldt, Erich, 159
Mussolini, Benito, 53-54

N

National [Alpine] Redoubt. *See* Alpine [National] Redoubt
Naujocks, Alfred, 65
Nazi Party
 civilian job losses due to association with, 93-94
 comments in Matteson's letters, 196, 198, 203
 common Germans' views of, 196, 198
 Gauleiters, 41, 51
 Kaltenbrunner's position, 1, 35, 36, 37
 Martin Bormann's position, 22
 mistresses in, 84, 235
 prewar ban in Austria, 44
Nebe, Arthur, 62, 275n34
Neurath, Konstantin von, 110
Normandy beach, 22
Nuremberg, 3rd Army advance to, 34
Nuremberg labyrinths, 94, 208-9, 210
Nuremberg trials
 charges and evidence against Kaltenbrunner, 104-9
 convictions and executions, 109-13

Kaltenbrunner's first appearance, 101-3
Matteson's mission, 87-95, 100, 237-38
opening day, 97-100
planning and testing security, 87-95
validity debated, 112

O

Odessa plan, 283n
Ohlendorf, Kathie, 105
Ohlendorf, Otto, 105
Ohrdruf concentration camp, 207-8
Olson, Sigurd F., 267
Operation Bernhard, 131-32, 147, 284n
Operation Cicero, 130-31, 132
Operation Harvest Festival, 159
Operation Reinhard, 270n1, 283-84n
Operation Sunrise, 125-28

P

Palace of Justice. *See* Nuremberg trials
Patton, George (General), 24, 27, 28, 33-34
Pavelic, Ante, 148
Pearce, Michelle Etcheverry "Chonty," 4, 5
Pearson, Ralph (Major), 48, 49, 71
Persinger, Robert B., 42, 243-44, 292n136
Plieseis, Sepp, 43
Pohl, Oswald, 159-160, 164-65
Pokrovsky, Y. V. (Colonel), 92, 94
Polish casualties, 34
Polish Jews, murder of, 271n9, 284n, 285n69
Porter, Sidney, 13
Praxmarer, Rudolf, 58, 60, 72, 84, 235-36, 241
prisoner of war camps, 85, 173-74
prisoners of war (Allied), 106, 174-75
prisoners of war (German), 27, 191, 192, 236

R

Rainey, Bob, 24
Ravensbrück concentration camp, 164
Red Army purges, 116
Regensburg, 210
Reich Security Main Office (*Reichssicherheitshauptamt*, or RSHA)

classified U.S. document describing, 60–63
functions of, 35, 44, 46, 61–63, 215, 270n1
Heydrich's leadership, 116–17
Höttl's account in *The Secret Front*, 119–125
Kaltenbrunner's leadership, 35–36, 178
Kaltenbrunner's plans to align with Western allies, 66
Werner Göttsch's role, 56–57
Ribbentrop, Joachim von, 84, 101i, 110, 235
Riedel, Walter, 242
Roach, Lloyd, 83, 87, 89, 253
Romanian casualties, 34
Rosenberg, Alfred, 101, 101i, 110
Rosenthal, Rolf, 163
Rudenko, Roman A., 92, 94–95
Runstedt, Gerd von (Field Marshal), 26–27
Russian army. *See* Soviet army

S

salt mines, art treasures in, 48, 57–58, 123
Sauckel, Fritz, 280n54
Scheidler, Arthur, 58, 70, 72, 78, 80, 167–69
Scheidler, Iris
  assessment of Kaltenbrunner, 134
  concern for husband in Kaltenbrunner arrest, 72, 80, 81
  final interrogation, 83–85, 234, 235–36
  friendships in Hitler's inner circle, 58–59
  photo with Gisela von Westarp, 59i
  Sydney Bruskin's recollections about, 261
Schellenberg, Walter (General)
  conviction and imprisonment, 123
  as Nuremberg trial witness, 46i, 46–47
  office layout described, 129–130
  relationship with Kaltenbrunner, 117–18, 133
  report of Bernadotte's contact with Himmler, 128
Schirach, Baldur von, 41, 59
Schumacher, Georg, 227
Schuschnigg, Kurt von, 45

Schutzstaffel (SS), 44–46, 84, 93
SD (*Sicherheitsdienst*), 1, 44, 119, 215
The Secret Front (Höttl), 119–125
The Secret Surrender (Dulles), 125
security at Nuremberg, 87–95
Seine River (Ontario), 12
Seyss-Inquart, Arthur, 45, 157
Shirer, William, 35
Sicherheitsdienst, 35
Silver Star award, 142–43, 143i, 145i, 223–24
Sixth SS Panzer Army, 47
Skorzeny, Otto (Colonel)
  under Kaltenbrunner, 27, 39
  role in late resistance scenario, 60–61, 122
  RSHA unit responsibilities, 44, 61, 63
  war activities and escape, 53–55, 54i, 128–29
Slovakia, Commission to, 106
snipers in Nuremberg tunnels, 94, 210
Soviet army
  German civilian fears of, 204, 206, 210, 212
  total casualties, 34
  U.S. linkup at Steyr, 34, 39
Soviet Jews, killings of, 271–72n9, 279n52, 281n56
Spanish Foreign Policy Association, 55
Speer, Albert, 280n54
SS Havelinstitut, 57, 274n30
St. Avold bombs, 25
Stalag Luft 3 escape, 174–75
Steyr, 34, 39
stonings, 108
streetcar prank, 11
Streicher, Julius, 84, 92–93, 235
Sutherland, Edwin Van Valkenberg (Lt. Colonel), 87, 91, 93
"Sword of Damocles" speech, 267

T

Thilges, Jean, 30
Thompson, Horace, 11
"Tin-Eyed Stephens," 90

totalitarian systems, Matteson's closing thoughts, 141–42
trench foot, 26
The Trial of the Germans (Davidson), 132
Truscott, Lucian (General), 91
Twelfth Army Group, 81–82

U
Ukrainian conflict, 6

V
Vajna, Gabor, 151–56
Vance, John, 30
Veesenmayer, Edmund, 151, 152, 291n121
Vietnam War, 267
vivisection experiments, 163–65
V-mail, 292n131
Volkssturm, 27

W
Waneck, Wilhelm, 55–56, 57, 64–65, 128, 241
Wannsee Conference, 53
War Crimes Trial Personnel Security Office, 92, 100
The War Years 1940–1946 (Matteson), 1
Warsaw ghetto massacre, 108, 281n58
Werwolves, 39–40, 47, 60
Westarp, Gisela von
  birth of twins to Kaltenbrunner, 5, 58
  earlier marriage, 126
  farewell to Matteson, 227
  farewells to Kaltenbrunner, 70, 81, 111
  final interrogation, 83–85, 234–35
  letter to Matteson at Nuremberg, 98
  note to Kaltenbrunner at Nuremberg, 102–3, 103i
  note to Kaltenbrunner in hiding, 71–72, 77
  opinions on leading Nazis, 84, 235
  photo with Iris Scheidler, 59i
  Sydney Bruskin's recollections about, 260–61
  transport to Hindelang by Matteson, 231–32

Westarp, Gräfin von, 235
Wildensee hideout, 68i, 69–74
Winkelmann, Otto, 150, 291n121
Winter, Paul (General), 40
Wippern, Georg, 161, 291n127
Wolff, Karl (General), 112, 121–22, 125–28
Woods, John C., 278n46

Y
Yugoslavian casualties, 34

Z
Ziereis, Franz, 36i
Zohrer (SS driver), 78

Printed in the United States
by Baker & Taylor Publisher Services